MALTA CONVOYS
1940–42

David A. Thomas has also written:

Naval History
WITH ENSIGNS FLYING
SUBMARINE VICTORY
BATTLE OF THE JAVA SEA
CRETE 1941: THE BATTLE AT SEA
JAPAN'S WAR AT SEA: PEARL HARBOUR TO THE
CORAL SEA
ROYAL ADMIRALS
A COMPANION TO THE ROYAL NAVY
THE ILLUSTRATED ARMADA HANDBOOK
THE ATLANTIC STAR 1939–45
CHRISTOPHER COLUMBUS: MASTER OF THE
ATLANTIC
QUEEN MARY AND THE CRUISER: THE CURACOA
DISASTER
(With Patrick Holmes)
BATTLES AND HONOURS OF THE ROYAL NAVY

Social History
THE CANNING STORY 1785–1985
CHURCHILL: THE MEMBER FOR WOODFORD

Bibliography
COMPTON MACKENZIE: A BIBLIOGRAPHY
(with Joyce Thomas)

Juvenile
HOW SHIPS ARE MADE

Malta Convoys 1940–42

The Struggle at Sea

by

DAVID A. THOMAS

LEO COOPER

First published in Great Britain 1999 by
Leo Cooper
an imprint of
Pen & Sword Books
47, Church Street, Barnsley, South Yorkshire S70 2AS.

ISBN 0 85052 6639

A catalogue record for this book is available
from the British Library

Typeset in 11/13pt Sabon by
Phoenix Typesetting, Ilkley, West Yorkshire

Printed by Redwood Books Limited, Trowbridge, Wilts.

CONTENTS

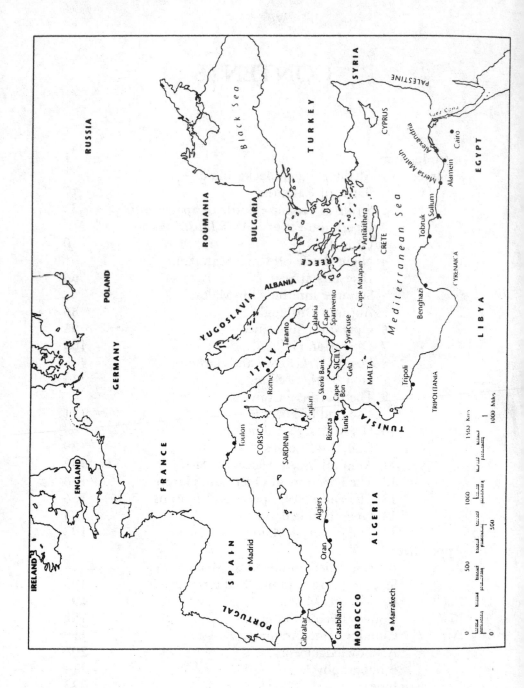

INTRODUCTION

Admiral of the Fleet Viscount Cunningham of Hyndhope KT
GCB OM DSO** was known less grandly and more affection-
ately throughout the fleet by his initials – ABC – Andrew Browne
Cunningham. He was admired, respected, feared and acknowledged by historians to be the greatest naval commander at sea
since Nelson. He was a master strategist and his campaign as
Commander-in-Chief in the Mediterranean for two and a half
years (1939–42) will be studied with admiration by generations
of naval officers throughout the world.

His period of command in the Mediterranean was marked by
thunderous and bloody air/sea battles and clashes at sea now
legendary: Matapan, Taranto, the Crete campaign, the convoy
battles of Operations Collar, Tiger, Substance, Halberd,
Harpoon, Vigorous and Pedestal, the battles of Sirte, Calabria
and Spartivento. He commanded the submarine flotillas operating from Malta with no geographical location to honour their
gallantry. He also commanded all the actions of Admiral Sir
James Somerville's Force H and the strikes of Force K. It was an
anxious period, an endless story of heavy losses of naval vessels
including splendid ships like *Barham*, *Ark Royal*, *Eagle*,
Manchester, *Fiji*, *Gloucester*, *Neptune*, *Cairo*, *Hermione*,
Southampton and *Welshman*, apart from all the smaller ships.

Heaviest losses in terms of personnel occurred aboard the
ponderous 31,100-ton bulk of the battleship *Barham* (8 × 15"
guns). She was torpedoed off Sollum by *U-331* and exploded
with dreadful loss of life.

1

Ark Royal (22,000 tons and 72 aircraft) was another loss, but, by contrast, suffered virtually no casualties when torpedoed by *U-81*. The carrier was taken in tow, but could not be salved, although nearly in sight of Gibraltar.

Eagle (10,800 tons and 15 aircraft) was another casualty when torpedoed and sunk by *U-73* off Algiers.

The cruiser *Gloucester* (9,400 tons and 12 × 6" guns) was just one of several cruisers bombed to destruction by skilled German and Italian dive bombers off Crete. On the very same day the cruiser *Fiji* (8,000 tons and 12 × 6" guns) was shattered by bombs from the same squadron of bombers. *Cairo* (4,290 tons and 8 × 4" guns), a small AA cruiser, also succumbed to the Luftwaffe pilots.

Cruisers seemed particularly vulnerable to air attacks. The 10,000-ton *Manchester* (12 × 6" guns) was attacked and torpedoed by two torpedo boats, *MAS 16* and *MAS 22*, off Tunisia in the Operation Pedestal convoy battle.* *Southampton* (9,400 tons and 12 × 6" guns) was bombed by German aircraft in January, 1941. Efforts to save her failed and she was scuttled the following day.

HMS *Hermione* (5,450 tons and 10 × 5.25" guns), a modern cruiser, barely a year old, was torpedoed by *U-205* in a hard-fought battle in June, 1942.

Yet another U-boat success was the sinking of the minelayer HMS *Welshman* by *U-617* a few days after the relief of Malta. The U-boat's commander, Albrecht Brandi, watched the death throes of the minelayer through his periscope: he claimed two torpedo hits, saw a huge boiler explosion and the capsizing of the ship before she disappeared.

It is not without significance that most of these sinkings were achieved by German forces and not Italian. But the Italians did enjoy one spectacular success, though they were unaware of its extent. It was a crowning indignity for the Mediterranean Fleet. It came in December, 1941, when six brave Italian human torpedo-men penetrated the Alexandria defences and mined the

---

* MAS = *Motoscarfi Anti Sommergibili*: Italian torpedo boat or E-boat.

hulls of the battleships *Queen Elizabeth* and *Valiant* (both 32,700 tons and 8 × 15" and 12 × 6" guns). Admiral Cunningham related the incident in his autobiography:

> "For some time we had suspected that the Italians contemplated an attack on the battleships. We had information that they possessed some sort of submersible explosive motorboat which could travel on the surface or underwater and was fitted with apparatus for lifting [torpedo] nets which enabled it to pass under the normal defences. On 18 December I warned the fleet by signal that attacks on Alexandria harbour by air, boat or human torpedo might be expected in calm weather. Besides the boom and net defence at the harbour entrance, each battleship was surrounded by a floating net as a protection against torpedoes whether human or otherwise. Furthermore patrolling boats dropped small explosive charges at the harbour entrance."

On 19 December at about 4 am the C-in-C was called from his cabin aboard the *Queen Elizabeth* to be told that two Italians had been found clinging to *Valiant*'s bow buoy. Mines had been secured to the hulls of the two battleships. Cunningham was on the quarterdeck when a violent explosion ripped open the stern of the tanker *Sagona* lying close to the *Queen Elizabeth*, with the destroyer *Jervis* (1,695 tons and 6 × 4.7" guns) lying alongside. Both were severely damaged. About twenty minutes later there was a heavy explosion under *Valiant*'s fore turret. This was quickly followed by another explosion while Cunningham was right aft by the *Queen Elizabeth*'s ensign staff. He was tossed in the air. Both battleships were badly damaged, *Valiant* down by the bows and the flagship with a heavy list to starboard.

However, both ships settled squarely on the bottom in shallow water, the damage disguised so as to deceive the enemy into thinking the ships were safely secured to their buoys, whereas they were both immobilized for several months. It was a severe blow to Cunningham. The navy had reached its nadir. The C-in-C commanded a phantom fleet, the majority of his destroyers, cruisers, aircraft carriers and battleships unfit for battle and no longer seaworthy. Without the navy the prospects for Malta's survival seemed grim. Abandonment of the island

3

had always been an option and its survival or surrender came as close as the toss of a coin. Cunningham's answer, however, was for action and battle. He took every opportunity to seek out units of the Italian fleet, so that every time they put to sea they did so at their peril.

The Luftwaffe air squadrons, however, posed different problems. They were looked upon less favourably by the Royal Navy and with a healthy respect.

But the enemy respected Cunningham too. He was known to have been a tough, relentless, demanding destroyer captain, with the award of no fewer than three DSCs. Years later he felt equally at home on the bridge of his 30,600-ton flagship *Warspite* commanding a battle fleet. It is only fair to mention that Cunningham commanded the capital ship *Rodney* (1929–31) but was never happy ship-handling her 33,900-ton bulk.

Tributes of the highest order have been paid to Cunningham. One of his biographers, Captain S.W.C. Pack, in *Cunningham: The Commander*, attributed to him "flair, brilliance, interest and integrity. [He] seldom used a loud voice but he spoke with deliberation and assurance." Pack refers to his "resolute and relentless determination to overcome the enemy whatever the difficulties". On the other hand some accuse him of bullying. Harold Macmillan thought that "many were rather frightened of him". But one compatriot has reported that "The enduring impression he gave was of force, a man intensely alive and brimming with energy and attention."

Admiral Lord Tovey, victor of the *Bismarck* pursuit, had no hesitation in referring to Cunningham as "the greatest sailor Britain has had since Nelson".

Admiral Sir Bernard Rawlings, himself a commander of some stature, who earned a fine reputation during the Crete campaign, went so far as to describe him as "the greatest sailor of all time".

Rear Admiral R.L. Fisher wrote of being comforted when ABC – "The Old Man" – was aboard the flagship:

"They knew everything would be all right. What's more the Italians knew it wouldn't be all right for them."

Paymaster Captain J.S.S. Smith, his acting secretary for many years, gave a description of Cunningham which ended with the exhortation: "God grant that such a commander comes when the Royal Navy needs him again."

As a Commander-in-Chief he dominated the scene by sheer force of character. To him goes the honour of promulgating the most dramatic naval signals in the Mediterranean theatre. At the time of the evacuation of the army at the defeat in Crete Cunningham signalled the hard-pressed flotillas and squadrons of the navy:

"STICK IT OUT. THERE ARE INDICATIONS THAT ENEMY RESOURCES ARE STRETCHED TO THE LIMIT. WE CAN AND MUST OUTLAST THEM."

During this same Cretan campaign, agonizing over the naval losses while rescuing the army from capture, he declared to his staff:

"IT TAKES THE NAVY THREE YEARS TO BUILD A NEW SHIP. IT WILL TAKE THREE HUNDRED TO BUILD A NEW TRADITION. THE EVACUATION WILL CONTINUE."

Some months later he drew up Admiral George Anson's first use of a signal in 1739, urging his ships "by sinking, burning or otherwise destroying all Spanish ships". It was a signal as appropriate to the modern ships of the Second World War as it was to the wooden walls of Anson's day. At the time of the defeat of Rommel's armies in North Africa and their evacuation across the Mediterranean Cunningham modified Anson's signal; with a little licence and no equivocation he *ordered* the fleet:

"SINK, BURN, DESTROY. LET NOTHING PASS."

And in so doing Cunningham gave support to the Desert Armies' chase of Rommel's fleeing divisions from North Africa.

He knew well how to dramatize a situation to glorify the Service of which he became Commander-in-Chief and in so doing enhancing his own status. To him went the honour of circulating the most dramatic signal in the Mediterranean: to the Admiralty he signalled on 8 May, 1943:

"BE PLEASED TO INFORM THEIR LORDSHIPS THAT THE ITALIAN NAVY LIES AT ANCHOR UNDER THE GUNS OF THE FORTRESS OF MALTA."

But it was to be a long haul before the events which gave rise to signals like sound bytes came to a victorious conclusion, before the Italian fleet surrendered and the bitterly contested naval campaign was played out, and before the Desert Army celebrated its victory.

During the two-and-a-half-year campaign in the Mediterranean masterminding the complexity of the Malta convoy operations, Cunningham's responsibilities were awesome. It was the Italians' misfortune to encounter a strategist of this calibre. Any lesser man might have lost the battle – with stunning consequences. At its worst the Royal Navy's and Cunningham's fortunes had sunk to rock bottom, with at times scarcely a seaworthy and undamaged ship left to defend the convoys and fight the satellite skirmishes upon whose safe arrival and outcome depended the survival of the brave people of Malta and their strategic island home.

Its story has been told many times by distinguished historians as can be testified by a glance at the Select Bibliography. Here are stories of eye-witnesses and participants from all Services. I have taken the raw material of unpublished or privately published diaries, personal experiences and accounts, most of them preserved for fifty years or more in the care of widows, sons, daughters and grandchildren. A linking narrative provides a background and gives a perspective against which the stories can be read and judged.

My appeal to the press for reminiscences received a substantial response from all over the British Isles, from the Channel Isles, Malta itself, South Africa, Belgium, Holland, France and even Australia.

What was also surprising was the variety of detachments,

services and special groups represented. Replies from Royal Navy and Merchant Navy personnel dominated, as was to be expected. The number from the army and DEMS (Defensively Equipped Merchant Ships) or the Maritime Royal Artillery was unexpectedly high. The trawl was comprehensive: naval officers, engineers, ordinary seamen, telegraphists, cooks, signalmen, Petty Officers, Chief Petty Officers, ERAs, mechanics from both the navy and RAF, navigators and air fitters. All were drawn together in extraordinary situations like soldiers manning RN ships' guns, Air Force personnel from HM carriers assembling Spitfires and Hurricane fighters, and even US sailors helping fly off reinforcements from the US carrier *Wasp*.

The letters demonstrated a remarkable recall of experiences, though checking them all exposed some limitations of old veterans' wartime memories. These memories, like a slipping clutch, have shown signs of fading. Some have mixed in their minds the dates and sometimes the convoy code names, the next ship in line, even the name of the corvette or escort ship which plucked them from an oily sea.

I have sought to correct all matters of fact and have endeavoured to present the stories as they have been written by the correspondents. I have not attempted to explain them except in the most general terms, nor to exonerate anyone, let alone pass judgement, but simply to let those who experienced the event relate their own part in the battle for the sustenance of the besieged island of Malta.

Much was written of the comradeship of those serving in the various services. Today phrases like privilege, service and pride are regarded as old-fashioned and outmoded, but are used here among my correspondents unashamedly and refreshingly.

Gilbert Taylor, an Able Seaman in the 10,000-ton 8 x 8" gun cruiser *Suffolk* and in the old destroyer *Vansittart*, (1,120 tons) recalls those grim yet glorious days in the Mediterranean so many years ago, and now wears the Malta Commemorative Medal "with pride", bravely earned in the "convoys to Hell and back".

Pride, too, was felt by G.D. Lindsey who served as an ERA in the light cruiser *Aurora*, one of the ships of the famous Force K Striking Force which took the sea war to the enemy in audacious forays against the Italian navy. "It was some sight to see the whole population (or so it seemed) lining the sea front and every available space, to cheer into Grand Harbour the *Aurora* and her chummy ships of the Force."

Ex-Leading Telegraphist (later Petty Officer) R.A.C. Green aboard the fleet destroyer *Fury* joined Vice Admiral Sir James Somerville's Force H at Gibraltar. He writes of one incident:

"We started with eight merchant ships and after a hazardous passage . . . we finally arrived with three. I was amazed that we were congratulated for a successful operation, which I suppose shows how desperate Malta's plight was in 1941–2. I came off watch at midnight on one occasion, walked on to the upper deck for some fresh air and, although I saw nothing, a merchant ship which was there when I went on watch had now disappeared. There was just a heavy stench of cordite. When you consider they were carrying aircraft fuel, munitions and a variety of highly dangerous cargoes, those merchant seamen did not get the recognition they deserved."

Green is keen to point out that he was not "a medal man". His medals have not been polished or worn since he left the navy. "However," he wrote, "I was proud of my Malta medal. . . . I am pleased and proud to have served with Force H and the merchant navy sailors who took such risks."

John Slader, author and naval writer, refers to

"the merchantmen and seamen who were lost in the defence of the island. They sailed from Gibraltar in the west and Alexandria in the east and etched as glorious a story as any in the annals of the sea."

Many of the correspondents, all now in their seventies and eighties, apologize for their unsteadiness, scrappy writing, fading eyesight and failing memory. Many encouraged their wives or daughters to write. So many of them remember the ordeals of the dive bombers and high-level bomber attacks, and especially the lack of sleep.

S.J. Mead served in the carrier *Eagle* and survived her sinking during Operation Pedestal in August, 1942:

> "A lot of what we went through on those convoys is a bit vague, but I still remember the peril and especially the sleepless nights we went through. I was on two convoys in 1942, one in June and the other in August when we were sunk."

A.H. Wilton served in the 10/7th Heavy Anti-Aircraft Regiment in defence of Malta, serving throughout the whole length of the island's siege, always on stand-by at the height of the battle, loading and unloading ships during the lapses in the bombing.

> "Myself, like a lot of others who served on the island lost many hours sleep, standing-by, knowing you lads [men of the Royal and Merchant Navy] were risking your lives to keep us fed and watered. . . . I salute you all . . . and all connected with you."

Leading Telegraphist Green found three consecutive nights without sleep enervating. "I realized how vital sleep is to recharge our batteries."

Gilbert Taylor wrote of his comrades, all of whom found sleepless nights debilitating. "Heroism on a grand scale was the order of the day during those convoys with death and destruction round the clock." Taylor want on: "O.Ds [Ordinary Seamen] showed the courage of martyrs." Taylor himself was exhausted by fear and lack of sleep. He recalls going down on his knees and praying for deliverance. His prayers were answered. He survived.

Asdic Operator and "lowly" Able Seaman Hector Macdonald experienced ordeals by bombs, shells, torpedoes and mines, and he admits to it all having been a horrendous experience.

He served for much of his sea time in the Tribal Class destroyer

Jaguar (1,690 tons and 6 × 4.7" guns) and later survived the sinking of his escort destroyer *Heythrop* (1,050 tons and 6 × 4" guns). He described the Malta experience in words like "depressing" and "apprehensive". He remembers his co-watchkeeping Asdic Operator and himself being "bloody terrified" at times. "Everybody was scared."

Fate followed Hector Macdonald in the eastern basin of the Mediterranean like an evil shadow. Both *Jaguar* and *Heythrop* were sunk within a week of each other, both of them by the same U-boat commander, Lieutenant-Commander Georg-Werner Fraatz in *U-652*. Macdonald reports that *Jaguar*'s sinking was during the middle watch; not one officer nor anyone in square rig was rescued. The only survivors were guns crews and men with stations up top.

Those servicemen stationed ashore, especially army personnel, suffered deprivations of all sorts. At the same time they endured intense and seemingly unending aerial bombardments both by day and night. They were denied even the most minimal human comforts, yet they wrote with genuine sincerity of their respect, appreciation and gratitude for the men of the Royal and Merchant Navies. One correspondent, ex-Corporal L. Newcombe, wrote from the heart:

> "I served in Malta throughout the siege in the 4th Battalion of the Buffs. As soldiers we had the task of unloading the ships that managed to reach port. We prayed for the convoys – and at times so few ships got through to be unloaded. They were constantly bombed at sea and were so badly damaged . . . One particular ship received a direct hit and had no interior left."

Newcombe recalled the *Pepperpot*, the nickname given to the 5,270-ton, 6-inch gun cruiser *Penelope*. She was struck by so much shrapnel that she resembled a pepperpot and the wooden plugs gave her the appearance of a hedgehog. Newcombe remembers the cruiser lying alongside the ship he was helping to unload and the intensity of the aircraft attacks even when the ships reached the so-called sanctuary of the harbour. He wrote:

"We waited for convoys to bring food and ammunition. We were told in1942 that two convoys were on the way – simultaneously – one from the east and one from the west . . . but so few of the ships made it. I can say of the convoys of brave ships and men that without them Malta would have fallen. As an ex-corporal in the army I thank the Navy and the Merchant Navy . . . I can never forget unloading those bombed ships."

The memory of those days linger on. Mrs Evelyn English recalls her late husband – their wedding banns were called while he was serving in the *Nelson* – experiencing the Malta convoys. "*Nelson* led Force H of Cunningham's fleet," she remembers being told. (It was Somerville, of course, who led Force H.) Mrs English remembers, too, being told about the horror of the clearing-up operations that followed. Later, English was drafted to the destroyer *Matchless* (1,920 tons and 6 × 4.7" guns), also very much involved with convoy work in the Mediterranean. "I only learned snippets of information about his service," Mrs English wrote. "We visited the War Museum at Valletta. . . . He would get very upset at some points on the island . . . so I refused ever to go back again." The scars even after fifty years were still raw and the memories emotional.

Another *Matchless* destroyer man, a regular RN serviceman of thirty-four years service which included a 2½-year stint in the fleet destroyer, was L.W. Munden. *Matchless* was seconded from Arctic convoy duties to the Mediterranean and he particularly recalls Operation Harpoon of June, 1942, during which *Matchless* was damaged, necessitating two months in dock to effect repairs. Like many sailors he felt safer at sea, with sea room in which to manoeuvre rather than secured alongside like a dog on a lead. Engine Room Artificer G.D. Lyndsey wrote:

"I served as an E.R.A. in [the cruiser] HMS *Aurora* (5,270 tons and 6 × 6" guns) and operated in and around Malta during a three-year period. Life was pretty hectic; air raids were counted in hundreds and being out at sea was a blessing at times. I remember one bombing raid with amusement. Myself and two mates set off for shore in a dghaisa [decoratively painted passenger boats not unlike Venetian oared canal boats] a matter of a hundred yards or

11

so away. The siren went and our boatman got going at a rate of knots. Ack ack opened up and Jerry arrived. We just made it ashore when a bomb exploded about sixty yards behind us. After the raid we crawled out from under a vehicle covered from head to foot in fine Maltese dust."

Edward Wright served in Malta for 2½ years as an RAF Armourer. "When the Spitfires arrived from the USS *Wasp*," he recalled,

"I was part of a ground crew made up of soldiers . . . and a number of Fleet Air Arm. The team spirit with soldiers, sailors and airmen was 100%. I shall never forget that team spirit in Malta."

Ex-Leading Aircraftman V.M. Leigh had a similar experience and expressed it in his Veterans' Association magazine:

"I was privileged to be there on Malta during such times as they were and to rub shoulders with such a wonderful crowd of lads who must now be old hands like myself. . . . We can all look back with some satisfaction, perhaps a lot of pride, at an experience never to be forgotten."

Yet another draft to Malta was a small RAF ground crew, mainly aircraft fitters, reputedly split into three parties: one went by submarine, another by Sunderland flying boat, and the final third in the cruiser *Newcastle*. This arrangement ensured, as far as possible, that one section at least would survive. Paddy Alton recalls his brief passage aboard the 9,400-ton cruiser (12 × 6" guns) and recalled, too, that *Newcastle* later sank. "I have often wondered if the kindly RN chaps we knew went down with her. I will always remember with gratitude the manner in which they accepted an extra twenty or so landlubbers under their feet." Paddy Alton was misinformed. *Newcastle* was torpedoed but did not sink. She survived the war.

One or two small technicalities deserve a word of explanation to make the nomenclature of the Malta convoys more understandable. "Malta convoys" technically refer only to convoys despatched specifically *to* the island. Clearly adherence to this limitation led to many anomalies. Obviously convoys *to and from* the island was a fairer definition. But even this left space for reasoning. The Battles of Spartivento, First Sirte, Second Sirte, Calabria, Cape Matapan, the FAA attack at Taranto, the bombardments of Genoa, Leghorn and Spezia, the evacuations from Greece and Crete and many other skirmishes are introduced, if only with a passing reference, to try to give a clearer perspective of the whole Maltese scene.

It is not the purpose of this book to cover the drama ashore except in so far as it impinges directly on the naval aspect of the siege. Thus, the bombing of the island, its heroic defence, dreadful devastation, its gallantry which earned the island the unique award of the George Cross, goes largely unrecorded or is dismissed in a flurry of statistics.

The sheer administrative complexity of planning the passage of a convoy from, say, Alexandria to Malta entailed the deployment of many squadrons of the Mediterranean Fleet (C-in-C Admiral Sir Andrew Cunningham) from its Egyptian base, and of Vice Admiral Sir James Somerville with covering forces. For a masterly presentation of all aspects of the planning and execution of the most bitterly fought Malta convoy battle see Peter Smith's *Pedestal: The Malta Convoy of August 1942.*

In November, 1940, the classification of M (for Malta) was rationalized. West-bound convoys from Egypt to Malta were numbered in the MW Malta (West-bound) series. East-bound (ie empty) ships being convoyed from Malta to Egypt were numbered in the ME (Malta East-bound) series.

The introduction of this system, as if to complicate matters further, was backdated to include previous convoys: So that MF 1, MS 1, MF 2, MF 3 and MF 4 were considered to have been MF 1, MW 2 and ME 2 and so on.

But this was not all. When the Mediterranean Fleet undertook a covering action for the passage of a convoy it was given an Operation code – eg Harpoon, Substance and so on. This fleet could, and did, operate as two or more separate forces: for example, part of the fleet might cover the Calabrian coast and be given a Force number. And Vice Admiral Somerville could well split his Force H into separate units each designated Forces, while the convoys themselves would be given code numbers.

Because of the variety of ways of defining time, it has seemed sensible to simplify matters by leaving times as quoted by the correspondents rather than try to standardize them. The guiding principle has been one of clear intention.

SUMMARY OF PHASES OF
MALTA CONVOYS CAMPAIGN

The Battle of the Malta Convoys 1940–42 conveniently falls into a number of phases which can be summarized as follows:

I ITALIAN PHASE (JUNE TO DECEMBER, 1940)

Italian aircraft from Sardinia, Cyrenaica and the Dodecanese attacked convoys and all shipping, but their high-level bombing, dismissed by many as ineffective, was accurate enough to be unnerving and frightening. This phase was characterized by a large number of movements of British warships across the entire Mediterranean, during which time advantage was taken to slip convoys to and from Malta. During this phase, too, the Fleet Air Arm attacked Taranto. Further, Covering Forces drove off an Italian battle squadron in the action off Calabria in July, 1940, and again in the action off Spartivento in November. The July action was in defence of Convoy MA 5 and the November skirmish resulted from the defence of the operation code-named Collar.

II FIRST GERMAN PHASE (SPRING 1941)

The *Luftwaffe*'s intervention in the anti-shipping offensive in the Mediterranean and, in particular, against Malta proved highly effective and was almost decisive in the central Mediterranean with the introduction of dive bombers from their Cretan and Sicilian bases. Operation Excess and the crippling of *Illustrious* featured in this phase.

III INTERLUDE (EARLY SUMMER, 1941)

Malta was given time to recuperate when Germany switched much of her air strength to the Balkans campaign and to the airborne invasion of Crete, and the transference of her Tenth Air Corps to the Russian front. Operation Barbarossa was launched in the summer of 1941.

IV ROYAL NAVY OFFENSIVE (JUNE–DECEMBER, 1941)
The Royal Navy's counter-offensive was foreshadowed by
Vice Admiral Sir James Somerville when his Force H
bombarded Genoa, Leghorn and Spezia earlier in the year
(in February), followed by the Halberd Operation. In
December the First Battle of Sirte was fought and an
Italian battle squadron was put to flight by a force of RN
cruisers and destroyers.

V SECOND GERMAN PHASE (JANUARY–JUNE, 1942)
This phase marked the re-launching of the offensive
against the island fortress and against the Royal Navy and
the merchant ships under its protection. The resulting air
battles and bombing raids seemed remorseless. Convoy
and fleet covering forces gave rise to the second Battle of
Sirte and the Operations named Harpoon and Vigorous in
June, 1942.

VI COMBINED ITALO-GERMAN PHASE
(SEPTEMBER–DECEMBER, 1942)
The battle surrounding Operation Pedestal in August,
1942, marked the culmination of the campaign embracing
Malta and the central Mediterranean. Pedestal did not
break the siege of the island as so many writers have
claimed, but it did lay the foundation for the next convoy,
and ensuing ones, to achieve that. Pedestal's escort forces
were the most powerful British fleet ever marshalled for a
supply convoy. The battle has been compared with the
Battle of Britain and described as the naval equivalent of
Alamein. Certainly the breaking of the siege was a
maritime victory of enormous proportions.

Operation Stoneage allowed the safe arrival of a
convoy to Malta in November, 1942, and this marked
"the final and effective relief of Malta".

The Italian fleet never came out again except to
surrender, while the land battles in North Africa also
brought that campaign to an end.

MEDITERRANEAN BACKGROUND: BATTLE OF CALABRIA

Nothing, nothing in the world, nothing that you may think of, or anyone else may tell you: no argument, however seductive, must leave you to abandon that naval supremacy on which the life of our country depends.

Winston S. Churchill
26 November 1918.

In the spring of 1940 Hitler embarked on his second trail of conquest and in a matter of nine months had rolled up the map of Europe. Poland, Holland, Belgium, Denmark, Norway, Luxembourg and France had all now been overwhelmed by German armies. Only the English Channel saved England from invasion. Hitler prevaricated. He baulked at the prospect; the sea seemed to mesmerize him. He turned to other plans and the invasion of England never materialized. It was a reprieve – and Britain took full advantage of it.

France signed an armistice on 21 June, humiliatingly in the very railway carriage at Compiègne where a defeated Germany had signed an armistice at the end of the First World War, the memory of which still rankled. France's humiliation was complete. Hitler pranced with joy.

Mussolini's opportunity came early in June, 1940. It had been clear to Britain during the past several months that Italy was building up to a declaration of war against Britain and France. Such an act would bring about a considerable change in the balance of power in the Mediterranean. An early opportunity needed to be taken to neutralize or even destroy the French Fleet. The British Mediterranean Fleet would have to be strengthened in order to match the Italian Fleet and British naval supremacy would need to be maintained in order to safeguard shipping, and, looking further afield, dispositions would need to be taken to protect communications with allies in the Indian Ocean and the Pacific.

Admiral Sir Andrew Cunningham, C-in-C of the Mediterranean Fleet, with his flag in HMS *Warspite* at this time, was feeling depressed. He recorded this anecdote: "I was walking up and down on the quarterdeck when I saw an admiral's barge approaching, and went to the gangway to receive the Vice-Admiral (D), John Tovey. A smiling figure ran up the gangway and greeted me with: 'Now I know we shall win the war, sir. We have no more allies.'" It was impossible, Cunningham commented, to feel downcast in the face of so much optimism.

Not only had Britain lost all her allies, she now gained another enemy; on 10 June Mussolini declared war on France and Britain.

It is apparent from the Table of Comparative Fleets that the Italian Fleet was markedly superior on paper to the British Mediterranean Fleet and the Gibraltar Squadron (which supplemented the French battle squadron in the Western Basin). Especially was this so in the destroyer, torpedo boat and submarine categories.

In the category of capital ships the British flagship *Warspite* (31,000 tons: 8 × 15" guns) had recently been modernized in an extensive refit. The other three battleships had been laid down either before or at the beginning of the First World War and had not been modernized. Two of the Italian battleships were just as old, while the other two had completed extensive refits comparable with *Warspite*'s. They had a main armament of ten 12.5" guns and a secondary armament of a dozen 4.7" or 5.3" guns. All had a designed speed of 27 knots, which was an advantage, the modern equivalent of the weather gauge in that

18

COMPARATIVE FLEETS 10 JUNE 1940

Ship	Royal Navy		Italy	Naval Bases	
	Alex	Gib			
Battleships	4	1	4* + 2†	Sardinia	Taranto
Aircraft Carriers	1	1	–	Naples	Messina
8" Cruisers	–	–	7‡	Augusta	Syracuse
6" Cruisers	8	1	12§	Palermo	Brindisi
Destroyers	20	9	57	Tripoli	Tobruk
Torpedo Boats	–	–	71		
Submarines	12		115		

Notes:

* *Cavour* } All four approximately 23,660
   Cesare } tons with 10 × 12.5" guns. Three
   Andrea Doria } WWI vintage. One modernised.
   Caio Duilio }

† *Vittorio Veneto* } Both due for completion in
   Littorio } August, 1940. 35,000 tons:
   } 9 × 15" guns.

‡ *Zara, Fiume, Gorinzia, Pola, Bolzano, Trieste, Trento*

§ *D'Aosta, Bande Nere, Attendolo, Abruzzi,
   Montecucclio, Garibaldi, Colleoni, De Guissano,
   De Barbiano, Savoia, Cordero, Cadorna*

they could choose when to chase or flee, to engage or not.

Captain Stephen Roskill, the official naval historian, provided the figures for the Table of Comparative Fleets and they differ in some respects from those appearing in Cunningham's autobiography. The C-in-C records that on 9 June, the day before Italy declared war, "the Fleet at Alexandria, on paper, was quite an imposing one." Cunningham named the capital ships as *Warspite*, *Malaya*, *Royal Sovereign* and *Ramillies*, the 7th Cruiser Squadron comprising *Orion*, *Neptune*, *Sydney* (RAN), *Liverpool* and *Gloucester*, the 3rd Cruiser Squadron comprising *Capetown*, *Caledon*, *Calypso* and *Delhi*.

The fleet destroyers Cunningham referred to a trifle disparagingly as "a mixed bag" of some twenty-five D, H, I, J, K and Tribal classes with the RAN's *Stuart* (commanded by the indomitable Australian Captain Hec Waller) and his four old V and Ws of the Australian Flotilla.

The carrier *Eagle* had recently joined the Fleet from the China Station, from which there also came a dozen P and O class submarines.

Within eighteen months these shortages were to bring the island of Malta to its knees and the navy to its lowest ebb. The disparity in numbers of destroyers was made worse by the realization that such warships as were available to the British Mediterranean Fleet would have to be shared between the Gibraltar Squadron and Cunningham's fleet at Alexandria.

Placed almost centrally between these two bases lay the island of Malta, 984 miles from Gibraltar and 822 miles from Alexandria. Malta was a strategically situated base of incalculable importance and had been so even in Nelson's day. Prime Minister Winston Churchill found a telling phrase:

"Since the days of Nelson Malta has stood a faithful British sentinel guarding the narrow and vital sea corridor through the Central Mediterranean. Its strategic importance was never higher than in this latest war. . . . The needs of the large armies we were building up in Egypt made the free passage of the Mediterranean for our convoys and the stopping of enemy reinforcements to Tripoli aims of the highest consequence. At the same time the new

20

air weapon struck a deadly blow not only at Malta but at the effective assertion of British sea power in these narrow waters."

The Prime Minister went on to explain that the superior air force of the enemy enabled them, by deterring our warships from acting fully in the Central Mediterranean except at much loss and hazard, to send troops and supplies to Tripoli.

It was at 7 pm on 10 June, 1940, the moment when Italy declared war on Britain, that Malta had thrust upon her an unwanted importance and responsibility of enormous proportions: on the one hand the British needed to sustain and maintain it as a vital thorn in the side of the Italo/German armies in North Africa; on the other hand the Axis partners needed to eliminate it to preserve their armies' fighting capability. Upon the result of this confrontation rested the outcome of the North African campaign, with staggering implications in other theatres of the war.

As soon as Admiral Cunningham received news of the declaration of war he brought his fleet to two hours' notice to steam. On the following day at 1 pm he followed the traditional combative naval policy of seeking out the enemy fleet and took his fleet to sea. Wearing his flag in *Warspite*, he led his battleships, screened by nine destroyers, from Alexandria. The AA cruisers *Caledon* and *Calypso* joined him at sea later that day. The plan was to steam north-west towards Crete, thence to a point about 80 miles south of Matapan, the cruisers sweeping west until dark, with an air search before them. The cruisers moved south to attack Italian patrols off Benghazi and Tobruk.

One of the aims of the evolution was to test the Regia Aeronautica. But Cunningham was disappointed and felt impelled to write to the First Sea Lord:

"I expected to spend most of the daylight hours beating off heavy bombing attacks on the fleet. Actually the battle squadron never saw a plane, though the best part of the day was spent 100 miles off the Libyan coast."

While Cunningham was trailing the fleet's coattails in an effort to induce the enemy to seek an encounter with the Royal Navy, two convoys were assembling in Valletta. One of the ships involved was the small 2,515-ton SS *Kirkland*, whose master, Captain Alexander Wilson, kept a diary of his ship's wartime record.

Kirkland put in to Valletta on 9 June. One of the first people Captain Wilson met on going ashore was his friend Captain Lancelot J. Brannigan, master of the *Zealand*. Their two ships earned them the nickname of the Siamese Twins for operating together so closely in the waters of the eastern Mediterranean over the next two years.

Even before the outbreak of war the British had been very active in the eastern Mediterranean. Ted Snowdon had been in Valletta some time before Captains Wilson and Brannigan. Snowdon has written:

"I was second mate on the Shell tanker *Trocas*. The Italian liner *Rodi* was in harbour. She had been intercepted off Haifa by ships of the Royal Navy exercising the ancient right of a belligerent of 'visit and search' for contraband: the *Rodi* was arrested and escorted to Valletta. Her passengers were Jewish refugees. When Valletta was abandoned as a naval repair base due to the bombing, the *Rodi* was loaded with naval spares and, with the *Knight of Malta* (the former Malta-Sicily ferry) and A.N. Other, formed the first east-bound convoy to attempt the passage to Alexandria. Half the crew of *Trocas*, including myself, manned the *Rodi* and after quite a 'heavy' passage made Alex without loss. We had no sooner anchored than the first bomb dropped on Alex, allegedly killing a camel."

Captain Wilson thought that Malta looked eerily deserted. He recorded:

"During the first day of war with Italy Malta was raided nine times, but the AA batteries, supported by HMS *Terror*, put up a wonderful defence, and the low-level bombing attacks soon came to an end and the Italians contented themselves with high-level attacks. During the first month I calculated that 83 raids were made on the island."

Captain Wilson recorded the number of merchant ships in harbour at this time. In addition to the *Kirkland* and the *Zealand* were the Egyptian passenger ship *El Nid*, the Malta ferry *Knight of Malta*, the Norwegian steamer *Novasli* and the tanker *Anglo-Saxon* with a broken tail-end shaft. Our naval forces brought in two Italian passenger vessels,one being the *Galilea*, with a prize crew on board. She left for Marseilles with Italian nationals and some corrupted Maltese whom the authorities thought should be removed from the island.

A week after the outbreak of war Captain Wilson was told that the authorities intended loading a quantity of HE and incendiary bombs aboard the *Kirkland*. About 200 tons of bombs were loaded, then a general cargo re-stowed on top.

Captain Wilson continued with his shipping movements:

"During the third week in June two more British ships arrived at Malta, the Brocklebank liner *Masirah* of 6,600 tons and the tramp steamer *Tweed*,both of them having successfully run the blockade from Tunisian ports. . . . About the 7th or 8th July all the masters were informed that the ships would leave the following day in two convoys. The slow ships *Masirah*, *Kirkland*, *Zealand*, *Tweed* and *Novasli* would leave at 3 pm and the fast ships *El Nid*, *Rodi* and *Knight of Malta* would leave at 10 pm. Although we did not know it at the time the first big naval operation in the Mediterranean was undertaken to cover our getaway."

Captain Wilson's report of the escape of two convoys from Malta to Alexandria gives a simplistic view of what became known as the Battle of Punto Silo or Calabria in which substantial British Forces giving cover to a wide range of merchant shipping movements not only ensured the safe arrival in port of the convoys of merchantmen but also brought about a skirmish of the opposing fleets. The prospects of an early clash of naval forces looked promising.

The C-in-C had led the fleet from its Alexandria base in three forces or groups:

FORCE A   Vice Admiral John C. Tovey (Second-in-Command and commanding Light Forces.) He flew his flag in the Leander class cruiser *Orion*

(7,100 tons: 8 × 6" guns and 8 × 4") with the cruisers *Neptune* (as *Orion*), *Sydney* (7,000 tons: 8 × 6" and 4" AA guns), *Gloucester* and *Liverpool* (both 10,000 tons: 12 × 6" and 4" guns).

FORCE B   The C-in-C flying his flag in *Warspite* (31,000 tons: 8 × 15" and 8 × 6" guns), screened by five destroyers.

FORCE C   Rear Admiral Pridham-Wippell with the two battleships *Royal Sovereign* (29,150 tons: 8 × 15" and 12 × 6" guns) and *Malaya* (as *Warspite*) with the aircraft carrier *Eagle* (22,600 tons) plus a destroyer screening flotilla.

All told twenty-one destroyers accompanied the Forces.

In addition two submarines, *Phoenix* and *Rorqual*, were allocated patrol areas in support of the operation.

These Forces set a north-westerly course with a speed of twenty knots. Throughout the whole of the second day they were subjected to Italian bomber attacks. These came from the Dodecanese in wave after wave. During the afternoon and first dog watches seven such attacks were directed at the flagship *Warspite*. About fifty heavy bombs were launched. Not one hit the target, although many were near misses. Similarly Force C escaped sinking or damage, although eighty bombs were released, only one hitting a target, that being *Gloucester*; she was struck by a bomb which caused considerable damage, killed eighteen of the crew and wounded another nine. The Captain was among those killed.

In the afternoon of 8 July a patrolling RAF flying boat signalled having sighted an enemy force of three battleships, six cruisers and seven destroyers about 100 miles from Benghazi, steering north. This fleet had been engaged in a similar operation to Cunningham, giving distant cover to the passage of a convoy.

Cunningham altered course to intercept the Italian force and to interpose his fleet between the enemy and his base.

At dawn on the 9th an RAF flying boat from Malta next sighted the enemy. Subsequent signals revealed another force comprising a large number of cruisers and destroyers in support.

At noon the Italian forces were about 90 miles to the westward of Cunningham's Fleet. A reconnaissance aircraft signalled that the enemy force comprised the two battleships *Cavour* and *Cesare*, twelve cruisers and twenty destroyers. The fleet was hugging the coast of Calabria. A clash seemed imminent.

A few minutes after 3 pm another force was sighted: six 8" gun cruisers with attendant destroyers steering east of north.

Minutes later the cruiser *Neptune* sighted the enemy to the westward and the privilege fell to Captain R.C. O'Conor, for the first time in the Mediterranean since the Napoleonic war, to make the signal: "ENEMY BATTLE FLEET IN SIGHT."

While the search for the enemy fleet proceeded, the *Kirkland* convoy was nearing Alexandria. Captain Wilson found himself the Commodore of the convoy. He reported:

"On the third day out everyone in the ship's company and in the convoy was heartened by the majestic sight of the C-in-C's flagship HMS *Warspite* and her flotilla of destroyers bearing down on the convoy. When a squadron of enemy aircraft approached from the direction of the Libyan coast a broadside of heavy AA guns from the flagship soon dispersed them. This proved to be the last attack of the day, and the only damage was shrapnel holes in the funnel of the *Novasli*."

Earlier in the day Captain Wilson had heard exchanges of gunfire which he thought might have been AA guns blazing away, but were undoubtedly the heavy broadsides of the 8" Italian cruisers engaging the British 6" cruisers.

Cunningham was determined to relieve the pressure on the cruisers and to engage the Italian battleships. To do so meant leaving the old and slow *Resolution*, while the faster *Warspite* sped to the sound of gunfire. *Warspite* got off a few salvoes of her 15" guns, discouraging the Italian cruisers which quite rightly turned away.

A feature of this skirmish should have been the use of the superior air squadrons aboard the *Eagle*. Captain A.R.M. Bridge launched a succession of flights of torpedo-carrying aircraft to find, fix and strike the enemy, but with no significant success.

This was one of the first times in naval history that a carrier had worked closely with a fleet in battle and the outcome was misleading.

After a brief lull the flagship and *Malaya* sighted and attacked the enemy battleships. *Warspite* succeeded in scoring a 15" shell hit on the *Cesare* at the incredible range of 26,000 yards (13 miles). This caused the enemy to turn away, understandably worried about the accuracy of the British gunnery. The Italians sought the sanctuary of a smoke screen. Whereupon the British cruisers and destroyers headed towards the smoke and towards the destroyers which appeared to launch torpedoes, but smoke now obscured the scene, firing became desultory and when the smoke had cleared there were no more enemy ships in sight.

The *Regia Aeronautica* marshalled its forces and launched a strike against the British battle fleet, the Italians realizing that they had a chance to disable some British ships, close by the shore and some distance from their home bases. Between 4.40 and 7.12 pm at least nine air strikes took place, upwards of one hundred aircraft being involved. All were fought off with barrages of AA fire while the British forces steamed close to the coast in a vain hope that the enemy might resume the engagement, but when Calabria came into sight Cunningham realized that the ships would put in to Messina. Further, *Resolution* was too slow to keep her place in the line and *Malaya* never got into range. The Italians wasted an opportunity to stand and fight with superior fire power.

Cunningham altered course to the south-westward to open the land, setting course for Malta at 9.15 pm. Finally, on arriving back at Alexandria, he was to find that the *Kirkland* convoy had arrived safely despite the heavy bombing. The navy could claim to have done its duty; the convoys had been fought through.

It had been a long-running skirmish hardly deserving of the title battle. Captain Roskill summarized it fairly:

"The Action off Calabria probably helped establish the ascendancy over the Italian surface forces which was to be so marked a feature of the naval campaign in the Mediterranean and was ultimately to reduce their theoretically powerful fleet to virtual impotence. As regards the air attacks, the Italian high-level raids were courageously carried out and sometimes unpleasantly accurate in aim."

Over a period of six days at the end of August, 1940, a convoy operating under the code-name Hats assembled in Alexandria. Naval reinforcements involving *Illustrious* and *Valiant* were passed from Gibraltar to Alexandria, the whole length of the Mediterranean. The handover from the western to the eastern fleet took place at the rendezvous point off Pantellaria.

While these naval movements were in train, advantage was taken to pass the first convoy to Malta from Alexandria. It was a small convoy of only three ships – *Cornwall*, *Volo* and the Royal Fleet Auxiliary *Plumleaf*. The convoy left Alexandria on 29 August, accompanied by a close escort of the fleet destroyers *Jervis* and *Juno*, plus the two old D class destroyers *Dainty* and *Diamond*. Old they may have been, but *Dainty* had already won acclaim by sinking two Italian U-boats. The first was the *Linzzi*, which was depth-charged to destruction on 27 June while patrolling off Crete, assisted by HMS *Ilex*. The second sinking occurred just two days later when the same two destroyers sank the Italian *Uebi Scebeli*.

The three ships of the convoy were subjected to air attacks, but they arrived safely, apart from the freighter *Cornwall*. She seemed to be singled out by a flight of five S 79 bombers. She was struck three times and was severely damaged. Both her guns were destroyed, her steering gear was totally disabled, her wireless put out of action, she was set ablaze aft and holed above the waterline.

Captain F.C. Pretty, master of the *Cornwall*, was still trying desperately to save the ship and get the damage under control when a magazine blew up with a thunderous roar and the fires spread. The master found that he could steer the ship with main engines, and without the rudder. He managed to get her on course again while ready-use ammunition exploded dangerously as the fires were got under control. The leaks were plugged and stopped, a task made more difficult by the heavy seas that were now running. But the ship managed to keep afloat and was salved by the tugs *Jaunty* and *Ancient* who towed her into harbour. Even then it was not over: an Italian E-boat was sighted, but she was driven off swiftly by patrol vessels.

Cornwall's survival was only achieved by a fine feat of seamanship. Captain Pretty had shown much courage. "I wish to report," he later declared in simple tribute, "that every member of the ship's company did their best under trying conditions."

Captain Mack, Senior Officer of the escorts, was more effusive: "The keeping of an accurate course with no steering at all constitutes . . . a most seamanlike performance."

It is calculated that this small convoy discharged about 40,000 tons of cargo.

It is a pity that the story of the *Cornwall* and her dedicated master did not end on a happier note. The ship was in dock for extensive repairs for six months. Captain Pretty was not allowed to await completion of the repairs. He was re-assigned to the captaincy of a brand new ship, the *Nottingham*. Six days out on her maiden voyage she was torpedoed and sank with all hands.

The fleet returned to Alexandria after attacks on two targets in the Dodecanese by aircraft from *Illustrious* and *Eagle*. These two small strikes were the overture to larger battles to come. An earlier attempt to assist Malta by delivering Spitfires and Hurricanes came when a dozen Hurricanes were flown off the flight deck of the old carrier *Argus*, based at Gibraltar. She accompanied convoys to Malta and enjoyed heavy escort. The exercise proved successful in transporting the aircraft to a flying-off position within range of the island.

But this first air-ferry experience in August, 1940, was deceptive. Twelve Hurricanes were flown off *Argus* at a point near Sardinia to relieve Faith, Hope and Charity, the three remaining Gladiator bi-planes. By October only one Gladiator and four Hurricanes were left. The decision was taken to repeat the air ferry in November. Admiral Somerville commanded Operation White with Force H, comprising *Renown* and *Ark Royal*, *Argus*, three cruisers and seven destroyers. The snail-paced *Argus* carried her cargo of a dozen fighters. Somerville flew his flag in *Renown*, slow, lightly armoured and no match for a modernized Italian battleship. *Ark Royal* gave some substance to the Force but even she had no armoured flight deck.

By sunset on 15 November matters were beginning to build up unfavourably. Somerville received intelligence of Italian ships concentrating south of Naples, a force comprising a battleship, seven cruisers and an unknown number of destroyers. By midday on the 16th the weather had deteriorated and was too bad for flying off the relief aircraft. In his subsequent Report Somerville explained:

> "The Italians were probably aware of our departure from Gibraltar. They might well consider engaging Force H with their superior forces in the hope of balancing record losses at Taranto."

He was anxious to fly off the twelve Hurricanes and two Skuas from a position as far west as weather and prudence would permit. He reported that Captain Rushbrooke of the *Argus* informed him that:

> "With the wind as at present the Hurricanes could be flown off from Latitude 27° 40' N, Longitude and 6° 40' E. . . . I decided to accept this as the flying off position."

This position was, in fact, about 40 miles west of the original one and it still gave the Hurricanes an acceptable margin of safety – something of the order of 100 miles. There was the added bonus of a following wind.

Force H arrived at the flying-off position at 5.45 am. Dawn came. The first sub-flight of Hurricanes and a Skua (commanded by Flying Officer J.A.F. Maclachlan DFC) started engines and at 6.15 the first aircraft flew off. Then the second sub-flight took off.

It soon became apparent that the meteorological and sea conditions were changing, and in particular the following wind had veered to almost dead ahead at 11 knots, and visibility, thickening sea mist and cloud intensity all worsened. In these conditions finding Malta would be difficult, but worse still was the fear of running out of fuel. The first casualty occurred 45 miles short of Malta. The first Hurricane spiralled out of control into the sea. Miraculously a Sunderland aircraft was guided to the surviving pilot. It landed on the sea and hauled him aboard.

The next pilot was less fortunate. He ditched his aircraft, but nothing was seen or heard of him again. Both the Sunderland and the Skua, aided by DF and radio, led the remaining aircraft to Luqa airfield. A few more minutes and all the fighters would have crashed through lack of fuel. As it was one Hurricane spluttered to a stop even before it had taxied clear of the runway. It had been a close-run thing.

The second sub-flight and its Skua also fell prey to the poor visibility, the mist, the cloud conditions and some faulty radio receivers. One by one the Hurricanes fell helplessly into the sea as their fuel dried up. An escorting bomber sent out to meet the flight never made contact. Last to crash was the Skua which was shot down by AA batteries and fell on to the Sicilian shore, 75 miles off course.

Of the original fourteen aircraft which flew off that morning nine, plus their pilots and observers, were lost.

Admiral Somerville has been criticized for excessive caution in his handling of this incident. Churchill was more accommodating: "Never again were the margins cut so fine, and though many similar operations took place in the future never did a catastrophe recur." He was right. The good to emerge from this tragic incident was the fact that lessons were learned, errors not repeated, aircrew protected and Malta sustained. Operation White's sacrifice had not been in vain.

During a period of fifteen months 333 Hurricanes arrived in Malta by this route. Actually, 361 were despatched, with twenty-eight failing to reach their destinations for one reason or another, a loss rate of about 8%. Tribute should be paid to these young pilots. For each one it was his first take off from a carrier's flight deck.

Spitfires, too, were delivered. Sixty were delivered in one such operation later in the war when the USS *Wasp* and HMS

Eagle together reinforced the island. All told 367 Spitfires were delivered. Their contribution to the island's final victory is incalculable.

Taking off from a moving flight deck for the first time was a complicated manoeuvre and a daunting experience. Ex-RAF serviceman S. Saggers tells of the technique required to fly off Spitfires:

> "Normally when checking Spitfire engines when they are tested at full revs on the ground, they have the brakes on, chocks in front of the wheels, and two erks [aircraftmen] laying on the tail planes to stop the tail from lifting. The wind from the props was so great that you were held across the tail plane whether you liked it or not. As this was warm air from the engine it was not too uncomfortable, unlike the Hurricane which stayed cold."

When taking off from a carrier the same procedure was gone through except that at a given signal the chocks were removed, the pilot released the brake and the airmen on the tail planes had to drop off onto the deck and lie flat so that the tail lifted and passed over them. Saggers added:

> "It wasn't easy against all that pressure, but we all managed except one small man, Jock, who was carried along the deck for some distance before he managed to fall off, unhurt except for a bruised bottom. On one occasion when the AA guns were going strong the airman with the radio which he had on deck in contact with the pilots was shocked when a piece of shrapnel hit it. 'Bloody hell!' he shouted, and promptly took off his helmet and held it protectively over the radio!"

Ron Williams also had experience of flying off RAF fighter aircraft from a carrier. He recalls two convoys when he served in the carrier *Furious* and on both occasions Spitfires were flown off:

> "They were engaged almost immediately they landed in Malta. The casualties were heavy because the pilots lacked combat experience. Their lives and their aircraft were wasted."

31

Williams also recalls the unpleasant air pollution aboard *Furious* which had to be endured:

"High-speed steaming with the flight deck funnel shut caused the inside of the entire ship to be contaminated with fumes and smut. High-speed steaming also required that the turbines took all the freshwater that could be condensed and water was severely rationed below decks."

Williams concluded on a more thoughtful note:

"It is amazing that the Royal Navy was able to find so many ships to protect the convoys and I think today, if the general public knew of the enormous casualties, they would find it difficult to understand the sacrifices made to support that little island."

STRIKE AT TARANTO:
BATTLE OF SPARTIVENTO

I again realize how much we owed to the magnificent spirit of our officers and men. Their enthusiasm and devotion were beyond all praise. Many times I had reason to thank the system and tradition that produced such fine seamen. No Commander-in-Chief ever had better subordinates. Never was the country better served ... we were able to forge a weapon that was as bright and as sharp as highly tempered steel.

Admiral Sir Andrew B. Cunningham,
C-in-C Mediterranean Fleet

Early in 1940 Admiral Cunningham led the Mediterranean Fleet to sea from Alexandria to cover a convoy operation involving the transportation of nearly 2,000 troops for Malta. They were embarked in the cruisers *Liverpool* and *Gloucester*. The Fleet's "First Eleven" (*Warspite*, *Valiant* and *Illustrious*), plus a cruiser squadron, were screened by a flotilla of destroyers.

A reconnaissance aircraft signalled having sighted an Italian battle squadron about 120 miles to the north. It comprised four battleships of which two were the modern vessels *Vittorio Veneto* and *Littorio*, both of 35,000 tons with nine 15" guns.

Cunningham was faced with the option of altering course to intercept the enemy squadron and bring it to battle or to give priority to the landing of the near-2,000 men aboard the cruisers at Malta.

The enemy ships had a numerical advantage, as well as an advantage in speed and fire power. It was also unlikely that the slower British force could intercept the Italians anyway. The incomparable asset of an aircraft carrier with squadrons of aircraft was not thought to outweigh the other factors. Thus the prospect of engaging four modernized or modern battleships was not an attractive one. To pursue them would mean jeopardizing the troops embarked in the cruisers. It could prove disastrous. So Cunningham decided that the safety of the troops, plus Malta's need for them, were his prime objectives and maintained a course for Malta. The Italian ships continued heading for Taranto, possibly unaware of the nearness of the British battle squadron.

The presence of these four battleships helps illustrate the enormous strategical advantage that Mussolini possessed, that of 'a fleet in being', and as long as he had it he could influence the balance of naval and even military power in the Mediterranean to a disproportionate extent.

It was a constant burden for Cunningham and his staff, trying to redress this imbalance either by increasing his naval and air strengths or by reducing the effectiveness of the enemy's capabilities. Simply containing enemy capital ships put a huge strain on a fleet's demands, as was evidenced by the German navy and its ability to influence seriously the dispositions of ships, squadrons and even fleets in striving to contain *Bismarck*, *Tirpitz* and *Scharnhorst*.

By adroit use of his superiority in capital ships Mussolini could exercise power such as was wielded by Hitler and his admirals, at which the German navy was adept.

It had been a long-cherished plan of Cunningham's to use his torpedo bombers to attack the Italian battle fleet in its base at Taranto and at a blow reduce the enemy's effectiveness. But he had been hampered by inadequate resources of ships, aircraft and trained personnel. A successful attack on Taranto, Cunningham knew, would bring about a drastic change in that imbalance.

The recent transfer of the carrier *Illustrious* and the battleship

Valiant to the Mediterranean Fleet brought nearer to actuality a projected raid on Taranto.

The Prime Minister, with his years of long interest in the Admiralty and the Royal Navy, kept a close eye on all events in the Mediterranean and he made clear his views to Cunningham in a prodding letter following the reinforcement of the Mediterranean Fleet with *Illustrious* and *Valiant*:

"I congratulate you upon the success of the recent operation in the Central and Eastern Mediterranean and upon the accession to your fleet of two of our finest units, with other valuable vessels. . . . It is of high importance to strike the Italians this autumn."

Such a strike on the fleet base at Taranto in the heel of Italy was already being planned. It was an ambitious operation entailing a nighttime attack by squadrons of aircraft from *Illustrious* and *Eagle* with torpedoes and bombs upon major targets of capital ships lying at anchor or at their moorings. It would be launched in the face of strong defences: the main units lay behind protective anti-torpedo netting, extensive AA batteries were well-sighted and a balloon barrage added to the pilots' problems.

11 November was expected to provide a clear moonlit night, ideal for the attack.

Supermarina, Italy's Admiralty, was caught by surprise, even though it was aware that something was afoot. Reconnaissance reports indicated much naval activity, but most of the intelligence was wrongly or poorly interpreted.

Commander Bragadin, then serving at *Supermarina*, reported later that on 9 November, two days before the strike,

"It was learned that the Gibraltar force, Force H, had reversed course, in keeping with the now classic British operational procedure. As far as the eastern squadron of the Mediterranean Fleet was concerned, the reconnaissance service gave various and conflicting reports. By that evening *Supermarina* could only conclude in a general way that the British Fleet must have been about 300 miles from Taranto and on its way to Alexandria at approximately 1500 that afternoon."

35

This was a gross error of judgement.

In addition to all this activity, it was known that *Barham* and her two cruiser consorts, and the *Ramillies*, now accompanied by the AA cruiser *Coventry*, were giving cover to a convoy. *Supermarina* ordered an extra nine U-boats to the general area, plus a number of MAS boats, and bomber forces were despatched; but without true knowledge of the meaning of all the movements *Supermarina* only brought her fleet to two hours' notice to steam, while it remained inside Taranto's protective defences.

While all this planning was in progress another routine but complicated operation was launched in the eastern basin in October, code-named Operation MB-6. It entailed the escorting of Convoy MF-3 from Alexandria to Malta, which consisted of the *Clan Ferguson*, *Clan Macaulay*, *Lanarkshire* and *Mermon*. It departed Port Said and arrived safely after a passage of three days on 11 October.

A second mini-convoy of two empty ships, the RFA *Plumleaf* and the *Volo*, were escorted back to Port Said from Malta, arriving safely on 15 October.

As four Italian battleships had been sighted at sea a month before, Cunningham decided to take his whole fleet to sea to afford both close and distant cover for these two convoys. The destroyer *Imperial* struck a mine and was severely damaged, and on the first night out (11–12 October) the cruiser *Ajax* (Captain E.D.B. McCarthy), which was in the line of cruisers spread to the westward, encountered an Italian flotilla. In a spirited, high-speed action in bright moonlight and with ranges down to 4,000 yards, *Ajax* sank two destroyers and damaged a third, setting her on fire. Two others were engaged, but escaped behind a smoke screen. *Ajax* herself suffered seven shell hits with severe damage to her bridge and radar equipment.

At daylight a Sunderland flying boat on reconnaissance sighted the damaged destroyer in tow of a consort. The *Illustrious* flew off three aircraft armed with torpedoes, while the cruiser *York* was despatched to finish off the damaged ship. When the aircraft attacked the tow was slipped and the towing destroyer fled at high speed. When *York* appeared on the scene the badly damaged *Artigliere* waved sheets in token of surrender.

Captain R.H. Portal of *York* was in no mood to transfer the crew as captives to his cruiser in case of retaliation by the *Regia Aeronautica*, but he released floats, persuaded the crew to abandon ship, then opened fire on the destroyer, which blew up with an enormous column of black smoke and sank rapidly.

Admiral Cunningham signalled the *Supermarina* in plain language giving the position of the survivors, an action for which he was chided by the Admiralty: "It might be well to exclude . . . reference to gallantry of the enemy or compromising our fleet's position for the benefit of the enemy."

Before the fleet returned to its moorings in Alexandria it was subjected to an attack by torpedo aircraft. The battleships put up a tremendous barrage which deterred the pilots. However, the *Liverpool* was struck by a torpedo which at first seemed to have caused little damage in the bows, but a fire started and soon gained control, spreading to the petrol tank which exploded, taking with it part of the foremost magazine, causing extensive damage to the foc's'le up to the bridge structure and leaving the bows hanging.

Orion went to her aid to try to secure a tow aft, but the bows tended to act as a rudder, or a huge drogue. After 100 miles or so the tow parted. A new one was rigged in the course of which the damaged bows broke away. Towing from the stern became easier and the crippled cruiser reached Alexandria safely.

The scene was now set for the pre-emptive strike against the enemy fleet in its protective anchorage. Crews from squadrons of aircraft in both carriers, *Illustrious* and *Eagle*, had practised evolutions with their aircraft, studied plans and maps, familiarizing themselves as far as possible with the positions of enemy defences, with their own routes of approach, and memorizing the Italian fleet anchorages and moorings.

Then came a grave setback and a terrible disappointment to the pilots and aircrews of the *Eagle*, as well as to the whole ship's company. The 22-year-old carrier, still suffering from the shaking by near misses in the Battle of Calabria a few weeks before, was not fully seaworthy and was therefore unable to take part in the raid. To ameliorate this disappointment some of the aircrews and aircraft were cannibalized into two striking forces. The first would comprise twelve aircraft and the second nine – squadrons 813, 815, 819 and 824.

At 1800 *Illustrious* reached the point where she detached herself from the C-in-C's *Warspite*. The carrier's cruisers which would accompany her took up station, flanking her with *Gloucester*, *Berwick*, *Glasgow* and *York*, plus four destroyers. Conditions for the attacks were excellent – sea, wind, weather and the promise of moonlight.

All six Italian battleships were shown by reconnaissance pictures to be in harbour, plus scores of other naval vessels. Cunningham observed with satisfaction: "So all the pheasants had gone home to roost."

The Admiral in charge at Taranto was Arturo Riccardi. He was, of course, aware of the possibility of an air raid on the harbour and especially of a torpedo attack in the broad sweep of the outer harbour, the Mar Grande, but believed he would get adequate warning of the approach of attacking aircraft and of an aircraft carrier, giving time to alert the defences.

The plan – its originator and planner was Rear Admiral Lyster – had been carefully prepared. It would take the Carrier Force to a point 270 miles from Kabbo Point, Cephalonia, passing through it at 2000 on 11 November. An hour later the second strike would be launched. It was planned that the carrier would begin recovery of the first aircraft at about 0100 on the 12th. Such was the broad outline of the plan.

All twelve aircraft of the first flight were flown off without mishap, except for one late starter. The pilot of the last of the torpedo-carrying aircraft of the first flight was Lieutenant M.R. Maund. His Observer was Sub-Lieutenant (A) W.A. Bull. Maund was able to record his experience in a dramatic diary of the raid. He remembered in particular the bitter cold.

"This thing is beyond a joke. . . . We are now at 1,000 feet over a neat residential quarter of the town. . . . Here is the main road that connects the district with the main town. . . . I open the throttle wide and head for the north of the Mar Piccolo . . . then it is as if

38

all hell comes tumbling in on top of us. It must have been the fire of the cruisers and the canal batteries – leaving only two things in my mind, the line of approach to the dropping position and a wild desire to escape the effects of this deadly hailstorm."

So low did Maund fly that he almost struck a chimney, barely skimmed the water in the outer harbour, twisted and turned to avoid merchant ships, almost hit a destroyer's foc's'le and could smell the acrid smell of tracer fire. It seemed unbelievable that he could get away from the maelstrom. Then with a shock he realized he was clear of the worst of it, that the sea meant safety and he zig-zagged away from danger. Unfortunately his was an unsuccessful attack, although his torpedo exploded on hitting the bottom below *Littorio*'s starboard quarter.

The second strike was launched at 2120. *Illustrious* turned into wind and flew off nine aircraft led by Lieutenant-Commander J.W Hale of 819 Squadron, with Lieutenant G.A. Carline as his observer. Like the first strike Hale encountered intense AA gunfire and found it difficult to identify his target, which was also the *Littorio*. From a height of only 30 feet he launched his torpedo at a distance of 700 yards. As the aircraft jerked upwards on release of the torpedo Hale banked to starboard, narrowly missed a balloon cable and managed to get away safely.

Lieutenant (A) C.S.E. Lea (pilot) and Sub-Lieutenant P.D. Jones (observer) selected a battleship as the target and released the torpedo at a range of about 800 yards. It struck the *Caio Duilio* on her starboard side abreast B turret.

Lea manoeuvred his aircraft past a fishing boat's mast, flew between the cruisers *Zara* and *Fiume* and escaped over the island of San Pietro.

Lieutenant F.M.A. Torrens-Spence (pilot) and Lieutenant A.W.F. Sutton (observer) had a narrow escape while skimming over the water; their aircraft's wheels actually struck the water, but Torrens-Spence managed to regain control, passed between two balloon cables and fled away over the harbour.

Another narrow escape was experienced by Lieutenant (A) J.W.G. Walham (pilot) and Lieutenant P. Humphreys (observer). Their Swordfish was damaged in their approach; they found themselves under heavy fire while scrutinizing four enemy battleships with no clear firing position for any of them. Walham selected the *Vittorio Veneto* and launched his torpedo at a range of about 500 yards, striking the battleship on her port quarter.

Aboard the carrier and in the flagship it was a time of agonizing suspense. *Illustrious* reached the recovery position at 0100 and turned into wind. Twelve minutes later the radar operator began to receive the blips on his screen signifying the safe return of the first flight, all except their leader. It seemed incredible that only one casualty should have been suffered considering the intensity of the opposition. By 0250 it was all over, the aircraft had been recovered except the Swordfish of Lieutenant G.W. Bayley (pilot) and Lieutenant H.J. Slaughter (observer) which failed to return.

Admiral Riccardi received the final count on the night's stupefying attack with despair. The results were as follows:

Battleship *Littorio*: 3 torpedo hits:

(1) Starboard bow: hole 49' × 32' abreast No. 1 6" gun turret.

(2) Port quarter: abreast tiller flat: hole 23' × 5'.

(3) Starboard side forward of first hit; hole 40' × 30' in bottom.

(4) A large dent marked a torpedo hit which failed to explode. Ship down by the bows and partly awash.

Battleship *Caio Duilio*:1 torpedo hit:

(1) Starboard side, low down abreast No. 1 5.25" gun mounting. 1 and 2 magazines flooded. Ship beached.

Battleship *Conte di Cavour*: 1 torpedo hit:

(1) Port bow under foremost turret. Hole 40' × 27'. Most seriously damaged of all ships. Adjacent compartments flooded, plus two fuel tanks. She was towed to shallow

waters and beached. The whole of her upper deck became awash.

Cruiser *Trento*: Hit by a bomb which penetrated the deck and side plating but failed to explode. Considerable blast damage.

Destroyers *Libiccio* and *Pessagno*: both near-missed but suffered considerable damage.

A seaplane hangar was burnt down and many other shore installations were seriously damaged.

Illustrious steamed at high speed to rejoin the rest of the fleet. *Warspite* flew the traditional flag hoist for a victorious flag officer with typical British understatement: "ILLUSTRIOUS – MANOEUVRE WELL EXECUTED".

The case for a repeat operation the following night fell flat when weather and sea forecasts indicated a deterioration.

Cunningham referred to the attack in his Report as "admirably planned and the determined manner in which it was carried out reflects the highest credit on all concerned".

The Prime Minister told the House, "The result affects decisively the balance of naval power in the Mediterranean and also carries with it reactions upon the naval situation in every quarter of the globe."

The Times caught the nation's mood and reaction:

"The congratulations and the gratitude of the nation are due in their fullest measure to the Fleet Air Arm, who have won a great victory . . . and to Sir Andrew Cunningham who is the first flag officer to handle the new weapon on such a scale and has used it triumphantly."

Count Ciano, Mussolini's Foreign Secretary, referred in his diary to "a black day" and recorded how seemingly disinterested Mussolini was at the awesome defeat. "I thought I would find the Duce downhearted. Instead he took the blow quite well and doesn't for the moment seem to have fully realized the gravity."

One of the immediate results of the raid was a dispersal of the remainder of Italy's fleet away from Taranto to Naples and La Spezia, conceding mastery of the central Mediterranean to the Royal Navy. Although the Italians could still operate in the central waters – for example, by cutting south through the Straits of Messina – they were brought under closer observation by aircraft on reconnaissance from Malta.

Cunningham expressed it clearly: the Taranto raid reduced, if it did not altogether abolish, the threat of the enemy fleet interfering with our never-ending succession of convoys to Greece and Crete. The raid also enabled our battleship strength in the Eastern Mediterranean to be reduced. And this had the knock-on effect of bringing relief to the hard-pressed destroyer flotillas as fewer were now required as an anti-U-boat screen for the smaller battle fleet.

Simultaneous with the Taranto strike was another operation carried out by the Second-in-Command, Mediterranean, Vice Admiral Pridham-Wippell, with his flag in *Orion*. He had with him in company the cruisers *Sydney* (RAN), *Ajax* (one of the victors of the Battle of the River Plate,) and the two Tribal class destroyers *Nubian* and *Mohawk*. These ships were designated Force X. Pridham-Wippell's orders were to detach Force X from the fleet covering the *Illustrious* raid and act as a diversionary squadron by raiding into the Straits of Otranto and to interrupt, if only temporarily, Italian communications in the area, especially the nightly convoy across the Adriatic from Otranto, Brindisi and Bari.

Force X passed the island of Corfu heading north at high speed. Conditions were ideal. The sea was calm, with barely any wind, desultory cloud cover and intermittent bright moonlight.

It was 0100 on the 12th (the first strike aircraft were about to be recovered by *Illustrious* after their raid) when Pridham-Wippell decided he had taken his force to the prudent limit of its northerly patrol and reversed course. *Mohawk*, (Commander J.W. Eaton) positioned on the port bow of *Orion*, sighted darkened ships off Valona, bearing about 120° at a range of about 8 miles.

The enemy convoy which had been sighted comprised four

merchant ships escorted by the torpedo boat *Nicola Fabrizi* of 650 tons (4×4" guns), accompanied by a sizable auxiliary vessel, the *Ramb III*, of 3,367 tons. The convoy was heading for Brindisi. It comprised the following: *Catalani* (2,429 tons), *Capo Vado* (4,391 tons), *Premuda* (4,427 tons) and *Antonio Locatelli* (5,691 tons).

As soon as *Mohawk* sighted the convoy she altered course and increased speed to 25 knots, accompanied by *Nubian*. She took the MTB as her target, opened fire at 0125 and hit the enemy at a range of 4,000 yards with her fourth salvo. The MTB made smoke.

Orion soon spotted the ships, trained her 6" guns on the third in line and her secondary 4" guns on the MTB. The merchant ship met a swift end, bursting into flames and then taking a torpedo hit. She was seen to sink. *Orion* shifted fire to the fourth in line, repeatedly hitting her and setting her ablaze. She was abandoned, as could clearly be seen in the brightness of the star shells. She, too, was torpedoed and was seen to sink.

Ajax sighted the convoy at 0125 and fired at the MTB which still managed to escape total destruction in the smoke. *Ajax* shifted target to a merchant ship, set it ablaze and then tackled the fourth ship. She was struck by two salvoes and appeared to be settling. A torpedo fired at her missed.

The *Sydney*, the last in line, according to her log sighted the ships at 0125, the same time as *Ajax*. She opened fire on the first merchant ship, but as she seemed to be well ablaze the cruiser shifted target to the second which managed to turn away, disappearing into the maelstrom of shell bursts.

The hapless MTB still did not sink and still tried desperately to make smoke to protect her charges. She came in for more attention from *Sydney*, but in all the confusion of the skirmish she made good her escape. *Sydney* herself was lucky to avoid severe damage when a torpedo passed under her at 0140. She engaged another ship, which was already ablaze and lying stopped, and fired two torpedoes at another.

Nubian and *Mohawk* had not been idle. Both had been engaging targets as they presented themselves in this confusing action.

At 0158, just thirty-eight minutes after *Mohawk*'s first sighting, Pridham-Wippell broke off the action, adopted a course of 166° and a speed of 28 knots to clear the area and distance Force X from any enemy forces by daylight.

It was subsequently learned that all four ships sank. The gallant MTB managed to reach port, although seriously damaged. *Ramb III* managed to escape undamaged. Cunningham was delighted by this success, in addition to the Taranto victory. He wrote in his Report:

> "The raid was a boldly executed operation into narrow waters where the enemy might well have been expecting to be encountered in force. It succeeded in doing considerable damage to the enemy and had a considerable moral effect."

The fleet returned to Alexandria with a feeling of great elation.

The Taranto attack had established that less than two dozen old aircraft could reassert Britain's maritime power in the central and eastern waters of the Mediterranean in dramatic fashion. The raid was to influence modern warfare in the decades to come.

While the bulk of activity in the Mediterranean at this time, November, 1940, was dominated by the Taranto enterprise and its associated fleet movements, convoys to and from Malta were alive with activity. While the Raid was in progress the opportunity was taken to pass Convoy MW-3 west-bound from Port Said to Malta, arriving at its destination on 9 November. The convoy comprised the merchant ships *Devis*, *Rodi*, *Volo*, *Waiwera* and the RFA *Plumleaf*.

On the 10th a convoy departed Malta for Port Said: It comprised *Clan Ferguson*, *Clan Macaulay*, *Lanarkshire* and *Mermon*.

With the strength of the Italian navy seriously depleted, it was considered safe to return *Ramillies* to Gibraltar. Accordingly the Mediterranean Fleet acted as escort as far as Pantelleria (Operation M-9). Force H from Gibraltar met *Ramillies* off Bizerta (Operation Collar) and carried on to Gibraltar.

At the end of November further developments occurred. A first attempt to pass a convoy direct from Gibraltar to Alexandria was undertaken. It was a fast convoy of just three ships: *Clan Forbes* and *Clan Fraser* (both destined for Malta) and *New Zealand Star* (bound for Alexandria). Some 1,400 soldiers and airmen were embarked in the cruisers *Manchester* and *Southampton* for passage right through to Egypt. Rear-Admiral L.E. Holland flew his flag in the *Manchester*.

The plan was for Force H, with *Renown* wearing Somerville's flag, with the carrier *Ark Royal*, the cruisers *Sheffield*, *Despatch* and nine destroyers, to accompany the convoy from Gibraltar. A significant proportion of Cunningham's fleet – the battleship *Ramillies*, the 10,000-ton cruiser *Berwick*, the 6" gun cruiser *Newcastle*, the AA cruiser *Coventry* and five destroyers – would meet Somerville's Force H in a position to the south of Sardinia. It was planned that Force H, the convoy and its escort, plus the detached squadron from Alexandria, would then keep company to a position between Sicily and Cape Bon. Force H with *Ramillies*, *Berwick* and *Newcastle* (all from Alexandria) would then steam for Gibraltar. The convoy and its escort would pass to the south of Malta to meet the remainder of the Mediterranean Fleet the next day.

Such were the intentions, and their complexity gives an indication of the closely detailed planning involved in the passage of even a relatively small convoy.

The three merchantmen duly passed through the Straits of Gibraltar from the Atlantic on the night of 24/25 November and were met safely by Force H the next morning. All went well till the morning of 27 November. By then *Ramillies* and her cruiser consorts had passed westward of the Narrows, but had not yet met Force H.

At 6.30 am on 27 November a Sunderland flying boat sighted an enemy squadron off Cape Spartivento, which gave its name to the ensuing battle. The force was steaming some 70 miles to the north-east of Force H and the convoy. This was confirmed by an aircraft from *Ark Royal*.

In fact the Italian force had quit its Naples and Messina bases. It comprised the battleships *Vittorio Veneto* and *Giulio*

Cesare, seven 8" gun cruisers and sixteen destroyers.

Thus, this battle squadron was superior to Somerville's Force H before he joined the ships from Alexandria (which were then about 50 miles away to the east) and would still enjoy a superiority even after the junction.

Somerville's prime duty was the safe passage of the convoy, but he also knew that this safety would best be achieved by an offensive manoeuvre. Accordingly at 11.30 am he ordered Rear-Admiral Holland's cruisers in the van to lead his squadron at speed towards the enemy.

Ramillies and her consorts from Alexandria joined Force H, but the flagship *Renown*'s slow speed hampered rather than helped the situation. Nevertheless, at 12.20 the most westerly of the Italian cruisers and the RN cruiser lines joined action. The Italian ships immediately fell back under a smoke screen and came under the protection of their capital ships.

Renown engaged with her main armament for a few minutes, but the Italian force continued to withdraw at speed to the northeast. The *Berwick* was struck by one shell but was not seriously damaged.

The Italian C-in-C, Admiral Campini, in the flagship *Vittorio Venito*, was unaware of the relative strengths of the opposing squadron, and *Supermarina*'s standing order made it clear that no engagement should take place if faced by a superior force. He feared, too, the danger of an air attack from *Ark Royal*. At 12.15 he ordered his cruisers not to become involved in a battle.

He was right to be worried about possible air attacks. At 11.30 am *Ark Royal* had got away eleven aircraft of 810 Squadron to strike at the battleships. They attacked at about 12.40 and claimed a hit, though in fact none was scored.

Meanwhile at 1 pm the enemy battle squadron was sighted ahead of Holland's cruisers and fire was opened. Holland retired to the safety of *Ramillies*' guns, then gave chase again as the Italian ships turned away to the north-east. By 1.15 the skirmish was virtually over.

Somerville's forces were getting uncomfortably close to the enemy shore and further pursuit seemed unrewarding. In the circumstances he abandoned the chase and all ships rejoined the convoy.

But it was not all over. At about 1.42 Somerville received a report of a damaged cruiser 10 miles off the Sardinian cost. He ordered *Ark Royal* to attack her. Accordingly a strike force flew off. Seven dive bombers were allocated to attack the supposedly damaged cruiser and nine torpedo aircraft targetted the battleships. The damaged cruiser could not be found so a secondary target of cruisers was attacked, but without success.

Nor did the attack on the battleships prove any more successful. Much, it seemed, still had to be learned both tactically and technically about air-sea fighting.

Later in the afternoon Somerville's ships came under attack from shore-based aircraft. By 5.0 pm the convoy was sighted and came under the protective umbrella of powerful forces. The skirmishes were over. The operation thereafter proceeded according to plan. Captain Roskill summarized:

> "Though the indecisive action was satisfactory to neither side, the Italians certainly failed either to hinder the passage of the convoy or to inflict appreciable damage on our weaker surface forces . . . [our] . . . failure to slow up or damage the retreating enemy was certainly disappointing,, but it was known that the *Ark Royal*'s aircrews lacked the high degree of training and experience necessary to achieve good results. Admiral Somerville was criticized in London for abandoning the pursuit."

This criticism seems, on reflection, to have been grossly mishandled. Instead of awaiting the Admiral's return to harbour and calling for a written report, the Admiralty sent Lord Cork and Orrery to Gibraltar to enquire into the circumstances of the skirmishes. A Board of Enquiry was set up even before the squadron – and the Admiral – reached Gibraltar.

Admiral Cunningham has recorded his profound dislike of this action. And Captain Roskill reflected:

> "Though the right of the Admiralty to criticize and if need be to chastise the flag officers is indisputable, the handling of the whole

matter was certainly unfortunate. The Board of Enquiry, once possessed of all the facts, entirely upheld Somerville's action."

The Battle of Spartivento had drawn to a close, but the precipitate Admiralty action left an unpalatable taste in the mouth.

Mid-December saw another rash of naval activity when *Malaya* was passed from Alexandria to Gibraltar. The battleship was escorted by the Mediterranean Fleet (Operation MC-2) as far as the Malta area, then Force H (Operation Hide) met her off Bizerta.

The opportunity was also taken to pass convoys to and from Malta as well as despatching two empty ships from Malta to Gibraltar.

Convoy MW-5 comprised the following: *Devis*, *Hoeg Hood*, *Lanarkshire*, *Pontfield*, *Rodi*, *Trocas*, *Volo* and *Waiwera*. It left Alexandria on 16 December and arrived at Malta on the 20th. On this day the two empty supply ships *Clan Forbes* and *Clan Fraser* left Malta, joined the *Malaya* squadron and made the passage to Gibraltar without incident.

Convoy ME-5 was the simultaneous east-bound convoy. It comprised the Royal Fleet Auxiliary *Breconshire*, the *Clan Ferguson*, *Clan Macaulay* and *Mermon*. The passage of this convoy was notable if only because it was the first convoy in which no British warship opened fire in anger throughout the operation. But that did not signify much. Indeed, if anything, it represented the calm before the storm which was about to be unleashed on the island of Malta and the ships of the Royal Navy with the arrival in Sicily of the German *Fliegerkorps* X whose objective was nothing less than annihilating Malta and seizing control of the central Mediterranean.

The end of 1940 marked the end of the Italian phase of the campaign and the beginning of the First German phase, and it will be seen how the Royal Navy came desperately close to disaster, how only by subterfuge was the enemy denied knowledge of his success in virtually sinking two battleships in Alexandria harbour, and how other disastrous events almost forced a withdrawal of the Navy from the central and eastern basins of the Mediterranean. Fierce ordeals and desperate situations still faced Cunningham and the ships and men of the Royal and Merchant Navies. The old antagonists, the British and the Germans, were to confront each other at sea, on land and in the air.

Malta, the centrepiece of the Navy's actions, had been replenished by the end of the year with approximately 60,000 tons of supplies. It was small enough, but it demonstrated the determination of the Navy to get supplies through to the beleaguered island.

OPERATION EXCESS:
HMS *ILLUSTRIOUS's* ORDEAL

The Admiralty Instructions to escort commanders left no room for equivocation: 'the safe and timely arrival of the convoy . . . is the primary object and nothing relieves the escort commander of his responsibility in this respect.'

Quoted by Captain S.W. Roskill,
The Secret Capture, Collins.

Captain Roskill, official naval historian of the Second World War, underscores this sentiment: it is one of the strongest traditions in the Royal Navy that no purpose whatsoever can supersede that of ensuring "the safe and timely" arrival of a convoy.

In the clamour of battle escort commanders were often subjected to competing claims for their attention in defence of the merchant ships in their charge. The Prime Minister, often seeming unaware of the remorseless aerial bombing of the Malta convoys, also acknowledged the dangers. In his postwar memoirs he explained how the island of Malta was under threat of invasion as well as suffering "constant and measureless" air attack, and he recorded how hostile air power imposed almost prohibitive risks on the passage of convoys through the Narrows, "condemning us to the long haul round the Cape". This was not a view he expressed at the time when under the extreme pressures of the war. At one stage he objected to

Admiral Pound's proposal to send AA guns and aircraft to Malta via the Cape, a proposal which earned a five-page riposte on the Admiralty's timidity: "Anyone," the Prime Minister admonished,

> "can see the risk of air attack which we run in the central Mediterranean. From time to time . . . this risk will have to be faced. Warships," he added tartly, "are meant to go under fire."

The fact of the matter was that the passage of a convoy through the central Mediterranean could not be categorized simply with the glib phrase "warships are meant to go under fire". Men who brought home the tanker *Ohio* through the ordeal of Operation Pedestal, the 860 who lost their lives in *Barham* and the survivors of *Illustrious* who battled their carrier through ferocious attacks during Operation Excess needed no prodding; if anything they were prodders.

Operation Excess was the code-name given to the passage of no less than four simultaneous convoys early in January, 1941, combining naval movements of awesome complexities throughout the whole of the Mediterranean. On the morning of 10 January the dispositions of the ships of the Royal Navy and of the Merchant Navy were approximately as listed. 10 January is taken as a pivotal point of time during a kaleidoscopic operation of shipping movements, coinciding with the date that *Fliegerkorps* X launched its intensive assault on the Royal Navy and the merchant ships in its charge.

OPERATION EXCESS

FORCE H

Vice-Admiral Sir James Somerville

Battleships:	*Malaya, Ramillies*
Battlecruiser:	*Renown* (flag)
Carrier:	*Ark Royal*

Cruisers:	Sheffield, Berwick, Bonaventure, Coventry, Newcastle, Manchester, Southampton.
Destroyers:	Duncan, Faulkner, Fury, Forester, Fortune, Foxhound, Firedrake, Hasty, Hereward, Hero, Hotspur, Jaguar, Vidette.
Corvettes:	Gloxinia, Hyacinth, Peony, Salvia.

Force H's duty was to escort a convoy (the Excess convoy) from Gibraltar to Bizerta. The convoy comprised the *Essex* (bound for Malta), *Clan Cumming*, *Clan Macdonald* and *Empire Song* (all bound for Piraeus). The convoy left Gibraltar on 6 January and the *Essex* arrived Malta on the 10th.

FORCE A

Major part of the Mediterranean Fleet.

Admiral Sir Andrew B. Cunningham.

Battleships:	Warspite (flag), Valiant.
Carrier:	Illustrious.
Cruisers:	Southampton, Glasgow, Bonaventure, Calcutta, Sydney.
Destroyers:	Dainty, Defender, Diamond, Gallant, Greyhound, Griffin, Hasty, Hereward, Hero, Hotspur, Jaguar, Janus, Jervis, Juno, Mohawk, Nubian, Stuart, Wryneck.
Corvettes:.	Hyacinth, Peony, Salvia.

This Force escorted a convoy (MW-5½) from Alexandria to Malta then met the Operation Excess supply ships off Pantelleria for Malta (the *Essex* convoy ME-5½). These were combined with a convoy of fast, empty ships, the *Rodi* and *Lanarkshire*, and escorted from Malta to Alexandria.

It was during this convoy operation that HMS *Illustrious* was severely damaged by German Stuka dive bombers and barely survived the ordeal. The cruiser *Southampton* was bombed, set ablaze, abandoned and sunk.

(The appearance of a ship under two or more forces was governed by the needs of the situation: *Southampton* and *Gloucester*, for example, were proceeding in company with Force H and Force A, technically 'in company', but in fact beyond fleet support. Both were severely damaged and *Southampton* had to be sunk on 11 January, 1941. Corvettes, too, had a wandering commission serving under Force A and Force D.)

FORCE B

Rear-Admiral E. de F. Renouf.

Destroyers: *Ilex, Janus.*

This small force passed through the Skerki Channel between Sicily and Tunis and joined the Excess Convoy on the last leg of its passage to Malta.

FORCE F

Cruiser: *Bonaventure* (Captain H.J.E. Egerton).
Destroyers: *Jaguar, Hereward, Hasty, Hero.*

FORCE D

Cruisers: *Orion, York, Ajax, Perth.*
Tanker: *Brambleaf.*
Corvettes: *Gloxinia, Hyacinth, Peony, Salvia.*

CONVOY ME-6

Comprised slow, empty ships from Malta to Egypt.

They were: *Devis, Hoeg Hood, Pontfield, Trocas, Volo* and *Waiwera*. It departed Malta 10 January and arrived Port Said on the 15th.

FORCE C

AA cruiser *Calcutta*. Cruiser *Sydney*, and destroyers *Defender, Diamond, Stuart.*

CONVOY MW-5½

Comprised *Breconshire* (RFA) and *Clan Macaulay*. It departed Alexandria 7 January and arrived Malta on the 10th.

CONVOY ME-5½

The empty *Lanarkshire* and *Rodi* departed Malta 10 January and joined Piraeus-bound Excess vessels. The latter were detached to Suda Bay in Crete on the 13th, while Convoy ME-5½ entered Alexandria on the 14th.

These widespread naval dispositions, drawing heavily on the maritime skills of its officers, help demonstrate the commitment of the Royal Navy not only to the merchant ships of the convoys but also the enormous lengths to which they were prepared to go in the protection and sustenance of the island of Malta.

Ranged against this broad deployment of shipping were squadrons of high-level bombers of the *Regia Aeronautica* and bombers and Stukas of *Fliegerkorps* X. The latter's arrival was the result of many representations sent to Hitler about the significance of Malta.

Admiral Erich Raeder first drew Hitler's attention to Malta. "The British," he exhorted, "have always considered the Mediterranean as the cornerstone of their whole position." He urged the conquest of Malta ("and to do it without delay"), also Gibraltar, and, for good measure, the Suez Canal as well.

Rear-Admiral E. Weighold, Liaison Officer at Italy's *Supermarina*, mixed his metaphor but struck the right chord. Malta, he declared, lay athwart the Axis supply route from Italian ports to those of North Africa, "like a thorn in the side of the Italian Naval Staff". Weighold also urged that Malta be occupied. Even Jodl urged Hitler to sanction an invasion of Malta.

They were all wasting their energies. The idea found no favour with Hitler. His mind had been made up. Other, lusher pastures beckoned. The glittering prize over the horizon was Russia. Malta was thus spared invasion. The island fortress remained in

British hands, a key position of incalculable strategic value.

By early January, 1941, the German and Italian air reinforcements were well in hand with squadrons amounting to ninety-six bombers and twenty-five twin-engined fighter aircraft assembled on Sicilian airfields. Air Force General Hans Ferdinand Guisler, a one-time naval officer, was given command and within a short time had increased his air fleet more than two-fold to 400 aircraft of all types, including 150 Ju 88 bombers and 150 Ju 87 Stuka dive bombers.

The *Luftwaffe Diaries* gave a brief account of the Excess Operation on 10 January. It was a day of ferocious fighting, the day when *Illustrious* was struck by seven bombs and a crashing bomber, emerging from the day's battle bloody, blazing and damaged almost beyond repair. *The Diaries* recount:

> "A British convoy with large escort of warships was heading westward for Malta. Staking all, the Stukas swept down from 12,000 feet to 2,000 into the concentrated fire of the ships. . . . On the following day Major Walter Enneccerus' squadron, guided by a Heinkel 111 pathfinder, gave chase to the British Fleet as it steamed back eastwards. At extreme range, nearly 300 miles east of Sicily, the Stukas attacked out of the sun and sank the cruiser *Southampton* with a direct hit in the engine room."

Eric E. Clark was one of a team of technicians who took passage in the heavily laden MV *Essex*, a modern refrigerated ship of the New Zealand Shipping Company of 11,063 tons. She carried 13,000 tons of war material, including 4,000 tons of ammunition, 3,000 tons of seed potatoes, torpedoes and sundry other items. Large crates clearly labelled Transit Malta gave the crew and passengers the first inkling of their destination – twelve Hurricanes for Malta.

The Excess convoy and some of the escorts began assembling in mid-December at Liverpool. Radio Officer H.A. Bruce of the *Clan Macdonald* recalls that the convoy comprised 5 or 6 [it was 5] ships; a fifth was to run aground on arrival at Gibraltar. They were all of a kind, similar in size and speed – and heavily escorted. The convoy slipped cables and headed for Gibraltar. En route it was intercepted in the Atlantic by the heavy German cruiser *Hipper* (Captain Meisel) and on Christmas Day the thunderous rumble of gunfire could be heard by ships of the convoy.

HMS *Berwick*, one of the heavy cruiser escort, was hit by two shells and two merchantmen were damaged. Shells fell between the carrier *Argus* and the *Clan Cumming*. Visibility was poor and gale-force winds whipped the sea into a fury. *Hipper* suffered gale damage and she broke away for Brest, sinking an independent ship of 6,078 tons on the way. Later *Berwick* sank one of *Hipper*'s supply ships, the *Bader*. The convoy scattered. *Clan Cumming* developed engine trouble but managed to make her way to Gibraltar.

Bombadier R. Rostron, an ex-territorial in the Royal Artillery, was a reinforcement for Malta in the *Northern Prince*. She arrived in Gibraltar at dusk on 28 December. Rostron recalls:

"What a spectacle it was, no blockade, everything lit up. . . . On 1 January a storm hit us causing the *Northern Prince* to partially slip the stern moorings which allowed her to drift slowly towards another ship that was carrying ammunition. . . . This caused a panic and we were all ordered on deck with life jackets . . . but the storm abated and the danger passed. Unfortunately [the *Prince*] had gone aground and was unable to proceed. We and the cargo were transferred to the *Clan Macdonald*."

Rostron had had no experience of action, but that was soon to be remedied. High-level bombers began the battle, but they were driven off successfully by the intensity of the AA gunfire of the escorts; all the bombs fell harmlessly into the sea. The Stuka bombers were another story. Rostron watched them as the pilots plunged through the barrage of fire, "like crazy men, I thought," concentrating their attacks on the aircraft carrier *Illustrious*. She seemed to start zig-zagging, Rostron said, but she was probably damaged in the attacks and lost her steering, if only temporarily.

Aboard the *Clan Cumming* was a nineteen-year-old cadet, Paul B. Stevens, who confesses:

"I was young and foolish and I really looked forward to being in action. And to be quite honest I found the whole thing rather exciting. However, I soon had all that nonsense knocked out of me long before we reached Alexandria. It was, of course, much more difficult for the older men with more sense and imagination. . . . When we were in action I was on a Hotchkiss machine gun. I cannot imagine I ever hit anything but it added to the noise and excitement."

Captain J.D. Matthews, master of the *Clan Cumming* and Paul Stevens' Commanding Officer, was described by the cadet:

"He was a Scotsman in his sixties, white-haired, and he seemed very elderly to me. He was strict on discipline but very fair. Although in awe of him I did not fear him. Looking back now, it must have been a great ordeal for him physically as well as mentally to go through all that we did at his age."

Stevens was right. Matthews had responsibility for a splendid ship, built only three years previously, with excellent accommodation, with a crew subjected to shot and shell, attacked by a surface raider, by high-level and dive bombers, by torpedoes and bombs, and, overall, the responsibility to get the ship's cargo to its destination. Captain Matthews reported:

"On 10 January the German dive bombers arrived and it was in the course of their persistent attacks in which most of the ships had narrow escapes that the carrier *Illustrious* was hit and set on fire. In this scrap we only had four casualties – three soldiers and Apprentice Robb. The apprentice got a piece of shrapnel in his arm while manning the high-angle guns but he stuck it out to the end of the action."

Both Radio Officer Bruce aboard *Clan Macdonald* and Cadet Paul Stevens recall how comforting it was to have the protection of such powerful warships as the battleship *Malaya*, who was near-missed six times. But the day that everyone remembers was the day *Illustrious* was bombed, remembered with horror but also with pride. Stevens wrote:

"On 10 January we were subjected to very heavy dive-bombing by Major Enneccerus' Stuka 87s which resulted in *Illustrious* being severely damaged."

January 10th 1941

The convoy received a new escort consisting of H.M. Battleships Warspite Valiant and Barham, H.M. Battle Cruiser Renown, H.M. Aircraft Carrier Illustrious, H.M. Cruisers Southampton, Gloucester, Perth, Orion, Bonaventure, Ajax and Calcutta and a dozen destroyers. In the morning the shore batteries of Pantellaria shelled the convoy and during the action between our forces and two Italian destroyers one of their destroyers was sunk while H.M. destroyer Gallant was damaged by a mine. Later on in the day the convoy was subjected to violent and incessant dive-bombing attacks by Junkers 87's and 88's as well as high level attacks by Italian bombers.

The convoy put up a terrific barrage, by far the biggest I have ever seen but this did not deter the German pilots who came down to 50 ft to deliver their attacks and then flew off between the ships making it impossible to fire on them. H.M.S. Illustrious was hit twice and each severely damaged but managed to reach Malta under her own steam. H.M.S. Southampton was hit and subsequently had to be sunk by our forces. Twelve enemy planes were destroyed and many other damaged. Just before dark the convoy was attacked by submarines but no damage resulted.

January 12th 1941

A few planes reached Piraeus

Paul Stevens of the mv *Clan Cumming* kept a diary of his adventures, a good contemporary record of war in the Mediterranean. (*Paul Stevens*)

Many others aboard the merchantmen and the escorts recall the day clearly. Able Seaman R.F. (Rimbo) Green was a 21-year-old in the fleet destroyer HMS *Hasty* in 1941. *Hasty* was his first ship and he writes of 10 January:

"It was my first experience of dive-bombing. The *Hasty* was part of the Mediterranean Fleet escorting our carrier *Illustrious* through to the eastern Med. My diary shows that we passed through the Narrows at 0600. At 0730 the fleet was fired on by two Italian destroyers. They were attacked by HM cruisers *Southampton* and *Bonaventure* and destroyers. One was sunk and the other damaged. At 0800 we formed up with the fleet and at midday were dive-bombed. They were frightening. The *Illustrious* was hit several times but did not sink – her steel flight deck saved her. She was a credit to British shipbuilding. . . . *Hasty* escorted her to Grand Harbour where she was bombed incessantly for days. She survived and slipped from Malta to the eastern Mediterranean, through the Suez Canal and on to the USA for permanent repairs. She lived to fight another day."

Able Seaman Green's timing was about right. At 0730, towards the end of his morning watch on 10 January when the convoy was to the south of Sicily, two of the escorting cruisers, the *Bonaventure* (Captain H.J. Egerton) and the *Southampton* (Captain B.C.B. Brooke) and the destroyer *Jaguar* sighted two enemy destroyers. It is believed that the encounter was quite providential: the destroyers "stumbled on the convoy inadvertently". The size of the Italian force suggests that it was unlikely to have been a deliberate attempt to intercept the convoy and its escorts. In the ensuing uneven contest, as Green reports, one torpedo boat was sunk and the other made good its escape.

Admiral Cunningham was some miles away to the eastward. On seeing the gun flashes he closed towards them. A few minutes later the destroyer *Gallant* struck a mine and the resultant explosion blew her bows off. Commander J.W. Eaton in *Mohawk* managed to get a tow secured, while *Bonaventure* stood by. A short while later Rear Admiral E.D.F. Renouf arrived with his two cruisers *Gloucester* and *Southampton* to give the crippled *Gallant* and the *Mohawk* a close escort and helped fend off intermittent bombing attacks.

Another memory of HMS *Illustrious* came from Shadrach W. Scommell. He wrote:

"In all my years of service in the Royal Navy the most horrific and the most pleasant memories were with the *Illustrious*. It was 10 January, late in the morning watch, when we were closed up at action stations at about 0730. We were informed that groups of aircraft were mustering about 20 miles away. The sun was already high in the sky. It was evident that something was coming. So the agony of waiting went on till 12 noon. Then the attacks began. As the bombs fell and exploded so the aircraft carrier of 23,000 tons started to bounce on the water, bombs bursting all around – three or four hits. One semi-armour-piercing went through the white line painted on the deck of *Illustrious* straight into the hangar, with enormous loss of life by men who thought it was safe with 5 inches of armour plating over them."

Scommell goes on to describe the events of this day to remember:

"At 1210 pm two Italian bombers made an approach to starboard. Fire was opened but they got to about 400 yards before releasing their torpedoes. Captain Boyd altered course sharply to comb the torpedoes, all of which missed. The bombers streaked away at about zero height."

Then came the dive bombers. They selected the carrier as their prime target. The fleet was in a position about 100 miles to the west of Malta, while the convoy and its escort was away to the south. Suddenly at 1235 a large formation of forty to fifty Ju 88s and Ju 87s approached from the north and attacked the fleet.

The evident skill and discipline of the attackers and the manner in which the attacks were pressed home brought a new dimension to determined bombing, surpassing anything so far experienced in the Mediterranean. Pilots and aircraft of *Fliegerkorps* X were making their presence felt.

The *Illustrious* was caught at her most vulnerable, while flying off and landing on aircraft, both Fulmars and Swordfish. They got away safely; then, almost instantly, the carrier disappeared behind a mountain of erupting and cascading water from near-miss bombs exploding alongside.

The bombers' resolute tactics were the result of practice and repetition. They had practised against mock-ups of the carrier to fine hone their skills. They approached their target from both port and starboard bows and from the starboard quarter, all simultaneously, diving in groups of three from each direction, dove-tailed neatly together "clover leaf fashion", through the 4.5-inch barrage and pom-pom screen. In the terrifying crescendo of crashing sound *Illustrious* disappeared in spray and smoke. The damage was severe.

When the mist and spray cleared it was seen just how severe the damage was. She hauled out of line and fires were seen to be burning fiercely. She was not under control, her flight deck was wrecked and then a second attack developed. Gun crews fought back strongly but it was a savage onslaught.

Another heavy bomb exploded in the after-lift well when the lift was half-way down. A Fulmar was on the lift with its midshipman pilot. The Fulmar was "obliterated", the pilot killed and the lift wrecked. Nearly all the armaments were knocked out and their crews killed. Dead and dying men lay everywhere; bloody remains littering the decks were heaved overboard.

At some stage a high-level attack developed. These pilots were less accurate, but then there came a blinding crash and a thousand-pound bomb struck the flight deck right on the centre line. It burst through the armoured deck and the hangar deck below, hit the after ammunition conveyor and exploded, killing or wounding everyone in the wardroom flat. The stench was overpowering, but the ship still remained afloat.

Rear Admiral Lyster's flagship, by all accounts, had little chance of survival or of reaching safety. Destroyers shouldered their way near to rescue the ship's company in case of abandonment. In the course of the next lull superhuman efforts were made by damage limitation and control. Commander Kenneth Edwards wrote of the incident:

> "With her flight deck wrecked and fires raging between decks another disaster befell the ship. Her steering broke down . . : she had to be steered by adjusting the speed of her engines, no easy matter in a severely damaged ship with an ever-increasing list due to the quantity of water which was being poured into her in an attempt to keep the fires under control."

Captain Boyd surveyed the wreckage of his ship and the scores of men who would never return home. The mangled remains of a sailor littered the flight deck. Boyd caught the eye of a Petty Officer and motioned almost imperceptibly. The PO threw the remains overboard.

Lyster referred later to the coolness and determination of *Illustrious*' crew:

> "From the fact that the ship was saved and brought into harbour it is evident that the entire ship's organization, the centralized control of damage and the initiative and energy shewn by all was of a very high order. The ship suffered damage in four out of ten attacks. . . . The two final attacks were on a very high scale with about 50 aircraft in each . . . seventy bombs fell in the immediate vicinity of the ship during the four large-scale attacks."

Miraculously, *Illustrious* survived and, her blackened hull and paintwork blistered, she was inched into Grand Harbour and finally into Parlatoro Wharf in French Creek, "an unearthly, terrible sight, glowing red within, trailing a pall of smoke, listing but somehow grinding on to safety". She came alongside the dockyard wall and stopped as lines were secured to bollards. The task of clearing up got underway.

A day later another casualty limped into harbour; the destroyer *Gallant* minus her bows had been towed 120 miles by *Mohawk* with only the foremost bulkhead standing between salvation or collapse and total loss. *Mohawk* and her cruiser escort slipped off to rejoin the fleet. *Gallant*, in fact, became a constructive total loss.

The loss of *Illustrious*, whether temporary or otherwise, was a serious blow, but another was yet to materialize. At 3 pm on 11 January Rear Admiral Renouf in *Gloucester*, overtaking the fleet after escorting *Gallant* and *Mohawk* to Malta, reported that his two cruisers, *Southampton* and *Gloucester*, had been attacked by a dozen dive bombers, suddenly appearing out of the sun. Both ships had been hit. *Southampton* had been reduced to a stumbling wreck and finally stopped. Fires raged out of control in the after engine room and in one of her magazines.

Gloucester was struck through the roof of the director tower by a bomb which failed to explode. But she was severely damaged and suffered nine killed and fourteen injured.

Southampton's hits were a different matter. She had been hit in the wardroom and the PO's mess, so all those best capable of leading the fire-fighting and damage control became casualties. The fires gained control and the ship had to be abandoned. All her ships' company were transferred to the *Gloucester* and the destroyer *Diamond*. There had been few casualties compared with *Illustrious*'s 126 killed and ninety-one wounded.

Rear Admiral Renouf was a lucky man. This was the second time that a flagship of his had been hit on the bridge by a defective bomb.

The main objective of this huge naval operation was the sustenance of Malta and Greece and that objective had been achieved, but the price was exorbitant.

The enemy were soon to learn the whereabouts of *Illustrious* and *Gallant*, and the supply ships of the convoys. Efforts were made to attack not only the ships but Malta itself and her AA emplacements.

On 16 January the dive bombers attacked the island and *Illustrious* was hit again. One of the supply ships, the MV *Essex*, was struck by a bomb and her engine room was smashed. There were thirty-eight casualties, but the 4,000 tons of ammunition she carried in her holds were left unscathed, as were the 3,000 tons of seed potatoes.

Malta was again heavily bombed on 18 January and on the following day when *Illustrious* was damaged once more.

Hundreds of dockyard workers scrambled over the wreck of the carrier and, after fourteen days of intensive care and attention, the carrier slipped out of harbour unobserved between the heads of the breakwater, still festooned with repair stages, scaffolding, dangling ropes, Irish pennants and even fishing nets, none of which could be jettisoned until she reached deeper waters. Soon she was making 25 knots, heading for the Suez Canal, then the long haul round the Cape to Norfolk, Virginia, for extensive repairs. In due course she was replaced in the Mediterranean by the *Formidable*.

While *Illustrious* was still alongside undergoing her ordeal by bombs, the island of Malta itself began to experience the full blast of the blitz.

Much of this is captured by E.F. Smith who served as an ordnance artificer aboard the AA cruiser *Carlisle*. Smith kept an unofficial diary which he added to later. This is his report of the January bombings:

"*17 January*: closed up at action stations all day and remained there till dark. Our aircraft shot down one plane. Another Ju 88 dropped bombs a long way off. Heard that the *Gurkha* had been torpedoed in convoy behind us.

"*18 January*: Attacked by Ju 88s. Another convoy joined us midday. Saw them being attacked. One merchant ship, *Thermopylae*, got engine and steering problems. We and two destroyers detailed to take her in to Benghazi. Arrived at entrance to the swept channel into Benghazi when told to return to Alex with her. At action stations all day.

"*19 January*: At 10 am attacked by 2 Ju 88s; one dived right through our barrage and hit *Thermopylae* amidships and set her on fire. Destroyers *Arrow* and *Havelock* took off survivors: 14 Norwegians; one RN rating; one army officer; 2 women; 26 other ranks; 4 dead. All these were taken off by *Arrow*. *Havelock*'s hoard amounted to: 9 officers; 230 other ranks; 4 merchant ship officers including the captain; 16 seamen; 1 steward. Total 265, later amended to 297. There were 33 lost. We were not allowed to stop to pick up survivors and it was harrowing passing chaps in the water. We were attacked ourselves but our barrage turned them away from us. Attacked again from astern but bombs droppcd well away from us. Very cloudy and a big swell – very bad for firing. *Arrow* put two torpedoes into *Thermopylae* and sank her. We set off for Alex at 24 knots."

It is generally accepted that 16 January, 6 days after the *Illustrious* was bombed at sea, marked the beginning of the air offensive against Malta. It was an attack of remorseless ferocity. Over the period 16 to 23 January the Germans had the inducement of sinking *Illustrious* while still secured alongside in harbour. It was a tempting target. To this end they launched eight massive air raids on the dockside area. More than 500 aircraft were employed. Sixty-one were destroyed either in aerial battle with the RAF or fell to the shore-based AA gunners.

Operation Excess safeguarded the supply of approximately 10,000 tons. It was a meagre amount and had cost the navy dear:

One cruiser sunk: *Southampton,*

One aircraft carrier damaged: *Illustrious,*

One cruiser damaged: *Gloucester,*

One destroyer damaged: *Gallant.*

NIGHT BATTLE OFF CAPE MATAPAN: DISASTERS AT SEA

Malta is of such importance as an air staging point and as important to the enemy reinforcement route to Africa that the most drastic steps are justified to retain it. . . . No consideration of risk to ships need deter you.

The Chiefs of Staff to Admiral Sir
Andrew Cunningham.

Two major events now intervened in the Mediterranean which deserve at least some passing reference in order to give a balanced view of the naval scene. The first was the victory of the Battle of Cape Matapan. The second was the series of disastrous events in the campaign for Greece and Crete.

The Battle of Matapan was fought on 28 and 29 March, 1941, between a British and an Italian Fleet, the main action taking place during the night of 28/29 March about 100 miles south-west of the Greek cape which gave its name to the battle. Events were put in train when the carrier *Formidable* joined an impressive-looking fleet resting alongside or secured to its moorings in Alexandria harbour, busy with the comings and goings of a major fleet anchorage. HMS *Warspite* responded to *Formidable*'s salute. *Valiant* and *Barham* were in harbour. The battered *Illustrious*'s crew gave a cheer, always a heartening greeting from a chummy ship. The elderly *Eagle* could be recognized. HMS *Medway*, the submarine depot ship, stood high and proud in the water, with submarines alongside in their trots. The harbour was full of moored naval vessels of every description, including immobilized French warships.

It was only a matter of days before the carrier and the battle fleet would seek out the enemy and cast long, protective shadows over the convoys to Malta. It is necessary to follow the fleet, firstly to Cape Matapan and then to the dreadful experience of the Battle for Crete. The British battle fleet left harbour soon after noon on Thursday 27 March. It comprised the following:

BRITISH FORCES

BATTLESHIPS:

Warspite	Flagship of C-in-C Admiral Sir Andrew Cunningham.
Barham	Flagship Rear Admiral H.B. Rawlings. 1st Battle Squadron.
Valiant	Captain C.E. Morgan.

AIRCRAFT CARRIER:

Formidable	Flagship Rear Admiral (Air) Rear Admiral D.W. Boyd.

CRUISERS:

Orion	Flagship Vice Admiral H.D. Pridham-Wippell, Vice Admiral Light Forces.
Ajax	Captain E.D.B. McCarthy.
Perth (HMAS)	Captain Sir P.W. Bowyer-Smyth.
Gloucester	Captain H.A. Rowley.

DESTROYERS:

Stuart, Greyhound, Griffin, Hasty, Hereward, Havock, Hotspur, Ilex, Mohawk, Nubian, Jervis, Janus

ITALIAN FORCES

BATTLESHIP:

Vittorio Veneto   Flagship C-in-C Admiral Iachino.

CRUISERS:

Trieste   Flagship Vice Admiral Sansonetti.

Trento
Bolzano
Zara   Flagship Vice Admiral C. Cattaneo.
Fiume   Captain G. Giorgis.
Pola   Captain M. de Pisa.
Abruzzi   Flagship Vice Admiral A. Legnani.
Garibaldi

DESTROYERS:

Da Recco, Pressagno, Maestrale, Lebeccio, Scirocco, Gioberti, Vittorio Alfieri, Oriani, Giosoe, Carducci, Corazziere, Carabinari, Ascari,. Granatiere, Fuciliere, Bersagliere, Alpini

Cunningham's fleet put to sea on the 27th heading north-west at 20 knots. It was believed that the Italian fleet had also put to sea. It was "a lovely night" and the expectations aboard the British ships were high. Aircraft searched for signs of enemy activity.

Pridham-Wippell's force of four cruisers and four destroyers was ordered to a position 30 miles south of Gavdo Island, a rocky outcrop 20 miles south of Crete. Thirty bombers of the RAF (Squadrons 84, 113 and 211) searched for the enemy. A quiet night at cruising stations was enlivened by an RAF sighting report of enemy cruisers steering east. A clash of fleets looked likely.

Soon after noon on the 28th the RAF gave another sighting report. Iachino realized that he had lost the element of surprise and altered course for base. It was not until the afternoon sighting that Cunningham knew this to be the *Vittorio Veneto*, nine cruisers and fourteen destroyers.

Formidable flew off a strike of torpedo aircraft to try to slow down the Italian battleship and at 3.15 pm a hit was registered on the *Vittorio Veneto*'s port quarter which reduced her speed. Lieutenant-Commander Dalyell-Stead, piloting an aircraft of 829 Squadron, scored the hit. Admiral Iachino described the attack:

> "We all had our hearts in our mouth and our eyes fixed on the [leading] aircraft. . . . It showed very great skill and courage in approaching so close before dropping [the torpedo]. . . . It was seen to fall in the water about 1,000 yards ahead of the ship as the flagship began to respond to the turn to starboard."

Iachino watched as the torpedo track approached. The aircraft was in obvious trouble. Every gun seemed to concentrate on her. Iachino reported:

> "Suddenly his aircraft staggered,dipped violently across the track a dozen yards ahead of *Veneto*'s bows, then dropped into the sea about 1,000 yards on the starboard side. And so died a brave pilot without the satisfaction of knowing that his attack had been successful."

Seconds later the torpedo struck, fifteen feet below the waterline, just above the port screws. Thousands of tons of water flooded in. *Veneto* settled by the stern, but remained afloat. The heavy cruiser *Pola* was also torpedoed during this action and was brought to a stop. Iachino ordered two of his heavy cruisers and a division of destroyers to stand by the *Pola* while he continued his westerly flight to safety.

At 9 pm that night the leading cruisers in the British fleet reported a darkened ship in sight stopped dead in the water. It was the crippled *Pola*. The scene was set for a mighty clash of powerful gunnery.

The British ships were prepared for action. Two more Italian cruisers suddenly appeared, crossing the British flagship's bows. *Warspite* turned to starboard to bring her 15-inch broadside to bear and opened fire at a range of 3,500 yards.

Searchlights exposed the *Fiume* and *Zara*, their guns still trained fore and aft. They were totally unprepared for action. Both these 10,000-ton cruisers were reduced to blazing hulks and sank.

The destroyer *Vittorio Alfieri* attempted a brave torpedo attack but was shot to bits, mainly by *Barham*'s 15-inch guns. The destroyer *Giosoe Carducci* was also sunk.

The cruiser *Pola* was then located at leisure and she, too, was overwhelmed by heavy gun fire. Captain P.J. Mack, in his destroyer *Jervis*, had found the *Pola* and managed to get alongside the wreck, take off the crew and sink her with a torpedo. At 4.10 am it was all over. The damaged battleship managed to elude discovery and slipped away in the night. Cunningham painted a graphic picture of the battle:

> "The plight of the cruisers was indescribable. One saw whole turrets and masses of other heavy debris whirling through the air and splashing into the sea, and in a short time the ships themselves were nothing but glowing torches and on fire from stem to stern. The whole action lasted no more than a few minutes."

Cunningham lamented the escape of *Veneto*, but the battle had an incalculable effect upon the maritime scene in the Eastern Mediterranean. *Supermarina*'s acceptance of British supremacy was now complete. It was never to be challenged again. Even during the agony of Crete, when Cunningham's resources were stretched to the utmost limit, the Italian navy resolutely refused to risk another rough handling such as it experienced at Matapan. It is true to say that such success as was achieved by the navy during its operations off Greece and Crete was made possible by the devastating broadsides of the battleships in the night action of Cape Matapan.

We must now turn our attention to the grave events in Greece and Crete, if only cursorily to contrast the heady feeling of victory and superiority after Matapan with the tragedy of Crete, its evacuations and convoys, all of which had a bearing on the

Malta convoys in the spring of 1941. No fewer than 58,364 British and Imperial (Australian and New Zealand) soldiers, complete with all their military paraphernalia, mechanical transport, equipment and stores, were rescued from the Piraeus, virtually the only port of any consequence in Greece.

Such was the confusion and fluidity of the campaign in Greece and Crete that at one stage Operation Lustre (reinforcements to Greece and Crete) was overlapping with Operation Demon (evacuation from Greece and Crete), with new arrivals being landed even while thousands more were being embarked.

An impressive assembly of vessels formed Operation Demon. It comprised four cruisers, three AA cruisers, twenty destroyers, two of the three Glen ships, the assault ship *Ulster Prince*, five escort vessels, six A Lighters, the RFA *Brambleleaf* and a number of merchant ships. Pridham-Wippell commanded this fleet. He delegated much to Rear-Admiral Baillie-Grohman. It was all a daunting prospect.

The first six days of Operation Lustre coincided with the passage of a vital convoy, code-named MC 9, from Alexandria to Malta. It comprised four supply ships with a substantial naval escort consisting of three battleships, one aircraft carrier, four cruisers and thirteen destroyers. The cost was heavy. Two of the merchantmen and one cruiser were damaged, but about 45,000 tons of cargo were safely delivered to Malta.

The whole of Operation Lustre was conducted smoothly, but again at a cost. From 22 March to 18 April twenty-five vessels had been sunk, eighteen of them in harbour and only seven while in convoy.

Rear Admiral Baillie-Grohman visited Athens where there had been a multi-explosion of several ships in the harbour during the night of 6–7 April. He was confronted by a scene of utter devastation in the Piraeus. Defeat hung over the port like a pall of smoke. In the chaos of a heavy night air-raid the ammunition ship *Clan Fraser* had not been removed to a berth of safety.

"All the decks and between decks had been cleared of motor vehicles and other stores. Her cargo of explosives had been partially removed; most had simply been unloaded into lighters still secured alongside – and the Greek tugmen went home for the night at sundown. Furthermore, 250 tons of TNT still remained aboard in No. 3 hold. At 2035 that Sunday evening the air-raid alarm sounded for the fifth time. The gang of stevedores left the *Clan Fraser* for shelter ashore."

Another ammunition ship, the *Goalpara* lay alongside. Also alongside was the *City of Roubaix* with a cargo of ammunition, and nearby was the *Clan Cumming*. Outside the harbour, lying at anchor in the Bay in the calm of a fine evening, were some of the escorts of Convoy ANF 24, the cruisers *Perth*, *Calcutta* and *Coventry*, and some destroyers.

Aboard the *Clan Fraser* was Paul B. Stevens, who had already survived a torpedoing in the *Clan Cumming* in January. He kept a diary and reported the events graphically. The first wave of planes arrived at 2100.Soon after 2200 the *Clan Fraser* was hit by three bombs. The first exploded on the foredeck. The second burst in the engine room killing the chief engineer and some crew. The third exploded aft. Stevens recorded:

"The resultant blasts wrecked the bridge and upperworks, showering debris over the ships and the buildings ashore. So great was the blast that it lifted *Clan Fraser* bodily, snapped her mooring wires and she drifted several yards from the quayside still with her lighters secured alongside. About five hours later she exploded."

Worse was to follow. Other ships in the harbour were to share a similar fate. *City of Roubaix* and *Goalpara* were reduced to blazing infernos with cargoes of ammunition in imminent danger of exploding. *Clan Cumming* was trapped and about to be engulfed. When *Goalpara* exploded, taking all sorts of harbour installations with her, Athens, seven miles away, was rocked by the blast. Devastation throughout the port was indescribable. Paul Stevens wrote in his diary:

"Every ship in the harbour caught fire due to large quantities of burning debris falling on them. The *City of Roubaix* which had a considerable amount of ammunition aboard blew up. . . . There were many burning barges floating about. . . . All the warehouses and the grain elevator were levelled. . . . It was impossible to see clearly in the harbour because of a dense pall of smoke over it. . . . We wore our gasmasks."

Stevens made good his escape after a series of adventures ashore, finally getting aboard HMS *Phoebe* and arriving in Malta. The Piraeus disaster deserves recording:

Losses: 41,789 tons of valuable shipping.

          60 Lighters.

          25 Motor Sailing Vessels.

          The port of Piraeus was closed for ten days due to mining.

          City of Roubaix, *Cyprian Prince* and *Patris* sunk at their moorings. *Cingalese Prince* and *Devis* damaged. *Clan Cumming*, also damaged, later ran into an uncharted minefield and was sunk. She had been torpedoed, bombed and mined over a period of twelve weeks.

It was soon after the Piraeus disaster that the SS *Paracome* attempted a solo run from Gibraltar to Malta. She was a 4,698-ton vessel whose 2nd Radio Officer was R. Procter. The Master was D.L. Hook. The ship carried a cargo of ammunition and twenty crated Beaufighters. Deception was used by flying, firstly, a Spanish flag, followed by a French flag when off the coast of Tunisia. As warned, the *Paracome* discovered mines. The first mine was hit by a paravane and the resultant explosion did some slight damage. A second explosion caused extensive damage. Procter writes:

"I struggled to get out on to the deck. . . . Flames were shooting up from the engine room. On reaching the after deck (and by this time the ship was ready for its nosedive into the sea) tracer bullets and shells were shooting into the sky. . . . I decided it was time to take the 60-foot jump into the sea. The ship was settling at an angle of about 50 degrees."

73

Procter survived the ordeal. Of the crew of forty-seven eighteen were rescued, some by a Fleet Air Arm flying boat and others by Vichy French in Tunisia. Procter was taken prisoner and not released until the Allied landings during Operation Torch.

Another single-ship adventure is recalled by H. Kay, a Leading Aircraftman in the RAF. He was a fitter embarked on the MV *Leinster*, variously described as a hospital carrier, a personnel ship, a supply ship and a transport, even a packet ship.

She had been assembled with four other ships to run a convoy from Gibraltar to Malta, but she ran aground near Algeciras and was badly holed:

> "The ship was heavily loaded with men. A few of us were below decks. I must have been asleep but was woken by the commotion. I was a non-swimmer and now here I was floating near the top of the steel deck above. We had our life jackets on all the time on the orders drummed into us. I managed to make the steel steps leading to the upper deck. I must say everybody was so calm, even myself. We managed to scramble into the lifeboats – but mine had a mishap. We dropped 25–30 feet towards the sea with the *Leinster* at a crazy angle. I still recall the hard jolt to my neck as I hit the water."

Kay and the rest of the passengers (numbering about 1750) were rescued after a few hours in the lifeboats by two corvettes from Gibraltar. He was re-kitted and he and the rest of the men were distributed among three cruisers which finally arrived at Malta.

Before we leave the Cretan scene there are some incidents which deserve recording because the battle for Crete marked one of the lowest points in the history of the Navy in the Mediterranean. The *Slamat* disaster was specially upsetting inasmuch as it was caused in all good faith by the Dutch transport evacuating troops from Nauplia in Greece. She should have sailed at 3 am, but, rather than leave some troops ashore, she waited till 4.30. It was a misguided decision. It meant that she would have more hours of daylight to endure bombing, and, sure enough, by 7.15 she had been bombed and set ablaze. The two destroyers *Diamond* (Lieutenant-Commander P.A.

Cartwright and *Wryneck* (Commander R.H.D. Lane) went to her assistance.

The *Slamat* sank and, while the destroyers attempted to rescue survivors, they were dive-bombed. Both were hit and both sank in a matter of minutes. Only one officer and eight soldiers were saved, while 500 troops were lost from the *Slamat*.

Other losses occurred. The troop carrier *Ulster Prince*, a fast motor ship from Belfast, was heavily bombed and she grounded in Nauplia where she was set on fire and gutted. Two days later a second bomb exploded in her engine room. She was towed to Suda Bay in Crete by the destroyer *Griffin* and then on to Alexandria by the sloop *Grimsby*, both masterly towing feats by ships ill-equipped for that purpose, particularly in the face of air attack.

In the first week of May there was a major operation to supply Malta, as well as to run a convoy from Gibraltar to Alexandria – Operation Tiger. It was a large-scale operation involving naval supplies, in contrast to the usual Malta convoys which mostly carried food supplies.

On 6 May a slow convoy of two tankers and a fast convoy of four cargo ships set out from Alexandria with an escort of five cruisers, mostly AA. Covering forces were powerful, including the Mediterranean Fleet at the eastern end and Force H at the western end of the Mediterranean. All ships came under air bombardment, but the forces were fortunate in having air cover from the carriers and heavy AA fire from the cruisers. However, the *Empire Song* was bombed and sunk and the *New Zealand Star* suffered mine damage.

Recording some of these events was Radar Operator Leading Seaman Terry Jackson, a nineteen-year-old senior rating who led a team of a dozen RDF operators and was responsible for half a million pounds worth of secret gadgetry aboard the cruiser *Dido*. He recorded:

9 May: Joined *Fiji*, *Naiad* and four merchantmen. One ship sunk by mine. Air attacks all day. One aircraft shot down.

10 May: Air attacks all day again. Gunfire incessant. Going cross-eyed on my RDF screen with aircraft approaching from every direction. Corned beef sandwiches yet again. Lucky to have survived. Captain an expert in dodging the bombs. He leaned back in his swivel chair watching the bombs fall.

Terry Jackson also recorded the events of the days immediately before the invasion of Crete:

17 May: Go to aid of Hospital Ship *Abba* being attacked by Ju 87. Two planes shot down by *Coventry* and us. . . . No sign of Allied aircraft.

21 May: Attacked by dive bombers off Crete. Four aircraft shot down. . . . In company with *Ajax* and *Orion*. We sink Italian destroyer, tanker and many caiques carrying German troops in Aegean. *Juno*, *Greyhound*, *Kashmir* and *Kelly* sunk.

22 May: *Gloucester* and *Fiji* sunk near Crete.

Leading Telegraphist R.A.C. Green remembers the first time his destroyer *Firedrake* approached Grand Harbour:

"I was shocked at the graveyard of ships outside the harbour. Even inside there was a sunken submarine, the *Pandora*: a bomb had gone right through her conning tower. *Firedrake* was also a casualty. She was damaged by a low-flying torpedo bomber, so low I could have thrown a cricket ball at him."

Early in May the movement of convoyed ships and of naval warships continued with bewildering complexity. The cruisers *Orion*, *Ajax*, *Perth*, *Dido* and *Phoebe* made a rendezvous with the Mediterranean Fleet. *Fortune*, of the 8th Destroyer Flotilla, suffered damage and a heavy list, while the rest of the flotilla oiled in Malta, then followed Force H. Two days later all the British forces had reached either Gibraltar or Malta. Only fifty-seven out of 295 tanks and ten out of fifty-three Hurricanes had been lost.

While Terry Jackson was experiencing his baptism of fire early in May aboard HMS *Dido*, E. Merrey was undergoing a different experience. He wrote:

"In January 1941 I was with the Royal Worcs Regiment and was sent with a detachment with landed in Egypt to reinforce our 1st Battalion in the desert. I had just passed an armoured truck vehicle course. Volunteers were needed to act as AA gunners on a merchant convoy to Malta. . . . I volunteered, although there was quite a lot of danger. At Alex I was put on a captured Italian 9mm Breda AA gun which was in the bows of the Norwegian tanker *Hoeg Hood*. I thought 'Blimey' – petrol etc. One hit and we could say our prayers. We sailed with convoy MW-7."

Joseph Caruana of the National War Museum in Valletta provided details which supplement Merrey's description of a bombing attack on the convoy. "All bombs missed," Caruana tells us, "but it was very hair-raising." Merrey's gun misfired and two torpedo bombers penetrated the screen. Caruana confirmed:

"At 1711 of the 24th *Hoëg Hood* was torpedoed. This happened SSW of Sardinia (approximately 37½N and 8 E) by an S 79 aircraft of the 278 *Squadriglia* based in Sicily. . . . The tanker fell behind but managed to follow at reduced speed. She limped into Gibraltar on 28 July 1941."

Many years later Merrey's son came upon a remarkable coincidence. The son, a long-serving RAF Flight Sergeant, managed to locate the original combat report of his father's experience by the pilot of the aircraft, Captain Amedeo Mojoli. It seemed incredible that the report should still be on file (see facing page).

Caruana also relates another Italian incident in Valletta at about this time. An ULTRA intercept had indicated that the Italians were planning an unusual explosive boat attack against some British island. This was believed to be Malta. As a result of a radar echo the island's gunners were ordered to sleep by their guns when not at action stations. Thus when the attack came at 0440 the guns were ready for action within seconds. Of

Stato Maggiore dell'Aeronautica

Roma: _____

3° Reparto

Rif. N. SMA/552/ __ __ /M. 85

_-1-_

Allegato

OGGETTO: Richiesta notizie.

In merito a quanto richiesto con lettera del 10 aprile u.s., trasmessa dal Comando del 14°
Stormo, si comunica che la petroliera HOEGH HOOD il 24.7.1941 fu silurata da due velivoli
della 280^ Squadriglia e non da quelli della 278^ Squadriglia; si allega fotocopia della
Relazione di combattimento redatta dal Cap. Amedeo MOJOLI.

La 280^ Squadriglia Aerosiluranti, costituita da velivoli S.M. 79, era dislocata
sull'aeroporto di Cagliari Elmas in Sardegna.

d'ordine
IL CAPO DEL 5° UFFICIO in s.v.
(T.Col. AArn(n) Giancarlo DE MARCHIS)

A.J. MERREY
HEADQUARTERS LOGISTICS COMMAND
SM (Tor) 10d2 (RAF), Swates Pavilion, Rm W 150,
HQLC Royal Air Force Wyton, PO Box 69,
Huntingdon, Cambs. PE 17 2DL

Translation of the covering letter.

In response to your letter dated 10 April, that you sent to the Commander 14 Stormo.
The petrol tanker was torpedoed on 24/7/41 by aircraft from 280 Sqn and not 278 Sqn.
Attached is a photocopy of the combat report raised by Capt. Amedeo MOJOLI.
The 280 Sqn aircraft were SM79's and were based at Cagliari Elmas airfield in
Sardinia.

Information on the attack.

a.   Date of attack   24 July 1941
b.   Type of attack   Torpedo
c.   Target (for boats it is neccessary to indicate the number, type and position)
                                                1 Auxiliary cruiser 7000 tonnes
                                                1 Petrol tanker 15000 tonnes

     Position   f   37-28
                                                R   270
                                                A   9.37

d.   Parent base of aircraft   Elmas
e.   Time of departure from parent base   16.25
f.   Number of aircraft   3 x SM79 aircraft from 280 Sqn
g.   Name of Commander of formation   Capt Amedeo MOJOLI
h.   Weather condition on route   V.Good
i.   Flight level   500-100-40-500
l.   Time of arrival on target   18.00
m.   Weather condition on target   V.Good
n.   Total height at target
o.   Number of aircraft arrived on target   3
p.   Type of formation   Patrol
q.   Ammunition used   3 x Torpedoes against Petrol
                                                tanker and Cruiser.
r.   Result of the attack.   2 Torpedoes struck the petrol
                                                tanker on the left side of the bow
                                                section. The petrol tanker leaned
                                                violently to the right and then
                                                drifted very strongly to the left
                                                while sinking slowly.

s.   Reaction from the air
     (indicate possible number & type of   nil
     opponent aircraft)
t.   Reaction   2 canons fired from the auxilliary
                                                cruiser.
u.   Defensive action   2 machine guns fired from both
                                                ships.
v.   Time of return to base   19.25
z.   Number of aircraft returned   3
Particular Event

     The petrol tanker and cruiser hoisted the italian flag and when the aircraft
approached a green flare was fire from the ship.

the eight boats which attacked two were destroyed in an attempt to blow their way into the harbour, four were sunk by gunfire and two by aircraft.

Before we leave the naval battle for Crete we must follow some of the disasters which nearly brought the navy to its knees. A whole series of bombings sank several cruisers and destroyers. The attacks were relentless.

One of the first to go was the *Juno*. She was struck by three bombs after having survived three hours of bombing. Two of the bombs blew the after boiler room and the engine room open to the sea. The third bomb detonated her after magazine and the resulting explosion broke the ship in half and in two minutes she had gone. Six officers and ninety-one ratings, shocked, dazed and oil-sodden, were rescued from the sea by the destroyers *Kingston*, *Kandahar* and *Nubian*. One survivor was the Medical Officer, who reported:

> "I have no recollection of any noise or great concussion. The lights went out and I could just see redness. My small first aid party and I climbed up ladders and quickly followed others who were jumping overboard. Looking up from the water I could see the bows sliding under as the ship sank with no suction and hardly a ripple. . . . We had sunk in under a minute."

The destroyer *Greyhound* was the next victim of the bombers. She was hit by two bombs and sank in fifteen minutes. Rear Admiral King ordered the *Kandahar* and *Kingston* to pick up survivors, with the two cruisers *Gloucester* and *Fiji* standing by. Both cruisers were low in ammunition. The *Gloucester* was an experienced 'ship of the line'. She had been struck by more bombs than any other ship, according to some. Then, just before 4 pm, she was hit again and was soon ablaze. The fires gained control and she became a wreck. The *Fiji* had exhausted her main ammunition and was reduced to firing practice shells. She soon followed the *Gloucester*. Both ships sank – two cruisers lost in one afternoon. Important, too, were the casualties, the numbers of which have been a matter of some dispute. It is believed that there were only eighty-two survivors; the losses amounted to 693.

Rear Admiral King was criticized for handling this situation as he did. He had fragmented his fleet into a number of individual units, thereby losing the mutual protection that concentration afforded. He was sent home and never went to sea again.

The day following the end of the *Gloucester* and *Fiji* it was the turn of Captain Mountbatten's Fifth Flotilla: *Kelly, Kashmir, Kipling, Kelvin* and *Jackal*. At about 8 am on the 23 May twenty-four dive bombers attacked and sank the *Kashmir*, like the *Juno* in two minutes. *Kelly* was then hit by a large bomb. She was steaming at 30 knots and was under full helm. She listed heavily to port, capsized and floated upside down for half-an-hour before disappearing. The *Kipling* picked up 279 survivors, survived more than eighty bombs on her way back to Alexandria, ran out of fuel and had to be towed into harbour with seventy miles still to go.

On 27 May the decision to abandon Crete was taken. The fleet's losses in just a few days amounted to two cruisers and four destroyers, with damage to two battleships and one aircraft carrier, the *Formidable*. Five more cruisers and four destroyers had been damaged. Cunningham and his staff set about planning and executing another evacuation, but now with fewer ships and far fewer resources, and in more difficult circumstances.

Seamen and ships were worn out to the point of exhaustion. Cunningham wrote that he had "never felt prouder of the Mediterranean Fleet".

Fierce ordeals were still to be endured. From 5 pm until dark on the evening/night of 28–29 May Rawlings led a squadron under remorseless air and high-level bombing attacks en route to Heraklion. The Rear Admiral wore his flag in the cruiser *Orion*. He had with him *Ajax* and *Dido*, and the destroyers *Decoy, Jackal, Imperial, Hotspur, Kimberley* and *Hereward*. Fortunately only *Ajax* and *Imperial* were damaged.

By 3 am 4,000 men had been embarked; then, before the watch ended, things began to go wrong. *Imperial*'s steering failed. Rawlings ordered *Hotspur* to embark her troops, then to

80

sink her. *Hotspur* should then rejoin the Admiral. In the grey light of dawn *Hotspur* was now crowded with 900 soldiers and two ships' companies, and there ahead steamed Rawlings' force. The Admiral reduced the fleet's speed to 15 knots to allow *Hotspur* to catch up. Speed was then increased, but the force was now about 1½ hours behind schedule, allowing the enemy five or six hours of daylight to bomb the force.

The raids began, predictably, at 0600 and continued intermittently throughout the day.

Hotspur was still speeding to her station on the starboard wing of the force and still had a mile to go when six Ju 87 Stuka dive bombers from Scarpanto, a mere 25 miles away, singled her out for the first attack. She lacked the multi-pom-poms of the more modern J and K classes, and the fact she was out of station increased her vulnerability. Lieutenant-Commander C.P.F. Brown handled the ship with skill, swinging her over to port then to starboard, threading the destroyer through the giant eruptions of water as the bombs exploded – "snaking the line" as some refer to it.

As the Stukas dived on the destroyer Brown employed the tactic learned quickly by the navy of turning the ship towards the diving aircraft to make its angle of descent steeper and steeper, forcing it to pull out of the dive early. The quicker a ship could move to achieve this the greater her chances of spoiling the pilot's aim and surviving the attack.

Aboard the *Hotspur* soldiers manned their Bren guns, others their Tommy guns and even rifles. Each Stuka was met with a hail of bullets and tracers.

"At 0625 when the force was in the middle of the Kaso Strait the *Hereward* on the port side of the force came in for the next attack. The first few Stukas were averted, but another, diving very low, let go a stick of bombs, one of which exploded near her foremost funnel. She swung out of line, her speed dropped away and she lost station on the screen. She was crippled . . . and she had 450 troops aboard."

Vice Admiral Rawlings was now faced with another grim decision, the second in only a few hours: whether to send another destroyer to assist *Hereward* or whether to abandon her to her fate. The fact that Crete lay just five miles away persuaded him to leave *Hereward* to her own devices. The crippled destroyer limped her way to the coast. Her feelings can be imagined. She was still firing her guns as Rawlings' force steadily drew away to Alexandria.

Commander Bragadin gives a different report of this incident. He claims that it was an Italian torpedo-carrying aircraft which torpedoed the *Hereward*, leaving her dead in the water. He goes on to say that patrolling MAS boats then approached the *Hereward*, there was an explosion and the British destroyer sank. The MAS boats then rescued the majority of *Hereward*'s crew and troops.

At 0645 the destroyer *Decoy* was hit and her speed reduced. Nearly an hour later, at 0735, the *Orion*'s captain, Captain G.R.B. Back, was mortally wounded by an explosive bullet. *Orion* was damaged by a near miss.

At 0815 the *Dido* suffered disastrously when she was hit on B turret. She had endured eight near-misses in rapid succession. The ninth hit the target. The blast of the detonation whipped through the marines' mess deck which was crowded with stunned troops. Dreadful casualties occurred. Fire swept through the area, hindering rescue work and damage control. First-aid parties were unable to reach the casualties until the fires were brought under control. Twenty-seven sailors and nineteen soldiers were killed and ten sailors and twenty-eight soldiers were wounded by this one bomb.

Hugh Hodgkinson, aboard *Hotspur*, witnessed the bombing and recalled:

"A great sphere of black smoke burst out from ahead of the bridge and a single stick-like object curled up into the air and dropped smoking into the sea. It was one of her guns from a fore turret. Then she seemed to come steering out of the blackness like a miracle, and she was engaging aircraft with her after guns and one gun missing from B turret with its twin bent nearly double."

Forty-five minutes later the flagship *Orion* suffered a similar blow when a Ju 87 dropped a bomb on A turret. The pilot made a suicide attack. The bomb burst with devastating results; the whole of the armour casing was blasted away, destroying the guns and crippling B turret too.

At 9.30 *Orion* was near-missed again and her captain was mortally wounded. By now Commander T.C.T. Wyne had taken command. Yet another attack developed later in the forenoon when eleven yellow-nosed Stukas selected *Orion* as their target. Bombs rained down. The last few bombers could only have aimed their bombs at the maelstrom of seething water spray and smoke. Clearly she was out of control. A large bomb pierced the bridge, missing two officers by a hair's breadth, continued through the signal deck, passing the torso of a signalman, through the sick bay, into the stokers' mess crammed with evacuated soldiers, and exploding on the crowded deck above the 4-inch magazine. The ship gave a sickening shudder. All communications between the bridge and the engine room and the after steering position had been severed. Compass, telegraphs and steering were all wrecked. Total darkness hampered rescue. One boiler room was out of action. Three out of five engine-room officers were killed.

The scene in the sick bay was one of indescribable devastation. Horribly mutilated bodies littered the cots and decks; nauseating smells pervaded everywhere below decks. The injuries were horrendous. The final count amounted to 262 men dead and 300 wounded. Valiant efforts were made by soldiers and sailors to get the wreck of the cruiser shipshape.

In time the ship recovered. She was got under control and, with only one shaft turning, with steering by hand, back on course.

Orion and the rest of the squadron survived the rest of the day's bombing, reached the sanctuary of Alexandria and discharged a total of 3,486 troops. Another estimated 600 were killed or captured. *Orion* arrived with only two rounds of her 6-inch HE ammunition and a mere 10 tons of fuel oil. Cunningham watched her enter harbour:

"I shall never forget the sight of these ships coming up harbour, the guns of *Orion*'s fore turret awry, one or two broken off and pointing forlornly skywards. . . . The ship was a terrible sight and the mess deck a shambles."

The evacuation of Crete continued until 1 June when yet another cruiser, the small obsolescent *Calcutta*, (Captain D.M. Lees) was sunk. The Germans, for what it was worth, had won the island. Never before or since has an island been conquered from the air. It was a fruitless victory, a damaging defeat for the Mediterranean Fleet and the Malta convoys. It was also a sign-post to the dominance of air power at sea and the destiny of Malta.

On 31 May the C-in-C informed the Admiralty that he was terminating the evacuation that night and even if Rear Admiral King's force returned unscathed from the night's operation, the Mediterranean Fleet would have been reduced to only two battleships, one cruiser, one AA cruiser (the AA cruiser *Calcutta* was sunk the next morning), one minelayer and nine destroyers fit for service. The cost of the operation had been:

British and Dominion:	1,742 dead
	1,737 wounded
	1,835 Prisoners of war

Unclassified others killed, wounded, captured: 800
More significantly the ship losses amounted to

Sunk:	3 cruisers and 6 destroyers
Damaged:	2 battleships, 1 aircraft carrier,
	5 cruisers, 7 destroyers.

It was the much-depleted and battle-scarred remainder that were now expected to concentrate their efforts on battling the convoys through to Malta.

This chapter must finish on another Prime Ministerial note of disapproval. When Cunningham announced that the losses being sustained were too great to justify further losses, Churchill retorted, "What do you think we build ships for? C-in-C must be made to take every risk. Saving Crete would be well worth the loss of half the Mediterranean Fleet." It was a comment much resented by the naval staff in Alexandria.

Commander Martin Evans who served at Malta's St Angelo for two years at the height of the blitz as Staff Officer (Operations) wrote that the impression of brave little Malta sticking it out gave an inaccurate picture:

"We never quite ceased to carry out offensive operations. . . . Malta was primarily and all the time an offensive operational base."

SUMMER INTERLUDE FOR MALTA: AUTUMN ONSLAUGHT

Nothing will make me believe that we shall not triumph in the end. . . . We are a kindly people, slow to anger and very tolerant. Our cause is a just one, probably the most just for which we ever engaged. We may not see it, but just as I know the sun will rise tomorrow, so do I know that we shall eventually win.

Admiral Sir Andrew Cunningham to
Rear Admiral George Hector Creswell, June, 1940

The long, dreary month of May, 1941, dragged on, bringing few developments for Cunningham to celebrate. Ashore in North Africa Rommel's battalions held a battle line roughly similar to Egypt's frontier. Tobruk stood like an island, still in British hands and a constant irritant to the German flank. At sea a major convoy was assembling. Malta and the North African armies sustaining Tobruk necessitated the provision of a regular supply of armaments, military paraphernalia and foodstuffs. It was especially necessary to minimize the losses in small craft; the losses in minesweepers were particularly irksome and an ever-present burden. These, Cunningham recorded, were the price to pay for the almost complete lack of air cover. His staff gave priority to the Tobruk situation. Orders were issued to all destroyers or other warships regularly going to Tobruk that they must carry stores to the garrison and bring away personnel. The average daily supply of stores was considered to be 70 tons. And to minimize losses, Tobruk was to be cleared between dawn and dusk.

An equally urgent necessity was the resolution of the use by the Germans and Italians of sea mines. These were proving extremely effective in the approaches to Malta and to a lesser degree to the harbour and approaches to Alexandria. Captain Mountbatten, on arrival in Malta to relieve Captain Mack's flotilla, was soon involved in a mining incident. Only five days after his arrival, the destroyer *Jersey* was mined in the entrance to Grand Harbour.

Gunner Cliff Drake of the destroyer HMS *Jackal* recalls the sadness of watching his sister ship, the *Jersey*, go down after the mining: "Three of our ships had passed over the acoustic mines: *Jersey* was fourth in line . . . yet it was she who detonated the mine."

Jersey's sinking bottled up other warships for some days, effectively closing Valletta's harbour and dispersing arrivals to other destinations. The Tiger Convoy became entangled in such a mining incident. Two of the transports were mined, one of them sinking. A similar incident occurred at Alexandria, bringing the harbour to a standstill.

A call for volunteers from the army personnel on the island to serve in Defensively Equipped Merchant Ships (DEMS) brought a good response. One such volunteer was J. Dean of the 1st Battalion, Bedfordshire and Hertfordshire Regiment, stationed in Alexandria. Gunners of all sorts were required to man guns aboard seven merchant ships about to leave Alexandria for Malta. Dean joined the Liverpool ship *Settler*. Once clear of the land the crew were told that the destination was Malta and that half the Mediterranean Fleet was to be the escort. Dean wrote of his experience:

"All went well until we were in the Straits of Pantellaria when all hell broke loose. The convoy was attacked by dive bombers, high-level bombers and torpedo bombers. On arrival at Malta we started to unload, but as the raids were pretty frequent it was decided that we should be billeted with the Cheshire Regiment where we were fed and paid until all seven ships of the convoy were unloaded, which because of continuous raids took three months."

James Miller was a Second Engineer Officer in the *City of Lincoln* (8,000 tons), "one of the best ships in the Merchant Navy". In Alexandria the ship was loaded with a large cargo of aviation spirit and ammunition, plus much general cargo. James Miller reported:

"The ship had a Lewis gun and an ancient WW I 4-inch gun mounted aft. This was manned by our own crew and trained by our naval gunner who carried out occasional practice firing at objects thrown overboard. . . . The lifeboat was lowered and we set off for Lux beach to fill sandbags to build gun emplacements, one each side of the funnel and around the monkey island above the bridge. We became the proud possessor of two captured Italian .22 Breda machine guns. . . . Apart from a few scattered bomb bursts on the far side of the convoy the trip to Malta was uneventful." The ship "slid into the historic harbour to the cheers of spectators on the Barraca, then anchoring at Parlatoro where we were soon surrounded by lighters and ready to discharge."

Miller relates how the ship was soon swarming with RAF, navy and army personnel to unload the "precious" cargo. While alongside

"we had a lookout posted. His job was to warn when a black flag was hoisted ashore, the warning of incoming enemy aircraft. They were not long in coming. We scrambled over the lighters into the safety of a nearby cavern. The sound of heavy gunfire followed by the sound of Stukas was dwarfed by the sound of bombs. We emerged from the shelter to find the lighters had been cut adrift. Those who had remained on board were visibly shaken and thereafter, on the lookout blowing his whistle, it was a case of abandon ship, then get ashore quickly. The second raid scored bomb bursts very close . . . it was debris everywhere. A bomb had hit our bridge and blown it and the monkey island to bits."

The *City of Lincoln* was soon back in business and equipped with a Bofors and two Oerlikons with a DEMS crew of gunners. On another visit to the island Miller remembered one evening:

"After we had discharged our cargo some peace and quiet had descended over this historic island. Nearby lay a cruiser and a Marine band started playing on the quarter deck – stirring music and a wonderful setting, and, as the sun descended, the lowering of the flag; the trumpets sounded clear and true signifying the end of the day, seeming to reflect the magnitude and magnificence of the British Empire."

On another passage from Gibraltar to Malta the *Lincoln* sailed under false colours and arrived totally unmolested. While discharging, the engines were running slowly as this was supposed to discourage Italian frogmen attaching limpet mines. Miller continues:

"By this time the area around the harbour was completely shattered and I remember climbing over ruins to get back to the ship after visits ashore. The labour of centuries had been destroyed."

Two army anecdotes deserve recording. Corporal Herbert W. Outen served with the Royal Hampshire Regiment and the Maritime Royal Artillery, taking passage to Malta aboard HMS *Ajax*. He recalls the Battalion being split up into company positions throughout the island in various villages. He remembers them quite well, but "I don't think I can spell them". His duties included a watch for parachute drops, but the most frequent role was to fill bomb holes in the airfield runways, and on occasions unloading cargoes from ships. Outen also carried out the duty of regimental policeman; at other times we find him manning a Lewis gun against low-flying Messerschmitts.

Sergeant A.J. Stevens, Royal Artillery, served aboard the MV *Clan Macdonald*. His most vivid recollection is of "watching Stukas dive-bombing and crippling the aircraft carrier *Illustrious* in January, 1941". Another duty was the protection his troop afforded HM submarines on Manoel Island.

"We were positioned on the very tip of the island . . . a few hundred yards from the submarines. We manned 3.7 inch heavy AA guns. In the six weeks we were there over 900 bombs landed within our perimeter wire. Fortunately for us our guns were on high ground, surrounded by a deep moat dug out by the Knights of Malta where many of the bombs exploded harmlessly. We suffered surprisingly few casualties. One, Sergeant Mullens, lost a leg and complained afterwards that his missing toes were itching."

Sergeant Stevens recalled another incident. It was the day Farson's Brewery at Hamrun was bombed:

"The news spread like wildfire and soon steady streams of service personnel were on their way with containers of all sizes and shapes. Our troop was lucky as we had a large mobile water tank drawn by our own transport – an ancient and extremely stubborn mule. The beer tasted terrible and there were many thick heads around for days afterwards."

Corporal Outen, the regimental policeman, was a witness to a near disaster during an air raid when

"the church at Mosta was bombed one afternoon. I actually watched this happen when a large bomb penetrated the roof, bounced off a wall two or three times, slid along the floor and failed to explode. What a miracle! There was a large congregation at the time. The actual bomb is now in the foyer of the church as a collecting box."

1. The Italian cruiser *Bartolomeo Colleoni* on fire and sinking during her engagement with the Australian cruiser HMAS *Sydney*, Mediterranean 1940. *(Norman C. Drake)*

2. The destroyer *Fearless* was hit by a bomb on the stern. She could not be saved and was sunk by her own forces. Note the battleship *Nelson* in the foreground. She suffered a torpedo hit for'ard. Malta convoy 1941. *(Norman C. Drake)*

3. Swastika souvenir Crete 1941. HMS *Dido*. *(R. Overend)*

4. Ron Overend and Jack Hootan of HMS *Dido*, Alexandria, May, 1941. *(R. Overend)*

5. Petty Officer Dick Richards DSC. (*Mrs D. Richards*)

6. Captain Nichol of HMS *Penelope* splicing the mainbrace after the action of 9 November, 1941. (*Mrs Bland*)

7. Everyone celebrated the action of 9 November by splicing the mainbrace. Here are some of *Penelope*'s crew. (*Mrs Bland*)

8. The destruction of an Italian oil tanker of 10,000 tons and a destroyer of 1,600 tons. The destroyer blew up. HMS *Lively* is going in for survivors. 1 December, 1941. *(Mrs Bland)*

9. Even between convoy operations ships' companies were encouraged to take part in boxing. Our correspondent W. J. Smith is the boxer on the right. This is aboard HMS *Rodney*. *(W. J. Smith)*

10. HMS *Centurion* was disguised to resemble a King George V battleship and so deceive the enemy. Note the dhobying on the fo'c'sle of the cruiser. Mediterranean, 1942. *(R. Overend)*

11. HMS *Illustrious* was almost crippled by seven bomb hits, many near misses and a crashed bomber. She is seen here almost obliterated by cascades of water on 11 January, 1941. *(Ronald Reed)*

12. Admiral Sir James Somerville was C-in-C Force H, based on Gibraltar. *(Somerville Collection)*

13. Rear Admiral H. B. Rawlings survived the bombing of two of his flagships, the battleship *Warspite* and the cruiser *Orion* during the Malta Convoys

14. The camp at Laghouat, Algeria, where Henry Hollington was interned. *(Mrs Ivy Hollington)*

15. Henry Hollington, who survived the sinking of the cruiser *Manchester* (see plate 14). *(Mrs Ivy Hollington)*

16. Corporal Goosey of the Cheshire Regiment helped unload ships at Malta. *(R. W. Goosey)*

17. The cruiser HMS *Aurora,* a member of the Force K Striking Force, leading a Malta convoy. *(H. A. (Bert) Rawlings)*

18. Photograph taken by a war correspondent aboard the light cruiser *Hermione* during the passage of a Malta convoy. *(L. A. Warnes)*

19. The destroyer *Bedouin* about to sink after being torpedoed 15 July, 1942. *(L. B. Clowes)*

20. The aircraft carrier *Illustrious* was crippled in the convoy battle of January, 1941. Even after limping into Malta she was still battered almost daily. She is under attack in this picture, beyond the crane by the tall plume of smoke. January, 1941. *(Mrs M. Bland)*

21. As she was not a front-line ship HMS *Argus* was used to fly off Spitfires and Hurricanes to Malta. *(Mrs D. Richards)*

22. One of the scores of German aircraft shot down during the convoy battles. *(Mrs I. L. Baker)*

23. The aircraft carrier *Eagle* sinking. Her flight deck can be seen to extend from the edge of the photograph to the merchant ship's foremast. *(W. J. Smith)*

24. Cliff Drake served in HMS *Rodney* and J and K class destroyers. *(C. Drake)*

25. Harry Kirkham's escape from his sunken ship and his escape in North Africa read like an adventure story. *(H. Kirkham)*

26. HMS *Indomitable* under fierce aircraft attack. *(Ronald Reed)*

27. *Rowallan Castle* in tow 14 February, 1942, during the passage of convoy ME-10. Photograph taken from the cruiser *Penelope*. The *Rowallan Castle* subsequently sank. *(Mrs Bland)*

28. One of the hundreds of Italian aircraft destroyed during the passage of the Malta convoys 1940-42. *(Norman C. Drake)*

29. The cruiser *Kenya* straddled fore and aft by bomb bursts. The high-level attacks were mostly Italian, the dive-bombing predominantly German. (*Norman C. Drake*)

30. HMS *Nelson*, a majestic capital ship of 33,950 tons and 9 x 16 inch guns, was used in Force H and gave cover to Malta convoys. (*A. F. Walker*)

31. Operation Pedestal: a merchant vessel is torpedoed. A destroyer is laying off. August, 1942. *(W. J. Smith)*

32. HMS *Indomitable* was seriously damaged in the Pedestal Operation of August, 1942. *(W. Bradshaw)*

33. Submariner Terry E. (Bish) Bishop. *(T. E. Bishop)*

34. The cruiser *Nigeria* near-missed during the Pedestal convoy. August, 1942. *(A. V. Ellis)*

35. The destroyer *Lance,* one of Force K's ships, damaged and in dry dock. Malta, 1942. *(E. Brown)*

36. Operation Pedestal – August, 1942. The tanker *Ohio* entered Grand Harbour lashed between two destroyers, towed by another and guided by a fourth. Hers was an epic convoy battle. *(National War Museum Association, Malta)*

37. An Italian torpedo-carrying aircraft has just released its weapon, attacking the British Tribal Class destroyer IIMS *Bedouin*. *(L. B. Clowes)*

38. The carrier *Eagle* was sunk during Operation Pedestal in August, 1942. *(A. F. Walker)*

39. The tanker *Ohio* being dive-bombed during an air raid. She survived and limped into harbour. *(W. J. Smith)*

OPERATION SUBSTANCE

It is seamen not ships that constitute a navy.

Admiral Sir Charles Napier
(1786–1860)

Operation Substance of July, 1941, was the code-name given to a convoy which had its origins in mid-June. Advantage was taken of Germany's preoccupation with the newly-opened Russian front. Germany had redeployed squadrons of aircraft from Sicily and Sardinia, providing Malta with a modest lull, and the need to run a convoy to Malta was self-evident. In particular Malta's stocks of food were depleted and the long, protracted campaign in Greece and Crete had drained the navy of its resources. AA shells and aviation fuel were at a point of near-exhaustion and in dire need of replenishment.

The withdrawal of Germany's air squadrons still left a formidable and violent enemy, comprising about 200 Italian high-level bombers, supplemented by some Junkers. They posed a serious threat.

But it was Italy's naval strength which posed the greater threat. In mid-June it was believed that the Italian navy had available for action five battleships, ten cruisers, twenty destroyers and thirty to forty MAS or E boats, plus numerous submarines. Later the Prime Minister found the words to describe the nation's fears:

"Amid the torrent of violent events one anxiety reigned supreme. . . . Dominating all our power to carry on the war, or even keep ourselves alive, lay our mastery of the ocean and the free approach and entry to our ports."

Prudently the island had been fully stocked before hostilities began, and during the first nine months of war twenty-four supply ships discharged a total cargo of 146,000 tons. A random example of what a typical ship carried in terms of food supplies was (in tons):

Wheat (787)   Beans (723)   Rice (164)

Salt (12)   Coffee (49)   Eggs (83)

Soap (17)   Olive Oil (12)   Onions (29)

Peanuts (30)   Oranges (13)

Other items carried a high-priority rating, such as cement for building gun emplacements and forage for the goats, on which the island's milk supply depended.

For the July convoy to Malta the Admiralty summoned six merchantmen and a troopship for special duties. The convoy comprised the following (displacement in tons):

Melbourne Star   (10,800)

City of Pretoria   (7,900)

Sydney Star   (11,000)

Durham   (10,900)

Deucalion   (7,800)

Port Chalmers   (8,500)

Leinster   (4,302)

We have already read of the *Leinster* which ran aground and whose 1,750 army personnel had to be transferred to three cruisers for the passage to Malta.

BRITISH FORCES
OPERATION SUBSTANCE

COVERING FORCE H

Renown	Flag Vice Admiral Somerville
Ark Royal	
Hermione	(temporarily replaced *Sheffield*)
Destroyers:	*Faulknor, Fearless, Foxhound, Firedrake, Foresight, Fury, Forester, Duncan*

HOME FLEET

Nelson	
Manxman	(minelayer)
Edinburgh	Flag Rear Admiral Syfret
Manchester	
Arethusa	
Destroyers:	*Cossack, Maori, Sikh, Nestor* (RAN), *Lightning, Farndale, Avondale, Eridge*

MEDITERRANEAN FLEET

8 Submarines off Calabria, Naples and N of Sicily. Also both sides of the Messina Straits.

Even as the Blue Funnel Line ship *Deucalion* began embarking stores at Swansea, the Fourth Engineer Stan J. Dodd guessed something special was happening. He wrote:

"It was sensed that this was a special voyage because we were loading general food supplies and *Deucalion* had limited but useful refrigeration cargo space, a lot of War Department equipment, loads of bully beef and endless 4 or 5 gallon drums of 'High Octane' aircraft fuel. The special voyage feeling was confirmed when a contingent of soldiers (I think about 40 or 50) embarked. They had very basic accommodation. They carried all their own gear including sleeping bags and were made as comfortable as possible. I learned later they were 'crack' AA gunners from the

Cheshire Regiment. *Deucalion* joined a convoy and headed south."

One of the ships was the *Sydney Star*. Six gunners and an NCO boarded her in Liverpool as a gun's crew. A. Cockburn recalls his experiences:

"We had of course been issued with naval clothes, lifebelt, tropical dress and civilian clothes. I was comforted when the *Sydney Star* broke out into the Atlantic with the rest of the convoy to find we were in company with the *Ark Royal* and quite a number of heavy cruisers and destroyers. Soon *City of Pretoria* and *Port Chalmers* joined up."

Captain W.G. Higgs was master of *Port Chalmers*. Higgs had watched the substantial cargo being loaded into the holds: 2,000 tons of aviation spirit in 4 or 5 gallon drums, cement, maize, wheat, flour, whisky, tobacco, cigarettes, corned beef and mutton, bales of cloth, guns, shells, cars, ammunition, lorries and aircraft components. Higgs, too, was comforted by the substantial presence of the navy.

Vice Admiral Somerville commanded the Operation. He sent a message in dramatic fashion via a destroyer to each master. The Force was still 150 miles off Gibraltar and the message was shot by rocket line. It was a personal message from the Admiral:

"For over twelve months Malta has resisted all attacks of the enemy. The gallantry displayed by the garrison and people of Malta has aroused admiration throughout the world. To enable their defence to be continued, it is essential that your ships, with their valuable cargoes, should arrive safely in Grand Harbour. The Royal Navy will escort and assist you in this great mission: you on your part can assist the Royal Navy by giving strict attention to the following points: Don't make smoke. Don't show any lights at night. Keep good station. Don't straggle. If your ship is damaged keep her going at the best possible speed. Provided every officer and man realizes it is up to him to do his duty to the very best of his ability, I feel sure that we shall succeed.

Remember that the watchword is: THE CONVOY MUST GO THROUGH."

Each Captain opened his personal package at midday.

The convoy approached Gibraltar in thick fog, so dense that the rock was invisible. Other troubles had developed. *Pasteur* failed to join the convoy and *Leinster*, as we have seen, ran aground.

Robert A. Hamilton was a radio officer aboard the MV *City of Pretoria*. She, too, had embarked a cargo of war materials, plus a small contingent of 130 soldiers and twelve officers. Hamilton was impressed by what he could see of the navy escort:

> "Our RN escort is amazing – *Nelson, Renown,* at least six cruisers and many other navy warships were in company. On 22 July the fun really began! Six torpedo bombers and many Italian high-level bombers attacked the convoy at intervals throughout the day. We lost three of our aircraft but shot down seven."

Unknown to Hamilton, diversions were being created in the eastern Mediterranean by the deployment of submarines off Italian ports, all designed to safeguard the ships of the convoy.

Despite all efforts, losses occurred. When Force H neared the Narrows the major fleet units turned about to return to Gibraltar, the usual procedure, so that the capital ships should not be subjected to unacceptable risk. Thus the convoy was left with only cruisers and destroyers to provide protection.

The first casualty was the *Manchester*. On 23 July two MAS boats, Nos. 16 and 22, launched torpedoes at the cruiser. Only a short while previously the *Port Chalmers* had been admonished by the *Manchester* for failing to keep up. *Manchester* had signalled her: "S STANDS FOR STRAGGLER – AND SUNK."

Port Chalmers was then two cables astern of station but coming up fast. That was at 9.15 am. Nineteen minutes later nine hostile aircraft came into sight. *Nelson* was still giving distant cover and when she opened fire. The air, Captain Higgs of *Port*

Chalmers reported, vibrated with thunderous crashes. Bombs exploded among the ships but none was hit.

Stan Dodd, aboard *Deucalion*, reports that the aircraft "rained down their bombs". He added: "*Ark Royal* seemed to be their chief target. We watched bombs dropping all around her but she was not hit, probably due to expert navigation and steady AA defences."

It was during this pause that the Italian bombers scored some successes. *Manchester* was hit by a torpedo or a bomb which severely damaged the cruiser. C.P.O. Hughes recalled the incident:

> "Before we could reach our destination the poor old *Manchester* was hit in an oil fuel tank. Adjacent compartments were flooded and as far as I can remember two of our engines were put out of commission but we managed to get back to Gibraltar."

Hughes confirms that the soldiers aboard were a great help in backing up the crew in a variety of duties such as damage control and dragging out survivors from the wreckage.

> "Our skipper, Captain Drew, broadcast a tribute to the ship's company and the Lancaster soldiers: 'Your courage and wonderful behaviour saved our ship'."

Almost immediately after this the destroyer *Fearless* was struck by a torpedo which disabled her. She was taken in tow but was unable to be saved. The *Forester* had to sink her sister ship. Stan Dodd watched the incident.

> "We were all depressed watching her crew jumping over the side. They would no doubt be picked up as there was plenty of help around. Some Italian airmen had been shot down and baled out into rubber dinghies. They were mockingly trying to thumb a lift from us. After seeing *Fearless* go down you can imagine how we were all feeling. One of the Cheshire Regiment soldiers standing alongside me had his rifle trained on the dinghy, but one of the officers walking past tapped him on the shoulder and said, 'We don't do that in the British army'."

Dodd recorded a skirmish with Italian MAS boats:

> "We could hear E boats in the pitch dark roaring through the shipping lanes and we could hear aircraft above. Frequently the destroyers exposed their searchlights and then 'let go' with all they had – all was acrid smoke, brilliant blue and orange as the big guns were fired and then a few seconds of dark and quietness until the next time. All this went on for quite a few hours. It was too exciting to be frightened."

It was during this last skirmish that *Sydney Star* was torpedoed and damaged in the bows. Dodd makes little of the experience.

> "By the expedient of her pumps she stayed afloat and made port. I don't think anybody was hurt."

Captain Horn was more expansive. He had nursed his ship for eleven days since leaving Liverpool:

> "Now at 3 am on the morning of 24 July he stood by the wheel watching the streams of blood-red tracers skimming the sea listening to the thunder of engines as the E boats at 40 knots tore in and out of the ships. Cordite fumes went streaming away down wind. Shells from a wildly firing merchantman scythed into *Sydney Star*'s starboard lifeboat. Searchlights tilted, swivelled and dipped. In the darkness torpedo wakes were almost impossible to see. . . . Captain Horn suddenly spotted the wake of an E boat running parallel to the *Sydney Star* less than 50 yards to port."

Ian Cameron also described the torpedoing of the *Sydney Star*. The E boat commander was raising his telephone tube to his mouth to order an emergency turn when the torpedo hit him.

> "It hit them . . . opposite No. 3 hold. For a second a pyramid of flame leaped funnel-high. Then the flame was doused . . . by the great cataract of water which came pouring through the shattered hull. A great cavern 40 ft × 20 ft was torn out of the ship's side." (Other sources suggest the torpedo exploded in the port bows, rather more for'ard than Cameron suggests.)

The *Sydney Star*'s engines stopped. She fell away. Within seconds she was down by the head and listing drunkenly as thousands of gallons of water flooded into her. Captain Horn felt his ship give a huge heave beneath him and wondered whether she was about to founder. He now had the prime responsibility of his human cargo to consider.

Sydney Star had embarked twenty army officers and 464 troops, most of them from the 32nd Light AA regiment, in addition to the grain, naval stores and ammunition which she carried. It was pitch dark and the soldiers were handicapped by unfamiliarity with the ship. As a precaution the Captain ordered everyone to their "abandon ship" stations. Discipline among the troops was excellent; they mustered at their stations while Captain Horn discussed with Chief Engineer Haig and Chief Officer Machie all necessary damage control. They organized the shoring and strengthening of bulkheads, but the prognosis seemed poor. Pumps were not coping with the rapid influx of water.

The 11,000-ton ship lay stopped and listing. She refused to answer the helm and she appeared to be settling by the head. She was also drifting with the tide, getting ever closer to Pantellaria, now only three miles away. Darkness would provide some safety but a few hours of daylight remained, so Captain Horn decided to take off the troops.

The Australian destroyer *Nestor* responded to Horn's signal for assistance. Commander A.R. Rosenthal RAN handled his destroyer skillfully, bringing her close alongside for transference of the troops, never an easy evolution even in the best of conditions. Gangplanks were secured to *Sydney*'s gunwhales and Jacob's ladders were rigged aft. The disembarkation began and troops swarmed aboard *Nestor* even while E-boat engines could be heard periodically. Fortunately sea and weather conditions held good.

Within half an hour something like 500 men had been transferred to the destroyer. Captain Horn and a few essential men from the *Sydney Star* remained aboard the freighter. The engines were nursed into action and Captain Horn gently increased speed until she was heading for Malta at a speed of 12 knots.

Dawn was breaking slowly in the east. It found *Sydney Star* with *Nestor* in company, the freighter down by the head in a deceptively smooth sea with E-boats over the horizon and torpedo-carrying aircraft ready for take off. Two reconnaissance aircraft appeared on the scene. Horn now felt more vulnerable than at any other time. Among those transferred to *Nestor* were the gun's crews of the four Bofors, 3 inch HA and three machine guns, their weapons now lying idle. Voluntary scratch guns' crews were summoned from the remaining crew and Captain Horn felt somehow comforted to have some weapons available, even though he realized their inefficiency.

The Savoia aircraft made a half-hearted attack at long range, but the evasive action taken by the crippled ship worsened her condition. She became heavier on the wheel, lower by the head and increasingly unhandy.

> "Still the water gained. *Sydney Star* yawed and wallowed. . . . Captain Horn estimated that she had shipped 7,000 tons of water."

An unexpected attack by a single aircraft occurred at 7 am, but the torpedo missed and exploded in the freighter's wake.

The cruiser *Hermione* made a welcome arrival and some Beaufighters dispersed an air attack. *Hermione* and *Nestor* added their barrage of fire. By now the main convoy had reached Valletta. Stan Dodd described the arrival:

> "Most of the navy seemed to have dispersed. . . . Sailing through the Valletta entrance the freighters were given a wonderful reception from the thousands of Maltese lining the slopes [of the Barracas] cheering and clapping. They even had a band playing *Rule Britannia*.The ships were unloaded almost immediately, dry-docked and put under repair."

Meanwhile the *Sydney Star* was still struggling to keep afloat and make headway. At 8 am she reached the swept channel. She entered Grand Harbour to rapturous applause. It had been an epic of survival.

One of the convoy, the *Deucalion*, departed Malta for

Gibraltar and made a successful run. On arrival a signal was received from HMS *Nelson*:

"JOLLY GOOD SHOW *DEUCALION*. INVITATION TO OFFICERS FOR PRE-LUNCH DRINKS."

Deucalion's venture ended in the Bethlehem Steel Shipyard, New York. The American shipyard workers were amazed and called the officers to the dockyard bottom to show where the near-miss had scraped the paint off the ship's side. Sadly the *Deucalion* was lost on a future Malta convoy.

When it was *City of Pretoria*'s turn to leave Malta Robert Hamilton remembers:

"We had large tarpaulins draped over each side of the ship painted with the Vichy flag and we also flew the tricolour from the mast. But they [the Italian aircraft] were not to be duped: later on the same day three Italian torpedo-aircraft and a U-boat attacked us. We hauled down the tricolour and hoisted the red ensign, and fired every gun on the ship. They fired their torpedoes at us but missed, and then they machine-gunned us, but with no casualties."

The *City of Pretoria* had an uneventful trip to Gibraltar and arrived safe, unscathed and happy. Hamilton concluded:

"The *Durham, Melbourne Star, Port Chalmers* and the *Leinster* (which ran aground at the start of Operation Substance) were all in harbour."

They all experienced the comfortably warm glow of achievement.

While *Sydney Star* was undergoing her ordeal one of the convoy's escort, an F Class destroyer, was struggling to ward off the enemy and to give herself a chance of survival. HMS *Firedrake* was a fleet destroyer of 1,350 tons (4 x 4.7 inch guns). Able Seaman George V. Dougall was serving aboard her on the afternoon of 23 July. In one of the air attacks of that afternoon off Cape Bon *Firedrake* received a direct bomb hit in No. 1

boiler room. The damage was extensive, from the waterline right down to the bilge keel. Dougall, a 12-pounder AA gunner, recalls:

> "Orders were given to stand-by to abandon ship. We were in the Narrows with the hills of Tunisia in the distance. Rather a long swim, I thought! The engineer officer warned the captain that he would try to raise steam in twenty minutes. And while *Firedrake* wallowed in the swell of the Mediterranean the convoy and the rest of the escorts proceeded on their course to Malta."

Dougall recalls that a Hunt class destroyer was detached from the convoy's escort to give assistance:

> "in towing us back to Gibraltar, a journey of about 800 miles. In the meantime engineers and stokers were working full out to shore up bulkheads and to repair steam pipes. Seamen on deck were busy, too, rigging collision mats over the damaged ship's side and arranging the tow to the Hunt destroyer."

By the next morning it could be seen that progress had been slow and *Firedrake* was a sitting duck in Mussolini's so-called "Lake". After about 36 hours the engine room staff were able to raise steam and make about 8 knots. Dougall recalls:

> "It was a great feeling when Vice Admiral Somerville in *Renown* caught up with *Firedrake* and steamed his fleet in line ahead and their companies gave HMS *Firedrake* a rousing three cheers!"

One other casualty deserves mention. She was the 9,351-ton tanker, the Norwegian *Hoëg Hood*. She was empty, heading for Gibraltar, having unloaded her cargo in Malta. She was travelling alone when attacked by a torpedo aircraft south of Sardinia. She managed to survive the attack and reached Gibraltar safely.

On this same day, 23 July, 1941, the cruiser *Edinburgh* continued steaming for Valletta. On board she carried the 11th battalion of the Lancashire Fusiliers packed like sardines. Every man in the battalion found jobs to do, lightening the burden on the navy. *Edinburgh* endured a long day of danger over a period of 13 hours of bombing and torpedoing. The Captain addressed the crew and soldiers:

> "While there is one gun above the waterline the ship will fight on. The convoy must get through and if by any chance the ship is sunk don't worry as you all have lifebelts and the destroyers will pick you up. And anyway the Mediterranean at this time of year is marvellous."

By 10 pm that night the casualty list read: *Fearless* sunk and another destroyer damaged; *Nelson* reduced by a torpedo hit to 11 knots; HMS *Manchester* with a battalion of infantry reinforcements aboard for Malta hit and dropped out of the convoy; the battle-scarred *Edinburgh* had been damaged as she fought throughout the long day. She entered the Grand Harbour manned by the navy – and the Lancashire Fusiliers.

We had left *Sydney Star* arriving at Grand Harbour to the plaudits of the watching crowds, but before she could be moored and secured she was to suffer the most strenuous and unremitting attacks by E-boats, by dive-bombers, by high-level aircraft, by torpedo-carrying aircraft, all of them pressing home their attacks and demonstrating the power of collective action. Yet even this parade of power could not match the single-mindedness of Captain Horn. One aircraft passed between the masts of the freighter. Another had to jink his wings to clear the stern. Torpedoes just missed her bows. Even the most optimistic mind could only see disaster ahead in the final hour or two.

The RAN destroyer *Nestor* fought back in defence of the convoy with typical Australian ferocity.

The *Daily Express* journalist Norman Smart was a passenger aboard the cruiser *Hermione* and he recorded his experiences of torpedo and bomber attacks on the convoy:

> "From the bridge I can see the torpedo coming straight for us, leaving a pretty green trail in the blue water. The lookouts shout in chorus and the captain skillfully swings the ship. The torpedo slides past 15 yards to starboard. We lean over and watch it.

...The bridge where I am is a kind of orderly madhouse of signals, shouts and orders. The commander, pausing a moment between ten other jobs, orders water for men in the stuffy gun turrets. ... Formations of aircraft are reported but some do not arrive because the *Ark*'s fighters are magnificent."

And then it was all over. Victory, in the main, belonged to Captain Horn. He was awarded an OBE, but the present he most treasured was the message sent to him from the naval officers who served with him in Operation Substance:

> "THE ROYAL NAVY OFFER YOU THEIR
> CONGRATULATIONS ON A VERY FINE
> PIECE OF SEAMANSHIP"

There are a few items of interest worthy of mention before we close the Substance story.

Colin Kitching was aboard the cruiser *Edinburgh*. At 2.15 am, during the middle watch, on 24 July the island of Pantellaria was sighted. Kitching recalled what followed:

"Fifty minutes later an enemy E-boat attack developed. *Edinburgh* was the flagship of Rear Admiral Syfret's 18th Cruiser Squadron. She exposed searchlights and illuminated an E-boat half a mile away. The E-boat was immediately struck by six 4-inch shells simultaneously and was blown apart. The remaining boats fled."

Edinburgh, accompanied by the cruiser *Arethusa* and the fast minelayer *Manxman*, shaped course for Malta. And so it was that at 11.30 am on 24 July these ships entered Grand Harbour. Kitching describes the occasion:

"We put on quite a show. The ship's company lined the guard rails, port and starboard. On the quarterdeck the Royal Marines played a selection of patriotic tunes – *Rule Britannia, Land of Hope and Glory, Hearts of Oak* and so on. We were given the most tremendous welcome by what must have been the whole population of Valletta. The emotion of the moment was so great that I found tears were rolling down by cheeks, a reaction which seemed to apply to everyone around me.

"At 5.15 pm that same day *Edinburgh* left Malta and by 7.30 am on 27 July we were back at Gibraltar, morale high from a sense of achievement."

Finally, we left the troopship *Leinster* aground at Gibraltar. She had to discharge her cargo and disperse the 1,750 army personnel before returning to Gibraltar. A.S. Potts of HMS *Hermione* related the cruiser's exploits:

"On our return to Malta, the *Hermione*, with the fast minelayer *Manxman* and the cruiser *Arethusa*, took aboard the troops that were destined for Malta, together with cargo and deck cargo, including torpedoes and bombs. This was to be a very fast run and rumour had it that *Arethusa* and *Hermione* were expendable so long as the *Manxman* got through. At daybreak we were steaming in line ahead – *Hermione*, *Manxman* and *Arethusa* – when we saw an Italian submarine on the surface. We increased speed from 300 revolutions to Full Ahead. The skipper, Captain Nigel Oliver, tannoyed, 'Stand by to ram!' Then we hit her just abaft the conning tower. We were followed by *Manxman* and *Arethusa*. . . . On arrival at Malta our diver identified a 20-ft gash in the bows and the loss of paravanes. The victim was, in fact, the submarine *Tambien*, sunk off Tunis on 2 August."

OPERATION HALBERD

You may be sure we regard Malta as one of the master-keys of the British Empire.

Winston S. Churchill, Prime Minister, to the Governor of Malta, 6 June, 1941.

Operation Halberd was another massive display of power at sea by the Royal Navy. Vice Admiral Sir James Somerville was still the commander of Force H operating in the western basin of the Mediterranean. He would lead his Force to the Narrows, the bottleneck in the Central Mediterranean between Sicily and Malta, before handing over responsibility of his powerful covering force to Cunningham's Mediterranean Fleet, and the supply ships of the convoy to the relative safety of Valletta.

Halberd entailed the passage of nine 15-knot ships from UK ports to Malta, now desperately in need of essential supplies. The Navy was committed to the pattern already established, assembling the convoy in the Atlantic so as to deceive the enemy of its destination. The convoy would then head for the Straits of Gibraltar, make the passage through the Straits at night, then set course for the Narrows and Malta. It was the pattern set by earlier convoys.

OPERATION HALBERD
BRITISH FORCES

CONVOY WS 11X

Breconshire	(9,776 tons)	Clan Ferguson	(7,300 tons)
Imperial Star	(10,700 tons)	Rowallan Castle	(7,800 tons)
City of Calcutta	(8,000 tons)	Clan Macdonald	(8,000 tons)
Ajax	(7,800 tons)	City of Lincoln	(8,000 tons)
Dunedin Star	(10,000 tons)		

CLOSE ESCORT GROUP 11

Prince of Wales	Flag of Vice Admiral A.T.B. Curteis
Rodney	
Kenya	Flag of Rear Admiral Burrough
Edinburgh	Flag of Rear Admiral Syfret
Sheffield	18thCruiser Squadron
Euryalus	
Destroyers:	Duncan, Legion, Lance, Lively, Gurkha, Oribi, Fury, Farndale, Heythrop, Piorun (Polish), Garland (Polish), Isaac Sweers (Neth.)

CONVOY GROUP 1

Nelson	Flag of Vice Admiral Somerville

FORCE H

Ark Royal	
Hermione	
Destroyers:	Cossack, Zulu, Foresight, Forester, Laforey, Lightning
Tanker:	Brown Ranger and corvette Fleur de Lys for refuelling destroyers
Submarines:	Utmost, Trusty, Sokol (Polish)

ITALIAN FORCES

Battleships:	Littorio	Flag of C-in-C Admiral Iachino	
	Vittorio Veneto		
Heavy Cruisers	Trento	Trieste	Gorzia
Light Cruisers	Duca Degli	Abruzzi	
Destroyers	Fourteen		
Submarines	Eleven		

The nine transports made an impressive sight; they were fast vessels, all crammed with tens of thousands of tons of important cargo – armaments, ammunition, military, naval and air force stores, vehicles and merchandise of every imaginable variety. In addition, the transports carried 2,600 service personnel to help garrison Malta. The Royal Navy cruisers, too, carried hundreds of soldiers and air force personnel.

F.W. Bennett was serving aboard the battleship *Prince of Wales* when his ship steamed through the Straits of Gibraltar under the cloak of darkness and into the Mediterranean. Only then did the ship's company know that Malta was their destination. Bennett remembers saying to some of his gun's crew, "Surely we are not expected to see this convoy through with so small an escort." He continues:

> "However, unknown to us up ahead was a sight I shall always remember . . . *Rodney, Nelson, Ark Royal,* City class cruisers and Dido class cruisers and the greyhounds of the fleet – destroyers. It was a breathtaking display of warships."

Bennett's AA station for repelling aircraft was on Y turret, aft, manned by Royal Marines. He wrote:

> "In charge of us in the turret was Captain D.L. Alwyn RM. He was an officer and a gentleman who I think we all respected. On the afternoon of the second day the air battle began. . . . Squadrons of torpedo bombers attacked the fleet and convoy, securing one hit on *Nelson.* She returned to Gibraltar down by the head."

On 26 September Italian air reconnaissance located part of the British forces south of the Balearics. Eleven Italian submarines patrolled their billets and E-boats were in readiness north of Pantellaria.

Admiral Iachino was at sea with his fleet, wearing his flag in the battleship *Littorio,* accompanied by the *Vittorio Veneto* and other warships as tabled. Iachino set out for south-east Sardinia, still within the umbrella of shore-based aircraft. But he was handicapped on two counts. While having the advantage of air cover, he was ill-served by intelligence. The strength of the British forces reported to him was badly underestimated. Furthermore, such was the shortage of fuel oil that other units of his fleet were unable to put to sea. It was to be a persistent worry for *Supermarina*.

The first significant success was the torpedo strike against *Nelson*. Although damaged, she reached Gibraltar safely. The two fleets, commanded on the one hand by Curteis and the other by Iachino, failed to get to grips with each other. Opportunities were presented, but shouldered aside. It was as if the two fleets were content to monitor the other's movements but not to risk all in an engagement.

On the evening of 27 September the transports separated in the Skerki Banks area and stood for Malta with Force X (five cruisers and the destroyers *Cossack*, *Zulu*, *Oribi*, *Laforey*, *Heythrop* and *Farndale*). Other F Class destroyers equipped with minesweeping gear were *Forester*, *Foresight* and *Fury*.

One witness of the day's activities was Able Seaman George Gilroy aboard the destroyer *Lightning*.

"Like many other convoys to come this was a blur of action – eat when you can, sleep when you can, fight and die with as little fuss as possible. I remember the almost continuous, intense, very accurate air attacks on the ships from dawn to dusk. We spent most of our time at action stations and got little rest or sleep. There was no time to wash and barely enough time to eat."

Gilroy related how the air attacks were a combination of all three types of bombing – high-level, dive-bombing and low-level torpedo. And there was always the risk of attack by German U-boats, by E-boats and by the Italian navy. The sky was often black with AA fire. The enemy gave them little rest.

Gilroy described how well co-ordinated were some of these attacks. He found the torpedo attacks the most frightening and reported one which missed the *Lightning* by perhaps twenty yards.

It was during that evening of 27 September that the transport *Imperial Star* was torpedoed off Cape Bon:

"The torpedo pilots would fly straight at you at masthead height, presenting an impossibly small target, below the depression of most of *Lightning*'s guns. The drill was to steer straight for the aircraft at full speed, and comb the track of the incoming torpedo. . . . The pilots were wise to this tactic and they often came in simultaneously from different angles. . . . I can quite clearly remember seeing the white wakes of the torpedo. We all knew that a single hit from a torpedo could kill a destroyer. The ship's steel skin was only a few millimetres thick and had no armour plating like the larger ships. I felt very sorry for the poor merchantmen; all they could do was chug along, and many would be carrying aviation spirit for Malta's fighter aircraft. They must have been like floating bombs."

Such was the case with the *Imperial Star*. S.K. (Ken) Laycock was trained as a gunnery officer and claims to have sunk more empty 40-gallon drums as targets than anyone else. His 6 inch "cannon" was put to good use in a brief encounter with a U-boat which dived after Laycock's third round got perilously close. Captain David R. Macfarlane was highly regarded by the crew of the *Imperial Star*. It was with great regret that he had to order abandon ship because of the severe damage. All the military personnel were disembarked into *Lightning* and *Laforey*, as were some salvageable stores before the 12,427-ton ship was sunk. Able Seaman Gilroy wrote:

"My 4-inch gun was captained by Petty Officer 'Slinger' Woods. We had no protection whatsoever from the weather and the shrapnel, not even a gun shield. Live, ready-to-use ammunition was stacked all around us: we would not have had a chance if this had been hit. To this day I shall never know how we never got hit by shrapnel from all the bombs that near-missed us."

Another witness of the loss of *Imperial Star* was RAF Sergeant John Omer Taylor, one of the 200 RAF passengers. He had watched the ship being loaded in the UK with a variety of dangerous, explosive stores and he remembers thinking that if the ship was hit and caught fire, "We will have some firework display, that's for sure."

Operation Halberd Dispositions of the convoy and escorts on 27 September, 1941. *Ark Royal* and her screening cruisers operated independently for the flying off/on of aircraft. Positions are not shown for the RFA *Brown Ranger* nor the submarines *Sokol* (Polish), *Trusty* and *Utmost*, which were also in company, nor the corvette *Fleur de Lys.* Source: *La Marina Italiana Nella Seconda Guerra Mondiale*, Vol. V.

GRAFICO N°5

OPERAZIONE "HALBERD"

DISPOSITIVO DI MARCIA DEL GIORNO 27 SETTEMBRE 1941

DUNCAN GARLAND LIVELY HEYTHROP FURY ZULU COSSACK FORESIGHT

GURKHA

ISAAC SWEERS

LANCE

FORESTER

LAFOREY

FARNDALE

LIGHTNING

ORIBI

KENYA
AJAX
RODNEY CLAN MACDONALD
IMPERIAL STAR
ROWALLAN CASTLE
PRINCE OF WALES CITY OF CALCUTTA

EDINBURGH
CLAN FERGUSON
DUNEDIN STAR NELSON
BRECONSHIRE
CITY OF LINCOLN

SHEFFIELD

EURYALUS
ARK ROYAL
HERMIONE

Operano indipendentemente per le operazioni di volo.

PIORUN

LEGION

Scala in yarde
0   300   600   900

NOTA: Nel caso che il gruppo Ark Royal dovesse dirigere si di là dello schermo, questo sara assunto in caso di accostata a dritta dalla sezione Lightning-Oribi, e dalla sezione Piorun - Legion in caso di accostata verso poppavia.

Taylor was comforted a little when he boarded the *Imperial Star*. As he climbed the gangway he realized he was boarding a well-armed merchantman with a large-calibre naval gun mounted on the stern. For'ard of this two Bofors AA guns were strapped to the main deck on the ship's superstructure above the bridge, on bridge extensions twin and single 303 barrels elevated skywards from many positions, and on the main deck at frequent intervals 20 mm Oerlikon cannon were mounted. It looked as if *Imperial Star* could look after herself.

It was especially sad for Taylor to watch all this weaponry go down with the ship. When it came to the point *Imperial Star* was unable to protect herself.

Another witness of the *Imperial Star*'s ordeal was a young ordinary seaman, Hugh Elias, aboard the *Dunedin Star*. He remembers some incidents as clearly as if they happened yesterday:

> "The main attack by torpedo bombers was in the afternoon. I was stationed at the stern of the ship in a hose party under the 6-inch gun platform. The noise from the AA gunfire was deafening. Flying level with our deck a twin-engined plane with Italian markings crossed our stern so close you could have thrown a stone at it. I have a vivid recollection of the pilot's white face staring straight ahead. As it passed, the navy gunners fired the 6-inch gun. I don't know where the shell went but it gave that pilot a shock. . . . He was a brave man."

Astern of the *Dunedin Star* was the *Imperial Star*. Ordinary Seaman Elias watched her go down, having fought bravely. He also reported the one casualty aboard his ship.

> "One of the gunners was hit in the leg by a 20 mm Oerlikon shell, probably crossfire from one of the other ships. Among the few troops being carried was an RAMC dentist. He amputated the poor chap's leg. He died, of course."

Dunedin Star reached Valletta safely and, after discharging her cargo, she left Malta at full speed flying the Vichy French flag during daylight hours.

RAF Sergeant Taylor gave a graphic account of *Imperial Star*'s last moments. He described the torpedo hit aft as "a muffled rumble . . . which travelled through the ship as if we were standing on jelly".

"The damage was extensive, the rudder and screws were destroyed. Twisted stern plates acted as a fixed rudder. She immediately pulled out of station and developed a list to port. The gun on the stern platform was damaged beyond repair. The Tannoy advised everyone that a destroyer was coming alongside: 'Troops to board the destroyer. Ship's crew and guns' crews to stand fast.' Attempts to tow were abandoned."

Taylor had rescued a cat and an accordion and found jumping on to the destroyer distinctly dangerous. But jump he did, aided by two helpful sailors: "Bloody hell! Another cat!" The cat shot away to the destroyer's interior and the accordion was returned to its rightful owner.

Taylor was ushered down to a mess deck where immediately a large bully beef sandwich and mug of tea were thrust into his hands. Taylor was transferred to the destroyer *Oribi*. He was told by one rating, "You are now a guest of the navy aboard the *Oribi*. Just make yourself at home." Taylor overheard two officers talking: "It's a terrible tragedy really. On board we had all the radar equipment for Malta."

Oribi sped off to Malta, overtaking the convoy.

At 1130 am on the 28th the cruisers arrived at Valletta, followed by the convoy at 1330.

LOSS OF *ARK ROYAL* AND *Barham*: FIRST BATTLE OF SIRTE

I appoint Field Marshal Kesselring . . . to secure mastery of the air and sea in the area between Southern Italy and North Africa, in order to secure communications with Libya and Cyrenaica, and, in particular, to keep Malta in subjection. . . . Also to paralyse enemy traffic through the Mediterranean and British supplies to Tobruk and Malta, in close co-operation with the German and Italian naval forces available for this task.

Hitler's *War Directive*, 2 December, 1941

The autumn of 1941 became a cauldron of activity, with the fortunes of the Royal Navy and the Axis powers fluctuating. Convoy protection was vital to both and successes were claimed by both sides. One such Italian claim was the defence of her convoy M-41 to Benghazi under the code-name Operation Perpetual. The intention was to provide escort for eight transports in three convoys with a close escort of seven destroyers and two torpedo boats.

The convoys were to be covered by the whole of the Italian fleet, comprising four battleships, five cruisers and eight destroyers. Cunningham was quite unable to raise a comparable force. Ranged against Iachino the Royal Navy could muster Vice Admiral Somerville's Force H comprising the battleship *Malaya*, the carriers *Ark Royal* and *Argus*, the light cruiser *Hermione* and seven destroyers, including *Laforey, Legion, Sikh* and the Dutch *Isaac Sweers*. The opportunity was taken to fly off thirty-seven Blenheim bombers, thirty-four of which reached Malta safely.

However, two German U-boats located the British force. U-boat *U-205* (Lieutenant-Commander Reschke) penetrated the destroyer screen and fired three torpedoes, one of which exploded in *Legion*'s wake.

Lieutenant-Commander Guggenberger was more successful. His *U-81* was ideally placed to attack the *Ark Royal*. He fired a spread of four torpedoes, one of which struck home.

G.S. Burlingham, aboard the new destroyer *Lightning*, witnessed the incident.

"I was on watch that afternoon, about twenty-four hours out from Gib. The captain of the carrier had just signalled he was going to exercise his planes and pilots in flying off the carrier. At 1545 I saw some smoke belch out of the funnel, then some time later she began to list and go around in circles. At this time several of her aircraft were in the air and unable to land on, so they made for Gib. It wasn't till midnight that a tug arrived to take her in tow. While on the next morning watch, about 0600, she started to sink. The tug was ready to chop the tow rope. Had the skipper of one of the destroyers been allowed to take her in tow at the start, she might well have made it."

It was a sad and sombre occasion to watch this fine ship disappear beneath the waves. However, worse was to follow.

The torpedoing of *Ark Royal* was one of the results of twenty German U-boats having entered the Mediterranean. Within ten or eleven days one of them scored a major success.

Force K, whose exploits we will follow soon, was formed as a striking force and was despatched from the UK to the Mediterranean. Force K comprised the two cruisers *Aurora* and *Penelope*, with the two destroyers *Lance* and *Laforey*. Their skill in attacking enemy convoys, plus the ever-improving intelligence available to Cunningham, resulted in some remarkable successes. The convoy of 25 October was a case in point.

It comprised seven merchant ships with a close escort of six destroyers and a covering force of two heavy cruisers, the *Trieste* and *Trento*, with another four destroyers. Air and submarine back-up was also provided. Surprisingly, the enemy were caught totally unprepared. The merchant ships totalled 39,000 tons. In the ensuing action all the merchant ships were sunk, along with one destroyer.

The submarine *Upholder* blew the stern off another destroyer, the *Libeccio*, which later sank in tow. The convoy's destruction was a grievous blow to Rommel's forces.

Another Force K success at this time was the strike against a convoy comprising the two transports *Maritza* carrying ammunition) and the *Procida* (loaded with high octane aviation fuel) of 2,910 tons and 1,842 tons respectively. They were escorted by two Italian E-boats. Force K sank both ships of the convoy, depriving the enemy of vital supplies.

So desperately needed was the fuel that the Axis had resorted to jettisoning 40-gallon drums of fuel overboard and allowing the tides to float them ashore to be collected on the beaches at Derna. This shortened the time in getting the fuel to the front line.

Heavy fleet movements took place at the end of November, partly to give support to Force K's sinking of *Maritza* and *Procida*. Cunningham hoisted his flag in the *Queen Elizabeth*. He had in company *Barham* (Pridham-Wippell), *Valiant* and eight destroyers. They comprised Force A. The cruiser squadron (Rear Admiral Rawlings) comprised *Ajax*, *Neptune*, *Naiad*, *Euryalus* and *Galatea*, plus four destroyers.

On 25 November Lieutenant von Tiesenhauson in *U-331* managed to penetrate the substantial destroyer screen and get to within 500 yards of the battleship *Barham*. This alone was a skilful achievement. He fired a salvo of four torpedoes, three of which were claimed to be hits. The battleship exploded and capsized, leaving an atomic-like pall of smoke. The destroyers *Jervis*, *Jackal*, *Nizam* (RAN) and *Hotspur* rescued about 450 men, including Pridham-Wippell. Altogether 861 men perished, including Captain Cooke, the commanding officer. *Barham* sank off Sollum at 1629 on 25 November.

Mrs H. Mitchell, daughter of Chief Shipwright Morrison, recalled that her father had survived an earlier occasion when

115

810 men died when *U-331* sank the battleship *Barham*. November 1941.

Barham had been torpedoed, making "a hole the size of a house". Two years later and here he was in a similar predicament. Mrs Mitchell tells of Morrison's thoughts:

> "He thought she would right herself like she did last time. But she didn't. The ship exploded, shooting my Dad into the sea and the suction of it going down took him with it. He felt he had touched bottom. Then there was another explosion which pushed him away from the drag. When he surfaced the *Barham* had gone."

With an injured arm and leg Morrison managed to swim toward a destroyer and was hauled to safety. Mrs Mitchell continued:

> "A friend of ours, Charlie Dudman, got off the *Barham* without getting his feet wet. As she rolled over he slid down the side and bottom and landed on one of the escort ships. He cut his back and bottom on the barnacles."

It was against this backdrop of disaster in the Mediterranean that the First Battle of Sirte was acted out. We have seen how disastrously weakened was Cunningham's fleet, albeit relieved and enlivened by the exploits of Force K. It is the movements of the two opposing fleets in the Gulf of Sirte to which we must now turn.

On 15 December, 1941, the British intention was to get the transport *Breconshire* (9,766 tons) safely from Alexandria to Malta. The forces opposing each other were as follows:

ROYAL NAVY

FORCE B:

Naiad	(Flag of Rear-Admiral Philip Vian).
Euryalus	
Carlisle	
Destroyers:	*Jervis, Kimberley, Kingston, Kipling, Havock, Hasty, Decoy, Nizam* (RAN)

FORCE K:

Aurora   (Captain W.R. Agnew)
Penelope
Destroyers: *Lance, Lively, Sikh, Legion, Maori,*
                  Isaac Sweers (Neth)
In Support: *Neptune, Jaguar, Kandahar*

ITALIAN FORCES

COVERING CONVOY M.42:

Three merchant ships ex Taranto.
Six Destroyers. One freighter. One Destroyer. One Torpedo
Boat.

CLOSE COVERING FORCE:

Battleship: *Caio Duilo* (Admiral Bergamini)
Cruisers: 7th Division (Div Admiral de
                  Courten)
11 Destroyers

DISTANT COVERING FORCE:

Battleships: *Andrea Doria*
                  Giulio Cesare
                  Littorio (flag Admiral Iachino)
Heavy Cruisers: *Goritzia*
                  Trento (Div Admiral Parona)
Ten destroyers.

These forces became engaged in a multiplicity of manoeuvres,
set against air attacks on both sides and some submarine activities, plus considerable use of intelligence matter which the British
were reading as soon as the Italians themselves.

The British were intent on securing the safe arrival of the
Breconshire and this became Vian's main duty, beset during
the day by more than twenty torpedoes and numerous bombing
attacks. His forces emerged unscathed. He had a good grasp of
all the Italian aspects of the encounter. He took the opportunity to detach *Breconshire* into the safer hands of Force K

which shepherded her to the relative safety of Valletta.

At sunset on 17 December Vian's cruisers and destroyers met Iachino's, who had overwhelming superiority. But Iachino was probably reluctant to engage in a night action, an aspect of naval warfare which had become synonymous with the Royal Navy in the Mediterranean since Italy's entry into the war.

Vian's destroyers attempted to deliver a torpedo attack on Iachino's force, but Iachino turned away and in the gathering gloom contact between the two fleets was lost. The Italian convoy resumed its course for Benghazi. Vian, realizing he could not intercept Iachino, returned to Alexandria. The Italian convoy made its way to Tripoli without loss. The first Battle of Sirte was over.

Another disaster needs recording at this stage in the epic of the Malta convoys – when six enterprising and brave charioteers totally immobilized the battleships *Valiant* and *Queen Elizabeth*.

Italy had pioneered the design of these two-man human torpedoes, designed by two engineer Lieutenants, Teschi and Tesei. Their slow-running torpedo was cigar-shaped, 21" in diameter and battery-powered to give a speed of 2 to 3 knots. The two-man crew sat astride the weapon. A detachable warhead carried 500 lbs of explosive. It was cumbersome and unreliable, hence the nickname "pig". A parent submarine carried the weapon to within striking distance of the target.

For the last stage of the approach the crew donned underwater gear and submerged completely. Once under the target the warhead was secured to the bilge keel and the fused detonator set.

Valiant and *Queen Elizabeth* were selected as targets. The mother-ship was to be the *Scire* (Lieutenant-Commander Prince Valerio Borghese).

Borghese navigated *Scire* to Alexandria, surfacing at 1840 on 18 December about 2500 yards from the Ras-el-Tin lighthouse. The attacks were carried out under fine weather conditions. By a stroke of great good luck Vian's force entered harbour, opening the boom gate, and the charioteers followed.

Two frogmen, De la Penn and Bianchi, penetrated the net defences around *Valiant* at about 0200, but Bianchi disappeared so Penn had to carry out the work on his own. On completion he surfaced and sought refuge on the battleship's bow buoy only to be surprised to find Bianchi clinging to it.

The C-in-C, Admiral Cunningham, had experienced many surprises during his career, but to be woken at about 0400 to be told there were two charioteers clinging to a bow buoy of his battleship in a defended anchorage needed some believing. The Italians were taken prisoner.

The first explosion occurred at 0550. It ripped a hole 80 ft long by the bilge keel and the ship settled on the bottom.

Queen Elizabeth's turn came at 0624 when a mighty explosion seemed to lift the flagship bodily, then shake her like a wet dog. A hole 40 ft square shattered the boiler rooms for'ard. She too settled squarely on the bottom.

In addition, damage was inflicted on the destroyer *Jersey* moored nearby, and the naval tanker *Sangano* had her stern blown off.

It was a stunning blow. All the charioteers were accounted for, including two who were arrested when trying to change out-of-date counterfeit £5 notes with which they had been supplied.

Cunningham was left with five light cruisers and some destroyers to face four Italian battleships and six cruisers. The Italians had demonstrated the power of chariots and their ability to take on capital ships inside a defended anchorage. It was a form of warfare the British developed in the brilliant attack on the *Tirpitz* later in the war.

The year 1941 ended on a note of near despair.

THE *DUISBERG* Convoy:
The End of Force K

Many congratulations on your fine work since you arrived at Malta and will you please tell all ranks and ratings from me that the two exploits in which they have been engaged, namely the annihilation of the enemy's convoys on November 8 and of the two oil ships on Monday last, have played a very definite part in the great battle now raging in Libya. . . . All concerned may be proud to have been a real help to Britain and our cause.

Prime Minister to Commander Force K, 27 November, 1941.

Events of stunning proportions cast shadows over the Maltese scene in the last quarter of 1941 and the beginning of 1942. Efforts had been made in April and May, 1941, to form a striking force specifically to attack enemy shipping in the central Mediterranean, but without the success anticipated. It was not until October, 1941, that a meaningful Malta Striking Force was formed. The Prime Minister had made it clear in a directive of 14 April that the main duty of the Mediterranean Fleet "was to stop all sea-borne traffic between Italy and North Africa. To this end heavy losses in battleships, cruisers and destroyers must, if necessary, be accepted. However, the destroyer flotilla which Captain Mack led failed to be as successful as had been hoped, though on his third foray he did

THE *DUISBERG* CONVOY

Ship/ Nationality/ Tonnage	Cargo	Tanker Freighter
SAN MARCO German 3,133	528 tons ammunition 47 Vehicles	Freighter
DUISBERG German 7,189	170 Vehicles Military Stores	Freighter
MINATILAN Italian 7,599	9,000 tons fuel	Tanker
MARIA Italian 6,339	3,000 tons general 360 tons ammunition 102 Vehicles	Freighter
SAGITTA Italian 5,133	2,500 tons aviation fuel 67 Vehicles	Freighter
RINA CORRADO Italian 5,180	621 tons munitions 807 tons aviation fuel	Freighter
CONTE DI MISURATA Italian 5,014	5,000 tons fuel oil	Tanker

Summary: The convoy totalled 39,587 tons of shipping and about 20,000 tons of fuel oil.

intercept an enemy convoy of four German ships and one Italian ammunition ship. The escort of three destroyers was totally inadequate and the convoy was overwhelmed. At the end of the engagement 1,271 men out of 3,000 were rescued. 300 vehicles and 3,500 tons of stores were destroyed. Four of the eight vessels engaged were sunk. The captain of the destroyer *Tarigo* had a leg blown off and he bled to death. The destroyer *Mohawk* was torpedoed and sunk and all but two officers and thirty-nine men were saved.

In the first three months of the year ten Axis ships had been sunk. In April and May the score was twenty-one, but still the majority of ships bound for North Africa were getting through.

Between March and the middle of May, 1941, convoys for Tripoli were leaving Naples every three or four days. It was imperative that these lines of supply should be stopped.

The abortive forays in search of enemy convoys were not helped by the absence of ULTRA. At that time the Italian naval code was not being read and there was as yet no information from the German Enigma in the Mediterranean theatre. But, as John Winton writes, "The best intelligence in the world is useless if the holder has not enough strength to act upon it." The Italians were using a medium-grade cypher known as C38m. The Government Code and Cypher School broke into this code in the summer of 1941. This supply of high-grade shipping intelligence, plus the formation of Force K, were, by the end of the year, to bring Axis supplies to Libya virtually to a halt.

Early in November, 1941, Force K comprised the 6" gun cruisers *Aurora* (Captain W.R. Agnew) and *Penelope* (Captain A.D. Nichol), both of 5,220 tons, and the two destroyers *Lance* (Lieutenant-Commander R.W.F. Northcott) and *Lively* (Lieutenant-Commander W.F.E. Hussey). On 8 November the newly constituted Force K left harbour in response to a Maryland bomber aircraft's sighting report and a C38m decrypt. Both reported a large convoy 40 miles off Spartivento. It comprised five merchant ships and two tankers. The Covering Force consisted of the 8 × 8" gun cruiser *Trento* and her sister ship *Trieste*, plus four destroyers. They were:

Maestrale	(Cap di Vasc Ugo Bisciani)
Fuciliere	(Cap di Freg Cerrina Feroni)
Bersagliere	(Cap di Freg Guiseppe de Angioy)
Alpino	(Cap di Freg Agostino Calosi)

These destroyers were joined later by:

Grecale	(Cap di Freg Giovanni Groprillo)
Libeccio	(Cap di Freg Tagliamonte)
Oriani	(Cap di Freg Chinigo)

Two corvettes then joined the fleet. They were:

| *Euro* | (Cap di Corv Cigala Fulgosi) |
| *Fulmine* | (Cap di Corv Milano) |

Two submarines gave additional cover:

| *Settembrini* | (Cap di Corv M Resco) |
| *Delfino* | (Cap di Corv Avogardra) |

The whole convoy, plus escorts, formed up in the Straits of Messina and set course for the south. The two heavy cruisers were commanded by experienced officers: Cap di Vasc Rouselle commanded the *Trieste* and Cap di Vasc Parmigiano commanded the *Trento*.

Force K had had a frustrating search with nothing to reward them. It was steaming in line ahead in the order *Aurora*, *Lance*, *Penelope* and *Lively*, about four cables apart. There was a friendliness between the destroyers and cruisers: *Aurora* 'adopted' *Lance* and *Penelope* adopted *Lively*. The Force was steaming at 28 knots on a course of 064 degrees in position 36° 55' N, 17° 38' E and was preparing to abort the search and return to Malta when, at 0039 in the early hours of 9 November, 1941, *Aurora*'s bridge personnel sighted ships. Radar proved invaluable allowing Force K to take up a position of advantage. The *Aurora*'s bridge log recorded the captain as exclaiming, "My God! There they are – bloody great haystacks!"

Aurora led round to the northward to silhouette the enemy against the moon and to attack from the starboard quarter. The

Force was well drilled in all its duties, so each ship, each gun's crew, each person aboard knew exactly what was expected of them.

Force K was now totally committed and pressed on with its approach "blissfully unaware" that they were soon to engage two 8" gun cruisers.

But if the British Force was unaware of the danger looming a few miles ahead the Italian ships were also unaware of the death and destruction about to be unleashed upon them.

Fire was opened at 0057. There followed a high-speed, intensive and savage exchange of gunfire in which the British had one major advantage – they were unencumbered by a convoy. Salvoes and broadsides of 6" and 4" shells found the range immediately and created havoc among the convoy. The destroyer *Fulmine* was struck right away, repeatedly hit about the bridge structure by *Lively* and *Penelope*. The Italian captain had an arm shot away. He went down with his ship.

The Italians suffered the loss of the entire convoy. The British losses were nil and casualties nil – except for five canaries which died of shock. The Italians lost close to 40,000 tons of shipping and all their valuable cargoes.

Two Italian officers were court martialled and deprived of their commands: Admiral Brivonesi, with his flag in *Trieste*, and Captain Bisciani aboard the *Maestrale*.

Italian destroyers managed to rescue 704 survivors in all.

A final footnote: The destroyer *Libeccio* was intercepted by Lieutenant-Commander David Wanklyn's submarine *Upholder*, torpedoed and sunk while attempting a tow.

In retaliation for the destruction of the *Duisberg* convoy Valletta was subjected to an aerial bombardment so intense that the ships' guns were manned all day and all shore leave was stopped.

Another small convoy came in for punishment early in December. It comprised two German ships, the *Procida* (1,842 tons) and the *Maritza* (2,910 tons), both bound for Benghazi. They were escorted by two torpedo boats, *Lupo* (Cap di Freg Mimbelli) and *Cassiopeia* (Cap di Corv de Gactamo) of 679 and 642 tons respectively.

Both German ships were severely damaged and set ablaze. They then collided, their cargoes exploding before they sank. No trace of them was left. The two torpedo boats managed to make good their escape.

December, 1941, saw the reinforcement of Force K by the addition of another similar force, ensuring that at any time one force would be at sea. Cunningham agreed to send two more cruisers and two destroyers to Malta. These four ships were:

Ajax   (Captain E.D.B. McCarthy)

Neptune   (Captain R. O'Conor)

Kimberley   (Lieutenant-Commander J.S.M. Richardson)

Kingston   (Lieutenant-Commander P. Somerville)

Rear Admiral Rawlings, commanding Force B, left Alexandria for Malta to bring the transport *Breconshire* to Malta. Rear Admiral Vian had with him the cruisers *Naiad*, *Euryalus*, *Carlisle* and the destroyers *Jervis*, *Kimberley*, *Kingston*, *Kipling*, *Nizam* (RAN), *Hasty*, *Havock* and *Decoy*.

The next day, 16 December, 1941, Force K set out for Malta with the cruisers *Aurora* and *Penelope*, and the destroyers *Lance* and *Lively*, as well as the destroyer division of Captain Stokes – *Sikh*, *Legion*, *Maori* and the Dutch *Isaac Sweers* – to meet the transport the following day. The cruiser *Neptune* followed with the destroyers *Jaguar* and *Kandahar*.

Admiral Iachino's force covering Italian convoys, and Admiral Vian's were both reluctant to pursue each other and after a desultory exchange of fire both were content to return to harbour. Vian's force returned to Alexandria and *Breconshire* reached Malta safely. Force K, however, ran into disaster. The force comprising the cruisers *Aurora*, *Penelope* and *Neptune*, with the destroyers *Lance*, *Lively*, *Kandahar* and *Havock* ran into an Italian mine barrage.

Some ships, especially the rearmost in the formation, were unaware of the disaster ahead. The first explosion struck *Neptune* on the port side. The time was 0106.

Commander Hussey of *Lively* knew nothing of the first explosion and was disconcerted to see *Neptune* pass down the port side at a distance of 4 or 5 cables – on an opposite course. Confusion reigned. *Kandahar* led the destroyer round to port. *Aurora* hauled out of line to starboard and within minutes felt an explosion to port abreast of B turret. She immediately listed to port and was down by the bows, but counter-flooding corrected the list. She was severely damaged.

Captain Agnew of *Aurora* realized they were in a minefield in an incredible depth of 80 fathoms. Captain Nichol of *Penelope* thought that both *Neptune* and *Aurora*, her next astern, had been torpedoed. *Penelope* therefore turned to starboard, away from a suspected submarine. A minefield in these waters was not countenanced. Within a few minutes *Penelope* suffered a thunderous explosion on the port side abreast of the bridge. The mine had detonated in her streamed paravanes, but her damage was not severe.

Aurora contrived to turn and steam out of the field, followed by *Penelope*. Meanwhile *Neptune*, drifting helplessly, struck two more mines in quick succession.

Captain Agnew in *Aurora* ordered Commander Robson in *Kandahar* to go alongside *Neptune* and render help, and to detach two destroyers to escort *Aurora* to Malta. *Penelope* was ordered to stand-by *Neptune* too. But on approaching *Neptune*, *Kandahar* herself was struck by a mine.

Even as attempts were being made to rescue something from this disaster *Neptune* detonated a fourth mine. With alarming speed she heeled over to port and sank. Only one man out of a crew of 550 survived.

Clearly there was no acceptable answer as to how to rescue over 1,000 men from ships sinking in a minefield. Help was sought from Malta. So *Jaguar* was despatched and found *Kandahar* still afloat. She rescued eight officers and 160 crew. But sixty-seven of *Kandahar*'s men were lost. She was finally sunk by a torpedo from *Jaguar*.

Lance was badly damaged while in Valletta harbour. She was put into dry dock alongside *Penelope* which was being repaired after the mine damage, a mass of shrapnel holes. Wooden plugs were hammered into the holes, making her look like a hedgehog. When watertight she was sailed to the USA for permanent repairs. *Lance* was damaged beyond repair. The crew lived in caves under the cliffs until they were drafted. It was altogether a harrowing time for the men of the navy. One participant was V. Healey of the light cruiser *Dido*. He joined her in Alexandria and sailed immediately for Malta:

"Four days of dive bombers, high level bombers, low level torpedo bombers, U-boats, E-boats. . . . I'm not a religious person but I used to pray on those convoys. I was on most of them from the eastern Mediterranean . . . we didn't have much air support in those early days – plenty for the enemy though. They were hard days, but things must have been harder on the Russian convoys. At least you could survive the water in the Med, and you had some good runs ashore when in harbour."

HIS MAJESTY'S SUBMARINES: GAINS AND LOSSES

It is seldom proper for Their Lordships to draw distinction between different services rendered in the course of naval duty, but they take this opportunity of singling out those of HMS Upholder under the command of Lieut.- Commander Wanklyn, for special mention. She was long employed against enemy communications in the Central Mediterranean, and she became noted for the uniformly high quality of her services in that arduous and dangerous duty. Such was the standard and skill and daring set by Lieut.-Commander Wanklyn and the officers and men under him that they and their ship became an inspiration not only to their own flotilla, but to the fleet of which it was a part and to Malta where for so long HMS Upholder was based.

Admiralty Communiqué, 22 August, 1942

In order to appreciate the successes and the trials of British submarines during the years of the Malta convoys, it is necessary to glance over our shoulders to recall some of the events already described.

It is important to remember that the French navy, with its substantial fleet of submarines and its political relationship with Britain, had been content to regard the Mediterranean as their zone of influence, as the British had regarded the Atlantic, the Home Waters and the Indian and Pacific Oceans as their theatres of control.

Thus, with the fall of France and the emergence of Vichy France the Mediterranean took on a more threatening countenance.

However, even before the fall of France the Admiralty had taken preliminary precautions, so that by May, 1940, the British had mustered at Alexandria the following submarines: *Olympus, Otus, Orpheus, Odin, Phoenix, Proteus, Pandora, Parthian*, and the two minelaying submarines *Grampus* and *Rorqual*. All were based on the 14,650-ton depot ship *Medway*. Two of the submarines, *Otus* and *Olympus*, were undergoing extensive refits at Malta. Submarines from the Far East had already been recalled. They were *Regulus, Regent, Rainbow* and *Perseus*, and later *Rover*.

Thus, with the breakdown of diplomatic relations with Italy, all submarines east of Suez, including the 4th Flotilla at Singapore and the 8th Flotilla at Colombo, were sailed from Alexandria to form the 1st Flotilla. Half of these forces went on to Malta.

The main objective of all the British naval forces in the Mediterranean had been defined quite clearly as the disruption of all enemy seaborne communications to North Africa. This applied especially to submarines.

The situation awaiting the arrival of these submarines was one of near-suicidal proportions. *Grampus, Odin, Orpheus, Phoenix* and *Oswald* had all been lost with nothing to show for their efforts. There was one exception. *Rorqual*, it was learned later, had laid mines, one of which struck an enemy ship of 4,000 tons.

Grampus was sunk by depth charges from E-boats. *Odin* was sunk by the destroyer *Strale*. *Orpheus* was sunk by the Italian destroyer *Turbine* off Tobruk. All these submarines were lost in their first patrols in three days. And the losses continued into July.

These submarines were large and conspicuous boats designed to operate in open seas. They were not intended for the confined waters of the Mediterranean. Even under ideal conditions they took about forty seconds to dive, usually a little longer, whereas T Class boats took about thirty seconds, and the smaller U Class were twice as fast – about twenty seconds. These are not the only criteria. An O Class submarine's silhouette approached that of a small destroyer. The older, bigger boats presented a larger Asdic echo. Further, they were more readily recognized from the air, through the relatively transparent waters of the Mediterranean.

Aircraft were never far distant from an enemy convoy and aircraft observation was much simplified. Although painted blue as camouflage, on a calm day with smooth waters the blurred outlines of submarines could still be detected at quite considerable depths.

On 1 January, 1941, the 8th Flotilla was formed at Gibraltar where it was shore-based (as HMS *Pygmy*) until the depot ship *Maidstone* arrived to mother the boats.

Captain (S) G.W. Voelcker (known to most as Vox) was in command.

> "This flotilla served an extremely useful purpose, operating as it did in the relatively peaceful Western basin of the Mediterranean. Boats being sent to Malta and Alexandria were attached temporarily to Voelcker and sent out to patrol a reasonably safe billet to gain first-hand knowledge of Mediterranean conditions without undue hazard . . . which possibly saved many submarines from being sunk by plunging them precipitately into the more treacherous Central Mediterranean zone without a preliminary canter from Gibraltar."

In September, 1941, the Malta boats were organized into the 10th Flotilla under Captain G.W.G. Simpson. Operational command was still retained by the 1st Flotilla at Alexandria (Captain S.M. Raw.) This month also marked a further increase in the flotilla's success, with 65,000 tons of shipping sunk.

U Class submarines were the most successful. Even though they did not have long endurance nor high speed, they were well suited to the warm waters of the Mediterranean.

Their successes mounted as they sought out enemy convoys from Italian ports to Tripoli, Benghazi or whatever ports were in Italian hands. As the totals of monthly sinkings mounted so Cunningham signalled the submarine flotillas:

"I wish to congratulate you and your command on the excellent results which have been obtained against the Tripoli convoys in the last few months. Your work is invaluable . . . and more than ever important in the present difficult times. Keep it up."

During 1941 Greece, Crete, Yugoslavia and the North African coast to the very frontier of Egypt all increased the number of terminal ports for enemy traffic. This spate of activity served the British submarines one useful purpose: it brought more Italian shipping into play. Mass movements ashore of troops entailed their supply and support by sea. These movements were seized upon by Malta's submarines.

The heaviest concentration of enemy shipping lay in the Central Mediterranean where supply ships, transports and troopships worked back and forth across the narrow Sicilian Channel in ever increasing numbers as the North African theatre increased in importance. Traffic also developed in the Adriatic and Aegean Seas.

During this period, mid-1941, there occurred an incident worthy of comic opera. All naval endeavours were being directed towards the evacuation of Crete and Greece. The submarine *Regent* (Lieutenant-Commander 'Hairy' Browne) was sent to Kotor with orders to evacuate the British Minister to Yugoslavia and his staff. *Regent* entered the Gulf of Kotor and steamed around in broad daylight on the surface, unaware that Yugoslavia had surrendered the port to the Italians. Nor could the British Mission be found. Lieutenant Lambert was sent ashore from the submarine as an envoy, while an Italian officer boarded *Regent* as a hostage. Lambert was actually in discussion with an Italian admiral when a German aircraft "swept out of the sky" and bombed the submarine, wounding Browne, the commanding officer, and others. Browne sought the sanctuary of the open sea and Lambert was exchanged for the Italian hostage.

A story, probably apocryphal, tells how *Regent* dived. Such was the confusion in the upper conning tower that a hatch was left open. The leading stoker at the diving panel having opened all the main vents cast a glance up the conning tower. Turning to the signalman he is reported to have remarked laconically, "Got your umbrella chum? It's going to be a rainy day." It was an attitude well suited to the temperament of a sumbariner.

Mrs G. Goodwin came of a naval family. She had two brothers in the navy, a younger one lost aboard the carrier *Glorious* and an older one in HMS *Hood*. They were both in their teens. "My son spent nine years as a Royal Marine Commando," she wrote. And she had a brother-in-law in HMS *Porpoise*. He was, she says,

> "a chief petty officer. The crew of *Porpoise* had to forgo all comforts in order to take food, petrol and oil to Malta. . . . The navy did not get much recognition for the help they gave to Malta. *Porpoise* was a lucky boat, though – she went through the war till sunk in the Malacca Straits.

Another submariner, P.J. Kellagher, wrote from Northern Ireland. He served in the *Tribune* and in the River class boat *Clyde*.

> "When supplies to Malta were virtually cut off for some time *Clyde* continued to ferry vital stores to the island, in small quantities, it is true, but welcome nonetheless."

Kellagher recalls, too, the frightening experience he had of being badly depth-charged in *Tribune*.

A submariner who served with distinction was the commanding officer of HMS *Unbroken*. He was Alastair Mars DSO DSC*. *Unbroken* joined the 10th Flotilla in Malta as the *P-42*, but the Prime Minister objected: "Men prefer to fight in ships with names not numbers." So she was re-christened *Unbroken*.

The 10th Flotilla fought the most concentrated submarine campaign of the war. They lost twenty-six boats and at one time it was reckoned that the odds of a submarine from the 10th flotilla surviving were no more than evens. But they sank a million tons of shipping, devastating the supply routes to Rommel's Afrika Korps.

Later in the campaign *Unbroken* had a spectacular success

when patrolling off the island of Stromboli. Lieutenant Paul Thirsk was officer-of-the-watch on the periscope when he sighted the masts of four Italian cruisers and eight destroyers steaming at 25 knots. Mars closed to attack. Thirsk subsequently reported:

> "Two of the escorting destroyers passed alarmingly close and a third, for which we should have gone really deep, literally thundered over our fore casing, missing the conning tower by only a few feet. Mars fired a bow salvo of four torpedoes and we went deep with a drastic alteration of course."

One torpedo hit the 10,000-ton heavy cruiser *Bolzano*, blowing a huge hole in her side. A second blew about 50 feet off the bows of the 7,000-ton cruiser *Muzio Attendolo*, finishing her service in the war. Mars' attack had been a spectacular success.

Because of the likelihood of sumbarines being damaged while in harbour, the decision was taken to submerge all boats in harbour with the exception of the one alongside the repair wharf. But even this precaution was no safeguard, for *Unbeaten* was damaged by a near miss even when dived.

> "*Pandora* was also lost during these dreadful days when a pall of smoke and dust almost constantly hung over Malta, flung up by the bursting bombs. *Pandora* had completed a Magic Carpet run to Malta from Alexandria. Before her cargo could be completely discharged she was hit by two bombs, water flooded in and she settled on the bottom."

Submarine crews were now being subjected to a life in harbour of irritating restrictions. There was need for shelter during the interminably long daylight hours of bombardment by bombs and land mines. Rest and relaxation was denied them. Yet efficiency and morale stayed high.

Early in 1942 the submarine *Thrasher* (Lieutenant Hugh Mackenzie) survived a life-threatening experience when she set out from Alexandria on her eighth war patrol, the fourth commanded by Mackenzie. A few days later Mackenzie was warned by Ultra Special Intelligence that a 3,000-tons Axis supply ship was off Suda Bay. He ambushed the target and sank it by torpedo. But it was well protected by five anti-submarine vessels which counter-attacked with bombs from support aircraft, machine-gun fire and no fewer than thirty-three depth charges, several of them too near for comfort.

Thrasher managed to get clear away and that evening surfaced to recharge batteries and ventilate the boat as she headed for her next patrol billet. Clearing the land, the boat began to roll in the swell. Mackenzie was awakened by "a rhythmic banging immediately overhead".

He ordered the watch to investigate and report. It was revealed that a 3-ft-long bomb was resting on the casing beneath the muzzle of the 4-inch gun, and there was also a jagged hole where it appeared that another bomb further aft had penetrated and lodged. Mackenzie called for volunteers to investigate thoroughly and to cast aside the bombs. The submarine was in grave danger. The first lieutenant, Lieutenant Roberts, and the second coxswain, Petty Officer T.W. Gould, clambered on to the casing. They had been briefed by Mackenzie that in the event of enemy aircraft or warships arriving on the scene *Thrasher* would have to submerge and the two volunteers would be sacrificed for the safety of the boat and her crew. And, of course, there was always the likelihood that the bombs may detonate at any time.

The two volunteers wrapped the first bomb in sacking, manhandled it for'ard to the bows and dropped it overboard while *Thrasher* went full astern. As the sea surged aft over the saddle tanks the bomb plummeted below.

The second bomb was more difficult. Roberts and Gould had to enter the cramped space between the pressure hull and the casing, gaining entry through the jagged hole created by the bomb. Once inside they were virtually trapped, with only seconds to escape before being engulfed. They pushed and heaved for seeming hours as they inched the bomb along the inside of the casing until they reached the grating.

The bomb was fitted with a large tail fin which made it very difficult to hoist on to the casing. It was then ditched overboard without trouble. They were then treated to a stiff drink in the control room. A more appropriate award came some months later with the gazetting of a VC to them both.

Mackenzie was awarded a DSO for his part in the incident, followed by a bar for having successfully carried out six war patrols, sinking nearly 40,000 tons of enemy shipping, including Mussolini's yacht *Diana*, and being almost sunk when attacked by a Fleet Air Arm Swordfish.

One of the advantages held by the older, larger submarines was their ability to load cargoes of supplies into every conceivable space. One such Magic Carpet run, as it became known, was carried out by the submarine *Porpoise* whose earlier exploit has been recorded. Chief Torpedo Gunner's Mate Joe Brighton reported:

> "Every corner of the boat was packed with dried food, ammunition, kerosene and mail. A false deck was lined with tins of soup and spam, and bales of dried cabbage. To allow for more stores and special personnel some battery cells in one section were even removed."

After sinking a 10,000-ton protected tanker, *Porpoise* took evasive action and suffered 87 depth charge explosions. Brighton said, "I have often been asked what it is like to be depth charged. Two words: Bloody awful." Brighton, incidentally, served for 18 years in the submarine service. He won a DSM and bar and was mentioned in despatches.

U class boats continued to take their toll of Rommel's shipping across the straits from Italy to the ports of North Africa. The 10th flotilla, made up largely of boats of this class, sank 650,000 tons of shipping at a cost of forty-six submarines in the Mediterranean, thirteen of them U class. In the brief period June to September, 1941, U class submarines based on Malta sank eleven enemy supply ships totalling about 75,000 tons.

Mines were the greatest danger for submarines. One mining incident involved the old, large submarine *Perseus*. She patrolled the island of Cephalonia and she carried a crew of sixty. Suddenly a massive explosion rocked the boat and ripped a hole in her bows. She flooded and settled on the sea bed at a depth of 170 feet. Only one man survived the sinking, Stoker John Capes.

He described how the compartment he was in was near the stern and it flooded last. He remembered being with three wounded sailors and sharing a bottle of rum while the compartment flooded, then, after equalizing the pressure, floating to the surface by using the Davis escape apparatus. When he reached the surface he saw he was alone. His shipmates were nowhere to be seen. He swam for several hours and managed to reach Cephalonia. He was discovered by villagers who hid him from German and Italian police and smuggled him into Turkey.

Divers located the wreck of *Perseus* in February, 1998, and confirmed Capes' story. Inside the hatch, lying undisturbed, were bones, boots, a boiler suit and an empty rum bottle. The compass still worked and a mine anchor gave silent testimony of the explosion which sank the submarine and killed all her crew except this single stoker.

A submarine officer of commanding achievements was Commander Anthony Miers with his celebrated boat *Torbay*. One of Miers' escapades occurred in February/March, 1942, when *Torbay* was subjected to a severe depth-charge attack by an Italian destroyer off Corfu. Miers took his boat into Corfu's anchorage, where he sighted a troopship convoy entering the roads from the south. He determined to follow it, negotiating the narrow channel and entering the enclosed roadstead at moonrise. He took up a position where he could watch the harbour entrance while charging his batteries. A small patrol vessel compelled Miers to submerge *Torbay* for a short while. With the dawn came the realization that the convoy had gone, so he selected a secondary target, the *Maddalena* (5,200 tons), a supply ship which he torpedoed but failed to sink. After spending twenty hours in the defended enemy harbour Miers made good his escape. It was an exploit which won him the VC.

Leading Stoker Harry E. Beale of the submarine *United* (ex-*P-44*) of the 10th Flotilla remembers:

"We were over-loaded with cans of food and other stores picked up in Gibraltar for the besieged island. Air raids were almost continuous at Malta and we were required to enter Grand Harbour submerged, with the exhortation 'accurate navigation is essential' to cheer us up . . .

"At times during convoy operations we in *United* and other subs of the flotilla were ordered to adopt the role of making ourselves as conspicuous as possible, to keep surfacing and diving, and generally acting as decoys to deflect the enemy's attention from merchant ships."

Beale pointed out that acting as a supply vessel was less attractive than attacking Rommel's supply routes.

A spectacular success was achieved by Lieutenant-Commander David Wanklyn in his submarine *Upholder*. In the Straits of Messina he stealthily approached a tanker and scored a torpedo hit. But the Italians salved the vessel and towed her to Messina. *Upholder* was then subjected to a savage counter-attack which destroyed her Asdic apparatus. Wanklyn only had two torpedoes left when he sighted three large troop transports south-bound with a strong destroyer escort. The transports were the *Vulcania*, *Oceania* and *Neptunia*. Wanklyn sank the *Oceania* and the *Neptunia*, both liners of about 19,500 tons. The attack on the third ship was aborted. In all 6,500 men were rescued and 384 lost by drowning. It had proved a stunning exploit.

Ernie Brown was a crew member of the submarine *Truant* and recalls operating from Malta:

"In addition to sinking a lot of enemy ships we were used as supply ships for urgently needed stores. Submarines of our class and bigger would go on patrol with the torpedo tubes filled and also carrying six re-loads of 'fish' as we called them, do our stint [patrol] and instead of returning to Malta after our patrol and use up the fish on enemy targets we would then go to Alex, have the outside tubes refilled with fish, but leaving the torpedo space (for reloads) empty, but instead carried supplies back to Malta."

Some of the larger boats which Brown referred to were the *Clyde*, *Olympus* and *Porpoise*. H.A. Rawlings was a submariner in two of the submarines mentioned, *Olympus* and *Clyde*. He was conscripted into the navy which was to his liking, but he was "a bit concerned about being drafted into submarines". Before long he found himself part of a spare crew in the depot ship *Maidstone* at Gibraltar. His daughter, Mrs Pat Grant, sent her father's report:

"Eventually I was drafted to the *Olympus* which was to be used for taking vital stores to Malta. It involved removing one of the battery tanks to stow supplies. We reached Malta, exchanged stores for spare crews of *P-36* and *P-39* and sailed at 0500 under very crowded conditions. We were about 7 miles out from Malta when we hit a mine. Luckily we were on the surface. 'Abandon ship!' was called. But we were struck by bad luck. Firstly, we had no lights throughout the boat. Next, we tried the Aldis lamp but it was too weak. So it remained to fire the gun to attract attention, but it jammed. We all plunged into the sea as the casing became awash."

Rawlings was a good swimmer. He looked about him:

"I could just about see the outline of Malta. I swam towards it, picking up a mate of mine on the way. He said he would swim for help. I don't think he realized how far it was. While I was swimming my mind wandered over all the places I'd visited – especially home. Whilst I was swimming there were two air raids on Valletta. Eventually I reached the shore with the help of several soldiers. I was packed off to hospital."

Chief Petty Officer Norman Drury served aboard the submarine *Unbeaten*, commanded by Lieutenant-Commander E. Woodward. He wrote:

"During our first patrol when 30 miles east of Tripoli we sighted a small merchant ship escorted by a small destroyer. We attacked with two fish. . . . The first hit bottom, blew up and lifted *Unbeaten* to the surface. She lost all trim and settled on the bottom. We had a lot of depth charges and everything was very tense. The depth of water was 90 feet and the area had not been surveyed since the last century. The Asdic operator was very shaky and, as I was a higher Detector Rating, I put on the spare headphones and sat beside him to give him back-up. The captain asked me what I thought. I said I thought she [the destroyer] had been heard to go. . . . Next day when trying to sneak away at periscope depth, being hopelessly out of trim, we broke surface. Nothing in sight – full speed and we were away. . . . The skipper said to me two days later, 'Thank you, Drury, for what you did'."

Drury relates that he felt six feet tall. Later Woodward was awarded a DSO for six successful patrols, and Drury was awarded the DSM. All or most of the patrols were 'scary' and Drury reckoned that "we lost a submarine about every three weeks from our flotilla – and more from the O, P, R and T class based at Alexandria." He described the occasion when *Unbeaten* sank a U-boat off Sicily:

"We were on patrol off the northern tip of Sicily. Etna volcano was clearly visible by its glow in the sky, and when we were submerged we could clearly hear creaking and groaning. It was about 10 am when the watchkeeping officer called, 'Captain in the control room'. The captain ordered up periscope, prepare a full salvo of four torpedoes. 'Target is an enemy U-boat.' One or two torpedoes hit. We, as usual, went deep in case a fish should circle and hit us."

When *Unbeaten* reached periscope depth someone was seen waving in the water. The submarine surfaced and picked up a German look-out, Able Seaman Hans Bloch. He was delivered to security on arrival at Malta. The U-boat was *U-374* whose captain's name was Fischer and she was sunk east of Calabria, Southern Italy. Her sinking won the award of a bar to the DSO for Woodward.

Less than five weeks later *Unbeaten*, with Lieutenant-Commander Woodward still in command, successfully challenged and sank the Italian submarine *Guglielmotti* off Sicily on St Patrick's day, 17 March, 1942.

Norman Drury related how when approaching Malta *Unbeaten* surfaced for the last few miles when it was observed that the "Imminent Warning" Red Flag was flying. The Captain ordered the bridge to be cleared. As the upper lid was being closed so a Messerschmitt's cannon sprayed the conning tower and machine-gun fire peppered the bridge. The C.O. missed death by inches.

On one notable occasion every available submarine was stretched across the Gulf of Otranto. Drury tells the story:

> "A large convoy of four merchantmen powerfully escorted by, I think, a battleship, two cruisers and eight destroyers was expected to leave Taranto. . . . The lights of the town could be seen."

Drury refers to the convoy and escorts as "the thundering herd which came and went over the top of us." It passed over *Unbeaten* who was unable to get in an attack and gave Drury his most scary experience.

Unbeaten returned home having successfully completed her commission. Her haul of decorations was impressive: three DSOs, five DSCs, fourteen DSMs and seventeen mentions.

A sad postscript to her brilliant record was the manner of her ending. She was subsequently sunk in error by the RAF over the Bay of Biscay on 11 November, 1942.

An equally dangerous incident almost put paid to *Thrasher* when Hugh Mackenzie sailed for Port Said on 26 July, 1942, for patrol. He was sitting at the wardroom table with immediate access to the control room. He reported:

> "I very clearly remember something telling me to get to the bridge and I got up and left the table without explaining why or in response to any request for me to go to the bridge. I was just going through the watertight bulkhead between the wardroom and the control room when there was a most God awful explosion. As I was picking myself up I heard the OOD (the First Lieutenant) give the order to dive and the drill was carried out."

Extensive damage was done to *Thrasher* by a Swordfish aircraft which had attacked with four 250 lb depth charges – in the middle of a submarine sanctuary. *Thrasher* not only survived the depth charging, she also survived the war. She was scrapped in 1947.

ADMIRAL VIAN'S SUCCESS
AT SIRTE

I shall always consider the Battle of Sirte on March 22nd 1942 as one of the most brilliant naval actions of the war, if not the most brilliant.

Admiral of the Fleet Viscount Cunningham of Hyndhope, *A Sailor's Odyssey.*

We have seen how the Battle of Sirte of December, 1941, developed anti-climactically into a watching game with neither side anxious to commit its forces to battle. The Second, the main Battle of Sirte, was fought in the same featureless Gulf about two months after the first, but under different circumstances and with a different outcome.

The supply position for Malta was getting critical by the end of December, 1941, and the prospects of running convoys to Malta were grim. Cunningham had tried to rush a convoy of three freighters to the island but they were savaged by aerial bombardment; two were sunk and the third reached Tobruk, then still in British hands.

On 9 March Cunningham received intelligence of two Italian convoys 200 miles from Tripoli, one homeward bound, the other outward.

Vian's cruiser squadron was sent to intercept. His squadron comprised *Naiad* (Flag), *Dido* and *Euryalus*, with nine destroyers. Separately, the brand new cruiser *Cleopatra* was at Malta, so the opportunity was taken to sail her with the destroyer *Kingston* to Alexandria.

Misfortune struck at 2001 when the cruiser flagship *Naiad* was torpedoed by *U-565* between Mersa Matruh and Sollum on 11 March. She sank in twenty minutes. Vian and his flag captain and chief of staff, Captain G. Grantham, were both rescued. A few days later Vian's flag was hoisted and broke at the masthead of *Cleopatra*.

Arrangements were being made to get another convoy from Alexandria to Malta. Four ships were soon loaded with 30,000 tons of fuel oil, armaments and food supplies. The *Breconshire*, veteran of five Malta convoys, was a naval auxiliary. She was accompanied by the freighters *Clan Campbell*, *Pampas* and the Norwegian *Talabot*.

The convoy was code-named MW 10 and it sailed from Alexandria on 20 March at 0700. The Battle of Sirte was beginning to take shape.

20 March was a day of numerous destroyer movements in the course of which the 1,050-ton *Heythrop* was torpedoed north of Sollum by the German *U-652*. Efforts were made to take her in tow but after five hours she sank at 1600 with the loss of fifteen men.

Vian's force met the convoy during the morning of the 21st. His force was strengthened by five of the six Hunt class destroyers. His forces were spotted by aircraft and an Italian submarine. Vian was a brilliant tactician and when commanding destroyers and cruisers he was in his element.

His first knowledge of enemy warship movements came from the British submarine *P-36*. He believed that 22 March, a Sunday, would be a crucial day. He was joined that day by the battle-scarred *Penelope* which passed close to the flagship. Vian was clearly seen to give a huge V sign welcome with his arms.

Sub-Lieutenant Terry Jackson DSM RNVR served in one of the cruisers, the *Dido*. He confessed:

"One thing which never ceased to amaze me is the fact that out of the ship's company there could be so many erstwhile civilians who

THE BATTLE OF SIRTE

BRITISH FORCES All forces from Alexandria unless otherwise stated

15TH CRUISER SQUADRON

Cleopatra	Captain G. Grantham DSO (Flag of Rear Admiral Philip Vian DSO)
Dido	Captain H.W.U.McCall
Euryalus	Captain E.W. Bush

14TH DESTROYER FLOTILLA

Jervis (D14)	Captain A.L. Poland DSO DSC
Kipling	Commander A. St Clair-Ford DSO
Kelvin	Commander J.H. Allison DSO
Kingston	Commander P. Somerville DSO DSC

22ND DESTROYER FLOTILLA

Sikh (D 22)	Captain St. J.A. Micklethwait DSO
Lively	Lieut-Commander W.F.E. Hussey DSO DSC
Hero	Commander R.L. Fisher DSO OBE
Havock	Lieut-Commander G.R.G. Watkins DSC
Zulu	Commander H.R. Graham DSO DSC
Hasty	Lieut-Commander N.H.G. Austen

AA CLOSE ESCORT FOR CONVOY

Carlisle (AA Cruiser) Captain D.M.L. Neame DSO

5TH DESTROYER FLOTILLA (HUNT CLASS)

Southwold	Commander C.T. Jellicoe DSC
Beaufort	Lieut-Commander Sir S.O'G.Roche Bt
Dulverton	Lieut-Commander W.N. Petch OBE
Hurworth	Lieut-Commander J.T.B.Birch
Avon Vale	Lieut-Commander P.A.R. Withers DSC
Eridge	Lieut-Commander W.F.N. Gregory-Smith DSC
Heythrop	Lieut-Commander R.D. Stafford

FROM ALEXANDRIA

*Proteus (*HM Submarine)	Lieut-Commander P.S.Francis

FROM MALTA

FORCE K REMNANT

Penelope (Light Cruiser)	Commander R.F. Jessel
Unbeaten (Submarine)	Lieut-Commander E.A. Woodward DSO
P-34 (Submarine)	Lieutenant P.R. Harrison DSC
Upholder (Submarine)	Lieut-Commander M.D. Wanklyn VC DSO

It would be difficult to find a better experienced set of officers in a convoy escort group as is indicated by their decorations.

in a very short time welded into a formidable fighting force and were accepted by the regular professionals. . . . The thought makes me tremble now."

Jackson kept a diary (like so many did):

"*20 March*: *Carlisle* leaves Alex with Convoy MW 10 0800. (*Breconshire, Clan Campbell, Pampas, Talabot*, with destroyers *Zulu, Hasty, Havock, Sikh, Hero, Lively, Dido* (Vian)). *Euryalus, Penelope* and destroyers leave 1800. Looks like another convoy. Malta is being heavily bombed by air. *Heythrop* sunk.

21 March: Overtake *Carlisle* and convoy. We had fighter escort at last. Italian fleet locates convoy.

22 March: Vian learns of Italian fleet threat and manoeuvres his force between Italian squadron and convoy. Many high-level and torpedo attacks. Italian ships sighted at 1400. Battleship sighted at 1630. *Carlisle* takes convoy south out of range. We decoy to draw enemy ships. Weather rough. When making tea in galley I see large shell splashes alongside and dash for my tin helmet. Destroyers make smoke to confuse all range finders. Battle breaks off temporarily with ships popping in and out of smoke. Air attacks severe throughout the day. Hunts with 6 x 4" and *Carlisle* with 8 x 4" guns particularly invaluable."

Able Seaman (later Leading Seaman) Ronald K. Overend served aboard *Dido*. His action station was in the ADP (Anti-aircraft Defence Position) on the port side of the bridge controlling the portside short-range weapons, the pom-poms and Oerlikons.

"I was very pleased with this position for the obvious reason that I knew what was going on and could see all the action. I would not have liked to be below decks like the stokers etc. . . . We didn't even close up at action stations when it was only high-level bombers. They were out of range, so we just had to wait for the bombs to arrive."

Vian ordered dispositions for surface action at 1230. *Carlisle* and the Hunt *Avon Vale* were positioned to lay smoke to cover

146

the convoy. The rest of the Hunts formed a close escort round the convoy. Vian's cruisers and fleet destroyers stood off to the northward to interpose themselves between the convoy and any approaching Italian force. The sea was rough, with a considerable wind.

Bright red flares heralded the enemy. Soon after 1400 Captain Bush in *Euryalus* sighted smoke. He tannoyed his ship's company: "Captain speaking. The Italian fleet is in sight. Masts and funnels of three big ships are clearly visible from here [the bridge]. Good luck everyone." The enemy were 24,000 yards away (12 miles).

From his privileged position in the ADP of *Dido* Overend was able to describe the scene:

> "There was the *Littorio* and I think three heavy cruisers. I remember someone on the bridge saying that you could actually see the 15-inch shells in flight. The sea was unusually rough for the Med. *Dido*'s bows plunged through the rising seas and the sea spray was coming over the bridge. After an hour or so the Italians turned away and we joined the convoy now being attacked by aircraft. But the surface craft came back again and we laid another smoke screen. In the confusion we kept nipping in and out of the smoke to fire off a few rounds and then back into the protection of the smoke. The destroyers went in to attack with torpedoes – without success I think. I believe the *Littorio* was hit by shellfire. The action went on for about three hours . . . the *Cleopatra* had been hit and two or three destroyers damaged."

The enemy force which Captain Bush sighted was, in fact, Admiral Parona's squadron of three cruisers and four destroyers. The *Littorio* came upon the scene, with her nine 15" guns and secondary armament of twelve 6". She was accompanied by three fleet destroyers, a fourth having had to return to base with engine trouble.

Admiral Iachino was well informed about Convoy MW 10 and Vian's Force. Vian was less well informed and knew he still had about five hours of daylight to get through before darkness. But he enjoyed what sailing ships called the weather gauge and also effective smoke screens.

After belching smoke and exchanging desultory gunfire Vian signalled the C-in-C in Alexandria: ENEMY DRIVEN OFF.

During this phase *Breconshire* and *Carlisle* were straddled with shellfire and damaged by near-miss bombs. Captain Poland in *Jervis* then joined the convoy, affording extra protection.

The battle continued, with every advantage other than smoke to Iachino. 6", 8" and 15" shells were screaming down upon the British cruisers and destroyers. The weight of Italian broadsides was 24,000 lb against Vian's 5,900 lb.

At 1650 matters had reached dangerous proportions. Vian's cruisers were still engaging the enemy. Captain Micklethwait in *Sikh* and her flotilla mates had six minutes' shooting at the Italians until *Littorio* appeared from the mist at a range of five miles. It was 1705. There were still two hours to sunset and Micklethwait's hopes of avoiding punishment were forlorn. At 1720 *Havock* was near-missed by a 15" shell. Seven men were killed, No. 3 boiler room was flooded, her speed fell away and she was ordered to join the convoy. *Havock* thus gained the rare distinction of being fired on by British and Italian battleships: she had been fired on by *Warspite* in the Battle of Cape Matapan.

Lieutenant Robert M. Richie RNVR served aboard HMS *Sikh*, Micklethwait's flotilla leader. He has left us with this impression of his time at action stations as communications supply for A gun. During bombing he was in the transmitting station (TS).

"We had been bombed regularly since leaving Alex. We were usually at action stations from dawn till dusk with a few rest breaks. We closed up at about 1400 and were kept fully occupied for nearly four hours. The ship was doing about 28 knots into a head sea. . . . The ammunition chute of A gun was open to the sea. We were passing ammunition with water cascading down on us. Our mess deck lockers were floating around because the water was as high as the mess deck coaming. I think we were more afraid of the lockers than the 15" shells being fired at us by the *Littorio*.

"As we were Captain (D) our bows were out of the smoke. *Sikh* with two other destroyers held off the Italian battleship for about two hours at a range of about 6,000 yards. We provided smoke through which the 14th Flotilla could attack with torpedoes. The only damage we suffered was an 8" shell through our for'ard funnel.

"The *Littorio* and cruisers eventually gave up and we headed back to Alex, mopping up mess decks between bombings. We got back at about 8 am, fully ammunitioned ship – 250 rounds per main gun. We only had eight rounds left. All told *Sikh* fired 450 rounds of 4.7"."

At 1735 Iachino was within an ace of destroying the convoy. The Italian ships were out of reach of the British cruisers, but the whole of the convoy lay within range of *Littorio*'s broadsides. But *Sikh*, *Hero* and *Lively* feinted with a torpedo attack and kept *Littorio* at bay. An Ordinary Signalman's view of the day's incidents has been given by John L. Mulligan. He was aboard the *Queen Elizabeth* when volunteers were called for to man the *Pampas* "for a hazardous operation". That evening with a Yeoman of Signals and a party of "bunting tossers" Mulligan joined the *Pampas* for the run to Malta. He remembers they were carrying a cargo of bombs, torpedo warheads and 100 octane aviation spirit in 40-gallon drums on the fore well deck. Mulligan confirmed that the first two days were given over to intensifying air attacks, deteriorating weather and sea conditions and the presence of Italian surface forces:

"Skirmishing between Vian's cruisers and destroyers and Iachino's flagship *Littorio* continued until Sunday when the convoy of four ships each with a Hunt destroyer as escort split up to make their own way to Malta. In the very heavy weather we lost our escort and, having no radar in those days, found ourselves alone several miles from our destination."

That same Sunday evening by 1805 crisis had been reached but peril averted by Vian's efforts. He relieved a hard-pressed Micklethwait by ordering all destroyers to make a torpedo attack. The time was 1759. All told twenty-five torpedoes were launched. *Kingston* had a narrow escape when making a torpedo attack: a 15" shell passed right through her and exploded outboard, killing thirteen. *Lively* also suffered from a near-miss

149

15" shell which caused some flooding. She managed to extract herself and made good her escape.

The time was now a few minutes before 1900 and the last shots in the Battle of Sirte had been fired.

Although the battle was over there was more fighting to be done before the convoy ended. Captain Hutchinson, the Convoy Commodore, knew that the scattered ships were still 240 miles from Valletta. By driving the convoy south, the Italian fleet had given the Luftwaffe a longer journey that last morning. Ordeals lay in store for both opposing forces. The worsening storm took its toll of Italian ships. The large destroyers *Lanciere* and *Scirocco* both foundered. *Littorio* shipped water by the thousands of tons and the cruiser *Bande Nere* was damaged. But the British forces suffered more.

On Monday 23 March between 0900 and 1000 the *Pampas* and the *Talabot*, with their escorts now practically out of ammunition, steamed into Grand Harbour during an air raid to the cheers of the islanders. They had gone directly through a minefield. *Pampas* had been struck by two bombs, both of which failed to explode. John Mulligan was aboard *Pampas*. He recorded the day's events:

> "One enemy plane found us, unprotected, and came in from ahead to finish us off. He was too confident. He came in so low, almost literally masthead height, and dropped a stick of three bombs which, because of his lack of altitude, hit us while still in a horizontal position. The first one hit the derrick over the aviation spirit drums and just disintegrated, showering us on the bridge with splinters and shrapnel.
>
> "The second hit the starboard side of the funnel just abaft the bridge about ten feet from where we were standing, ricochetted across the boat deck and over the side. The third one missed the ship by a yard or two. The Gods were certainly with us that day because if any one of these bombs had exploded on board, with the cargo we were carrying, there wouldn't have been much left of *Pampas*."

The convoy duly arrived at Grand Harbour. The *Breconshire* remained outside:

"Her engine room was flooded. She was without power, light, cooking or water services. Her steering was out of action. . . . After an unsuccessful effort to tow her in she drifted inshore and came to with both anchors. . . . at the extreme end of the island. She had not yet disembarked her passengers or unloaded her cargo. The next day she was bombed again, without result."

But it was essential to bring her into harbour and she was eventually towed into the great bay of Marsa Scirocco. Nevertheless 26 March was a black day. One ship after another was lost: *Pampas* caught fire and landed only 310 tons of her cargo: *Talabot* sank having landed only 497 tons. *Breconshire* was bombed again and again. Her loss was agonizingly sad after having come so close to her destination.

Another freighter in the convoy was the *Clan Campbell*. Second Mate (later Captain) John H. Harman had already experienced the February convoy. The Battle of Sirte embraced Passion Sunday, hence the name it is sometimes given. Harman recorded:

"We had a terrible day with torpedo, high-level and low-level bombing. As the *Clan Campbell* was the slowest ship in the convoy we were left with a small escort to continue on our own. The other three ships continued to Malta; one was sunk in the entrance to Grand Harbour [*Breconshire*]. The other vessels were bombed and sunk in the harbour after discharging their cargoes. The *Campbell* was found by the bombers 12 miles from Malta at 0800 on the Monday. One of the bombers dropped a bomb which exploded under the stern, knocking off the rudders and propellors. She sank by the stern in just fifteen minutes. Of the crew, which included naval personnel and a Roman Catholic priest, 37 were lost. The naval escort managed to pick up the rest and land them at Malta."

The arrival of the convoy marked the beginning of an all-out series of reprisal air raids on the island. From 24 March to 12 April there were recorded 2,159 bomber sorties, and during the same period it is estimated that 1,870 tons of bombs landed in the harbour, sinking ships, devastating docks and installations, blocking quays and roadways and cutting off light, water and communications.

Before we leave Admiral Vian and his successful defence of a convoy in the Gulf of Sirte there are some items of interest to put on record.

Another casualty of the MW 10 convoy battle was the loss of the Hunt destroyer *Southwold*. On entering Grand Harbour she struck a mine, killing five of the ship's company while she was giving assistance to the *Breconshire*.

Able Seaman M. Wally served aboard the destroyer *Kingston* when she was hit by a 15" shell from *Littorio*. He has never forgotten the incident, nor the intensity of the bombing they were subjected to on the second and third days out. His views of the engagements were limited by the fact that his action station was in Y gun magazine, but he remembers being told by the commanding officer, Commander Somerville, that enemy ships had been sighted – that is the Italian Fleet. As he remembers:

> "We were still closed up at action stations when our destroyer was ordered by Admiral Vian to attack with torpedoes. . . . The second attack was not so good for *Kingston* as we took a shell amidships in the engine room and we came to a standstill . . . a sitting duck for the Italian ships. Admiral Vian stood off our starboard side and engaged the enemy until we got under way again. . . . We were ordered to make for Malta at best speed. We entered Grand Harbour next day and secured alongside the quay. On looking around our ship the damage seemed devastating."

The following day Wally watched the Norwegian *Talabot* enter harbour. No sooner had she arrived and secured than she was sunk by an aircraft bomb. "As you can understand," Wally said, "at the time, it was all very scary."

H. Franklin had recently been drafted to Vian's flagship *Cleopatra*. He was a rangefinder in the Director Control Tower throughout the Battle of Sirte. He wrote:

> "I had my head out of the tower, as my duty was taking angles of the other ships. I saw shrapnel screaming past and when I looked

down I could see that we had been hit by an 8" shell wiping out all the lookouts on the starboard side and exploding on the after part of the bridge killing about 20 ratings. . . . It was a ghastly scene."

Another *Cleopatra* witness to the battle was Leading Stoker (later Petty Officer) E.R. Bell. He refers to the Passion Sunday battle and enclosed a news cutting by J.L. Cooper, the *Daily Express* Naval Correspondent. Cooper wrote describing the shell burst which struck the bridge:

"Before they [the Italians] turned we hit a battleship and my last glimpse of the fleet showed red flames . . . they came from somewhere aft. It was little more than a spark, but a spark at 13,000 yards meant a pretty big fire in the ship. . . . We were hit under the bridge, five feet from where I stood. . . . The Maltese can thank the admiral: we had five hours of torpedo bombing and about sixteen torpedoes fired at us by 1410 in the afternoon. . . . Vian stood unprotected on the bridge with his shoulders hunched and elbows on the windbreaker as if trying to get inches nearer the enemy. He rapped out orders. . . . A south-east gale was whipping up the seas and the spray drenched us."

Cooper painted a graphic picture of Vian and the other officers on the bridge:

"At 1642 I found myself knocked to the deck. A mountain of sea spurted up, and soot showered me. We had been hit. Smoke from our screen blinded me. But there on the bridge was the Admiral, straining over the wind barrier, his whole body taut as a ship going into action. And there was the Captain still with a pipe in his mouth though he had seen a shell coming towards him like a football. And the gunnery officer at his speaking tube as calm as if it was a Mediterranean cruise."

Cooper's article was written in the *Cleopatra*'s charthouse as the shells continued to flow:

"At 1745, as we dashed toward the enemy in battle formation, white ensign ironed out in the gale, comes the whining of the shells over our ship. This is much bigger stuff. 'Fifteen inchers,' shouts the gunnery officer who controls nothing larger than 5.25s. . . . Our ships are hopelessly out-matched in fire power. The Axis must have devoted 150 aircraft dropping bombs and spotting for the navy. . . . *Cleopatra* had fired 98 shells non-stop. . . . We reached port to the welcoming sirens and to the flags run out in our honour."

Derrick Stephens was an Ordinary Signalman (later Leading Signalman) who was drafted to HMS *Dido*. His normal watch position was on the flag deck, as was his action station, immediately under the bridge with voice-pipe control both ways.

"Our duties were to maintain strict lookout, to answer any incoming signals and to transmit signals as required by flags, morse by various lamps and semaphore by hand. We were a very well-disciplined ship. . . . As soon as we cleared the harbour we worked two watches – four hours on and four hours off for the rest of the trip. It was a tough routine and it further exhausted the weary crew."

A few statistical items make interesting reading. On the side of the Royal Navy, the Hunt destroyer *Eridge* rescued 112 survivors from the *Clan Campbell*. From the British point of view the convoy battle was a failure: of the 25,900 tons of stores fought through to Malta only about 5,000 tons finally came ashore. The cruiser *Euryalus* fired no fewer than 421 rounds of 5.25". *Littorio* fired 181 15" shells, 445 6" and 21 3.5". In reply she took an unknown number of hits to no ill-effect, but the storm and flooding put one 15" turret out of action.

Following the Battle of Sirte the Prime Minister was generous in his praise. He signalled Admiral Cunningham:

"I shall be glad if you will convey to Admiral Vian and all who sailed with him the admiration I feel at this resolute and brilliant action by which the Malta convoy was saved. That one of the most powerful and modern battleships afloat, attended by four heavy and two light cruisers, should be routed and put to flight with severe gunfire and torpedo injury, in broad daylight, by a force of five British light cruisers and destroyers, constitutes a naval episode of highest distinction, and entitles all ranks and ratings concerned, and above all their commander, to the compliments of the British nation."

THE DISASTERS OF
OPERATION HARPOON

This much is certain, that he that commands the sea is at great liberty. . . . The vantage of strength at sea . . . is great.

Francis Bacon (1561–1626) *Essays*

It was a towering, ambitious enterprise, hedged about with fears and complex possibilities, and an enemy alert, remorseless and ruthless. It was a meticulously planned operation, more complicated than a jigsaw puzzle and as unpredictable as a bomb blast.

Harpoon lacked the "glamour" of Pedestal, if one can associate the naval/air battle with such a word. It has been dubbed "the forgotten convoy". It deserves better.

June, 1942, saw the passage of two convoys to Malta simultaneously, one from the west – Operation Harpoon, and the other from the east – Operation Vigorous. Both were destined for Malta.

OPERATION HARPOON
SHIPS INVOLVED   JUNE 1942

FORCE X

Freighters:	*Troilus*(7,422 tons)
	Burdwan (5,601 tons)
	Chant (5,601)
	Tanimber (8,619 tons)
	Orari (10,350 tons)
Tanker:	*Kentucky* (9,308 tons)

CLOSE ESCORT

AA Cruiser:	*Cairo*
Destroyers:	*Bedouin, Marne, Matchless, Ithuriel, Partridge, Blankney, Middleton, Badsworth, Kujawiak* (Polish)
Minesweepers:	*Hebe, Speedy, Rye, Hythe*
Motor Gunboats:	Six
Fast Minelayer:	*Welshman* (Operated with Force X)

COVERING FORCE W

Battleship:	*Malaya*
Carriers:	*Argus, Eagle*
Cruisers:	*Kenya* (Vice Admiral Curteis) *Charybdis, Liverpool*
Destroyers:	*Onslow, Icarus, Escapade, Wishart, Wrestler, Vidette, Antelope*

FORCE Y

Corvettes:	*Coltsfoot, Geranium*
Tanker:	*Brown Ranger*
Submarines:	*Safari, Unbroken, Unison, United*
Motor Launches:	*121, 134, 135, 168, 459, 462*

157

On 12 June the Western Convoy passed through the Straits of Gibraltar and met Force W. Action started on the 14th when the Harpoon Convoy was attacked by high-level and dive bombers. It was the first of four major attacks that day. At about 1130 the Dutch became the first casualty with the loss of the *Tanimbar* (8,619 tons). About forty bombers were involved. Roy Maber aboard the *Argus* witnessed her sinking:

"A violent explosion occurred. . . . I looked over to see one of the saddest sights of my life: a merchantman [the *Tanimbar*] carrying ammunition had been struck. . . . The ship had been rent apart and I saw lifeboats, people and debris hurtling upwards; flames shot hundreds of feet into the air. The hull of the vessel separated amidships and within no time she had disappeared from sight, leaving only a few smouldering relics."

Another casualty was the cruiser *Liverpool*. Maber saw her in dry dock later "with an enormous gaping hole in her bottom. It was large enough to drive a bus through. The engine room had been struck and twelve bodies had to be got out. Volunteers had been requested. . . . I enjoyed the reward of an extra tot of rum, but not that much."

Action began at 0635 on the 15th when Italian surface craft appeared on the scene: two 8" gun cruisers and sundry destroyers. Commander Scurfield of HMS *Bedouin* ordered *Marne*, *Matchless*, *Partridge* and *Icarus* to follow him and engage the enemy, leaving the Hunt destroyers and the *Cairo* to give the convoy close support. The latter made smoke and the MGBs fired smoke canisters.

Bedouin and *Partridge* were both damaged and fell astern, and an Italian destroyer was damaged. At 0715 the US oiler *Kentucky* was disabled. She was taken in tow by the minesweeper *Hebe*, but she became a total loss and was sunk by gunfire.

Partridge was now able to take *Bedouin* in tow, but she was sunk by a torpedo bomber. *Partridge* suffered further damage but managed to limp back to Gibraltar.

Ordnance Artificer Arthur (Jim) Green (Later Sub-Lieut

158

RNVR) served aboard *Liverpool*. When he got back to Gibraltar he, too, was amazed at the sight of the cruiser's damage. He was also stunned by the Stuka dive bombers:

> "With their fearsome scream, they seemed to fill the sky, and the barrage put up by the convoy escorts was ear-splitting and awesome. As O.A. on the multiple pom-poms and Oerlikons I had a front line view."

A.L. Baker in the destroyer *Partridge* remembers the enemy striking force taking shape as the British destroyers closed the range. *Bedouin*, as we have seen, became an early casualty and sank. *Partridge*'s commanding officer, Lieutenant-Commander Hawkins, announced that they would engage the cruisers and two destroyers and, when they had finished them, they would take on the other four.

Baker reports how *Partridge* managed to reach Gibraltar. "We eventually arrived and, to our surprise, we were met with a reception of all the ships with their guard rails lined with crews cheering *Partridge* in."

Another casualty of this fateful day was the oiler *Chant*. She was dive-bombed and, listing, was well ablaze. Captain Rice watched the incident:

> "Knowing what she was loaded with . . . we thanked the powers for that extra touch of speed the *Orari* can produce in a tight corner. . . . The *Chant*'s crew got out and over by all available means, but she sank so rapidly that the water reached her ammo first. Her oil tanks burst as she went down, leaving a terrific pall of smoke and fire that was visible for most of the day. The fight continued throughout the day. *Orari*'s gun crews stripped to the waist in the heat. . . . A great cheer went up when we sighted Malta about 4 pm . . . just a blur on the horizon on the port bow."

The Third Officer aboard the *Kentucky* was P.K. Fyrth. He has left us with this brief report: "At 0800 a Ju 88 flying in swiftly from the quarter straddled the poop with two heavy bombs, one so close a giant column of water crashed aboard. The *Kentucky*

159

lay motionless like a stranded whale. . . . The remaining ships of the convoy swept past."

By early afternoon matters were at crisis points. *Cairo* had come under sustained attacks and she had been hit twice by 6" shells from the Italian cruisers. *Ithuriel* considered towing the *Kentucky*, but this would have reduced the convoy speed to an unacceptable limit. *Burdwan* had been near-missed and disabled. Rather than towing, she decided to scuttle. Captain Hardy then decided to cut his losses by sinking *Kentucky* and *Burdwan* and concentrate on getting *Troilus* and *Orari* through to Malta. At about this time *Partridge* rejoined the convoy with *Bedouin* in tow. The situation deteriorated with five bombers attacking and the re-appearance of the Italian surface forces. Hardy decided to steam ahead with the remainder of the convoy, leaving *Bedouin* and *Partridge* behind and *Hebe* and *Badsworth* deputed to sink *Kentucky* and *Burdwan*. They were hard decisions to have to make.

Marne, *Matchless* and *Ithuriel* had left the *Partridge* and her tow to fend off the enemy cruisers. They launched torpedoes and scored a hit on one of the cruisers.

Commander Scurfield has left us his diary describing his reactions while leading fleet destroyers into battle. He was exhilarated by the experience. His training of twenty-two years was brought to a head as he and his five destroyers in line ahead read his signal: ENEMY IN SIGHT. FORM SINGLE FILE AHEAD. TWENTY-FIVE KNOTS.

> "There, quite plainly, were enemy ships. The light was improving rapidly and we could make out two 8" cruisers in line ahead with two destroyers screening ahead and two more astern."

Bedouin was badly mauled. After the engagement Scurfield took stock: he reckoned that his ship had been struck twelve times by 8" shells. Two of them were duds and had passed through the ship without exploding. The main and steering engines were out of action and there was no power for lighting. Magazines had been flooded, the primary fire-control system had been destroyed and the mast shot away. The ship's side was holed in

160

several places, but her guns were ready for action.

She took more punishment early in the afternoon when a Savoia 79 struck her with a torpedo in the engine room. The ship sank in about five minutes. Help for the survivors came in a curious way. An Italian float plane or rescue aircraft alighted near the crowds of men, hoisted nine aboard and called up a small rescue hospital ship. All the survivors became prisoners of war of the Italians. When the Germans were moving PoWs away from advancing Allied troops in Italy a party of British prisoners was bombed by Allied aircraft and Commander Scurfield was killed.

Leslie W. Munden was an Electrical Artificer 3rd class (later Lieutenant (E)) aboard the fleet destroyer *Matchless* and he witnessed much of *Bedouin*'s end. His action station in the Transmitting Station allowed him to get up top periodically. On the day of the battle he recalls:

"I remember gazing astern where the whole convoy was spread out. It seemed as if every ship was belching flame and smoke with a pall over everything and screaming dive bombers and the thud of exploding bombs. The next morning the Italian cruisers made their appearance. I nipped out from the Transmitting Station and there was the splendid sight of sunlight on blue water and the destroyer force steaming flat out with creaming seas at bow and stern and battle ensigns standing out stiff and straight. . . . We passed *Bedouin* stopped, on fire and in her death throes. While *Matchless* and her consorts were away the convoy suffered more air attacks and when they returned they passed through the shattered wreckage of a sunken ship. . . . It was during this action that we rescued a ditched Italian flyer. I remember seeing him winched aboard and observing dispassionately that one of his legs appeared to be partially severed just above the ankle. During a lull in the action the crew were in a heavy, deep sleep: nervous tension left everyone frayed. A voice shouted at us, 'If anyone's interested we've struck a mine'. We had all slept through the explosion."

The mine had not caused much damage to *Matchless*. But she was in good company. *Badsworth*, *Hebe* and *Orari* had been damaged as well and the Polish *Kujawiak* sunk, all attributed to a new minefield. Munden remembers gazing over Grand Harbour and seeing the sad sight of mastheads protruding above the water like grave markers and noting the acres of flattened buildings ashore. He walked aboard *Lance*, leaning over drunkenly in the dry dock where she had been bombed.

Another Harpoon survivor was Able Seaman (LR 2) (later Sub-Lieutenant RNVR) Monty Veale aboard the Hunt destroyer *Blankney*. The intensity of the air raids on the fleet, the torpedoes, gunfire and bombing was startling. Like Munden, Monty Veale enjoyed the blue skies and the warm Mediterranean weather. And morale was high. It was comforting and impressive to see such powerful escort forces. Veale was alarmed, though, to see all the action going on on the far side of the convoy. He wondered what it would be like when it came over his side. He recorded:

"A wave of a dozen or so Italian torpedo bombers came in at sea level. We could not fire for fear of hitting the ships in line with the targets. . . . The planes were quickly obliterated by a curtain of shell bursts through which they had to fly. Some of the bursts were beyond any of my previous experience, creating huge black clouds like a smoke screen. As the planes dropped their torpedoes and tried to gain height we were all able to open fire and our targets were buffeted up and down. I can't imagine how they survived. One pilot baled out over the convoy and drifted down into the flames. . . . We could feel the heat of the cruiser *Kenya*'s salvoes as she fired over us."

But *Kenya* had returned with Force H, and anyway a couple of Kenya class ships would still be heavily outgunned by the two 8" gun cruisers now approaching over the horizon. They marked their arrival with salvoes of 8" shells. A number of the escorts were torpedo-carrying destroyers.

"They peeled off from the screen whilst we all made smoke and without hesitation they belted towards the enemy at full speed raking them at close range and firing their torpedoes. We laid smoke screens between the enemy and our charges and when the enemy closed the range we would dash out from the cover of

162

the screen and fire as many rounds as possible and dash back out of sight again."

Veale commented on the tragic end of HMS *Bedouin* and how she had sustained damage to her engine room. He confirmed that, after attempts to tow her, it was decided to take her crew off and sink her. Veale remembers that as night fell:

"We suddenly heard the captain's voice over the Tannoy: 'We are now safely under the protection of the Malta barrage. The ship's company may stand down at their action stations.' I think we all dropped with utter exhaustion only to be awakened to stand-by to go to the assistance of the Polish-manned Hunt destroyer *Kujawiak* which had hit a mine. When we got to the scene she had already sunk. We went in amongst her life rafts, boats and swimming survivors and they clambered aboard."

Monty Veale ended his report on a high note. "Our entry into Grand Harbour," he recollects, "will forever be in my memory":

"We weighed anchor, changed into clean uniforms and shortly after dawn were led in by a minesweeper. As we drew nearer to the ramparts we could see them crowded with people, men, women and children. Little union jacks were being waved to us and a loudspeaker was blaring *There'll always be an England.* Whilst we were standing to attention I cast a side glance at my neighbour, a hardened three-badge AB and like me he had a tear trickling down his cheek."

The Harpoon story is not finished yet. Lieutenant Gray's experience as commanding officer of the Hunt class *Badsworth* needs touching upon. It was during the raid at midday on the 15th that *Badsworth* went to the assistance of the *Burdwan*, disabled by a near miss. Lieutenant Gray had been deputed to sink the *Burdwan* because her rudder was jammed hard over and the engine room was flooded.

Gray concluded his story of the 15th with the comment:

"It was sad to see the convoy reduced to only two merchantmen and a bitter blow that we had been forced to send so much precious cargo to the bottom. Ships lost were the Dutch *Tanimbar*, the US *Chant* and *Kentucky* and the British *Burdwan*. . . . Approaching Malta during the night of 15/16 June the remaining ships ran into a minefield now believed to have been British-laid. The Polish destroyer was struck first and sank. *Badsworth* was damaged under the bridge and the other three, *Matchless*, *Hebe* and *Orari*, were all damaged but were able to proceed into harbour."

Operation Harpoon ended with a melancholy list of ships sunk, damaged, mined, bombed or torpedoed by about every weapon available to man. But the battle of the convoys was not over. While Harpoon was experiencing its fierce ordeals Vigorous had another tale to tell. So we must re-trace our footsteps a few days to follow the dangers of that convoy. But before we leave Harpoon we need to glimpse back at some of the activities of HMS *Argus* and HMS *Eagle* both of which have earned little mention, yet are deserving of praise.

Air Mechanic Roy Maber served aboard both ships in the Mediterranean. He had a front-seat view of the West-to-East Operation Harpoon. He remembers the flying on and off of Hurricanes and Spitfires from *Eagle*. Several pilots were lost even before they set foot in Malta. One aircraft reported technical problems after take off. He was instructed to fly at 1,000 feet and bale out ahead of the fleet; someone would pick him up. He did so. Maber reports, "and we watched him but no parachute was seen. He was picked up dead. It was said that his parachute had been stolen and a blanket packed in its place."

Another pilot suffered mechanical failure of some sort. He signalled, "Mayday: Engine failing". He just managed to land as the engine failed completely.An inspection showed that sugar had been put into the oil tank causing it to seize. The pilot, of course, was a particularly offensive character. "Right bastard", was the phrase used.

Roy Maber and his squad of six joined HMS *Argus*. He reports that "she used to roll like a pig and earned the nickname 'The Floating Ditty Box'." The ship was unusual in that her bridge was located in the centre of the flight deck, and when flying was taking place it would retract below the flag deck while the bridge crew hot-footed it over to a conning position in the port or starboard side.

The captain tannoyed the ship's company what they already had guessed: Malta was the destination. They were urged to get as much rest as possible for the convoy of six had to be fought through in the face of fierce attacks from aircraft, surface vessels and submarines.

As we have already learned, 14 June was a beautiful Mediterranean day, blue cloudless skies, warm, and the sea like a millpond. Speed was at *Argus'* topmost – 18 knots [actually it was probably about 16 knots].

The precious merchant ships were in the centre of the convoy, screened on either side by the two carriers and the battleship *Malaya*. The destroyers were the real workhorses of the convoy, zig-zagging at high speed ahead while others circled the convoy.

HMS *Argus* and HMS *Eagle* became heavily engaged in the ensuing engagements:

> "The sky was filled with black puffs of smoke as every gun of every calibre opened up and splashed in the sea indicating where the shrapnel landed. Three aircraft dropped their torpedoes when about half a mile from us, then climbed to clear our flight deck which they only missed by a few feet. I could make out the pilots' faces quite clearly as they passed over. The ship did a violent turn and the torpedoes ran past harmlessly. The pilots showed great courage."

Maber saw the Dutch *Tanimbar* explode and disappear, learned how to survive six hours at a time of action stations, saw the *Liverpool* in dry dock and helped fight through the convoy, now much depleted and battered.

THE FAILURE OF
OPERATION VIGOROUS

*If anyone wishes to know the history of
this war, I will tell them that it is our
maritime supremacy gives me the power
of maintaining my army while the enemy
are unable to do the same.*

Attributed to the Duke of Wellington.
21 September, 1803.

Simultaneously with Operation Harpoon (12–16 June, 1942)
the Royal Navy, supported by the RAF and aircraft of the Fleet
Air Arm, mounted Operation Vigorous. While Harpoon
covered the West-to-East operation from Gibraltar to Malta,
the convoy code-named Vigorous sailed from Haifa, Port Said
and Alexandria. The intention was to fight through to Malta
no fewer than eleven fully laden merchant ships. The escort
and covering forces totalled sixty warships: one dummy battleship, two rescue ships, four corvettes, two minesweepers,
twenty-six destroyers, eight cruisers, four MTBs and thirteen
submarines.

The use of a dummy battleship calls for some comment. HMS
Centurion was an ancient and virtually unarmed target practice
vessel of 25,000 tons. She had been launched in 1911 and was
converted into a target ship in 1924. She was altered to give a
silhouette of a dummy battleship, rather like the *King George V
class*.

While the Harpoon convoy had been battling its way through

OPERATION VIGOROUS
SHIPS INVOLVED   JUNE 1942

EASTERN CONVOY MW11 (Commodore Rear-Admiral England)

Freighters:	*City of Pretoria* (7,900 tons)
	City of Calcutta (8,063 tons)
	City of Edinburgh (8,000 tons)
	Potaro (5,410 tons)
	Aagtekerk (6,811 tons)
	Bhutan (6,104 tons)
	City of Lincoln (8,000 tons)
	Ajax (7,800 tons)
	Elizabeth Bakke (5,450 tons)
	Rembrandt (8,126 tons)
	Bulkoil (8,071 tons)
Dummy Battleship:	*Centurion*
Rescue Ships:	*Antwerp, Malines*

CLOSE ESCORT

Corvettes:	*Delphinium, Primula, Erica, Snapdragon*
Minesweepers:	*Boston, Seaham*
2nd Destroyer Flotilla:	*Fortune, Griffin, Hotspur*
5th Destroyer Flotilla:	*Dulverton, Exmoor, Croome, Airedale, Beaufort, Hurworth, Eridge, Tetcott, Aldenham*

COVERING FORCE (Rear-Admiral Philip Vian)

15th Cruiser Squadron:	*Cleopatra, Dido, Hermione, Euryalus, Arethusa, Coventry*
4th Cruiser Squadron:	(Rear-Admiral Tennant) *Birmingham, Newcastle*
7th Destroyer Flotilla:	(RAN) *Napier, Nestor, Nizam, Norman*
14th Destroyer Flotilla:	*Jervis, Kelvin, Javelin*
12th Destroyer Flotilla:	*Pakenham, Paladin, Inconstant*
22nd Destroyer Flotilla:	*Sikh, Zulu, Hasty, Hero*
MTBs:	Four (Towed by merchant ships: returned because of stormy weather)
Submarines:	*Proteus, Thorn, Taku, Thrasher, Porpoise, Una, P31, P34, P35* (All patrolling off Taranto), *P 211, P 42, P 43, P 46,* (Patrolling between Sicily/Sardinia)

to Malta the ships of the Vigorous section of the operation were similarly engaged in a savage series of skirmishes approaching Malta from the Alexandria end of the Mediterranean.

It fell to Admiral Sir Henry Harwood, victor of the Battle of the River Plate, December, 1939, to accept the challenge of overall command of the operation. He had succeeded Cunningham as C-in-C of the Mediterranean in April a few weeks previously. Vigorous was a heavy inheritance.

Commander of the operation at sea was Rear Admiral Philip Vian whose responsibility was almost as heavy as Harwood's. Vian hoisted his flag in HMS *Cleopatra*. He viewed his charges and his fleet of sixty warships with his customary brooding silence which some took to mean satisfaction but others found discouragingly frightening. Vian, master tactician at the Second Battle of Sirte just a few weeks beforehand, now handled an armada of naval vessels.

We must now see how the navy coped with "the catalogue of all known forces of attack" to which it was being subjected.

The first casualty was the freighter *City of Calcutta*. She was damaged in a Stuka attack. She was detached to Tobruk with the Hunt destroyer *Tetcott* and *Grove* as escorts. *Grove* ran aground but managed to get herself clear and was able to proceed at slow speed. She was sighted by *U-77* (Lieutenant Schonder) who sank her with two torpedoes off Sollum. *Tetcott* picked up survivors.

The Dutch *Aagtekirk* suffered engine trouble and was left making way for Tobruk with an escort of two corvettes, *Erica* and *Primula*, but later in the afternoon she came under attack from about 40 Ju 87s and Ju 88s. She was overwhelmed and sank.

The First Lieutenant of *Tetcott* was alarmed at the intensity of the operation. D.L. Devonport recorded:

"We arrived in the Med on the 4th June and in ten days had lost three of the four ships in our charge and one consort, the *Grove*."

On the same day the convoy endured air and E-boat attacks. Three merchant ships were hit and two of them sank.

On the following day intelligence warned of two Italian heavy units sailing from Taranto. The convoy altered course many times for safety's sake. But so intense had been the engagements that already in the first day of battle the escorts' ammunition was depleted to dangerous levels. This fact alone determined the course of the operation. It could not proceed with such fast-diminishing ammunition. At this rate another day of fighting would see escorts without shells.

On this day, too, two cruisers were damaged and the destroyers *Hasty* and *Airedale* sunk. *Airedale* went in an especially tragic manner. During the afternoon flights of dive bombers set upon the convoy. Twelve of the bombers selected *Airedale* (Lieutenant-Commander A.S. Forman) as their target. She was swamped and, when the smoke and spray had cleared, she was seen to be dead in the water, a smouldering wreck, her X gun and after end completely gone. It was all over in a matter of seconds. She was near-missed by at least six large bombs, hit by one, and probably several smaller ones. It was believed that her 4" after magazine or her own depth charges exploded. What was left of her was sunk by her consorts.

On the 15th it was confirmed that the enemy fleet had put to sea. It was seen to comprise two battleships, four cruisers and seven destroyers, a powerful force which Admiral Harwood judged to be too powerful for Vian's fleet to cope with, hampered as it was with the responsibility of the convoy.

At 0145 Harwood ordered the whole force to return to Alexandria. It was a dreadfully complex manoeuvre to get nearly sixty ships to reverse course, and at night. The Italians took the advantage just before dawn of targeting the *Newcastle* which was disabled. However, she soon managed to get up to 24 knots.

The destroyer *Hardy* had to be abandoned and sunk. Intelligence advised Harwood that the run to Malta would, in fact, be clear and he had the courage to order the whole force to turn about again and head for Malta. Further, more accurate information came to hand directly, threatening the convoy, which impelled Harwood to alter course yet again and the whole operation was turned once more for Alexandria.

Almost continuous attacks by E-boats on the sea and aircraft

AXIS FORCES
OPERATIONS HARPOON AND VIGOROUS
JUNE 1942

Cruisers: 7th Division:	(Divisional Admiral da Zara)
	Eugenio de Savoia, Montecuccoli
Destroyers:	*Oriani, Ascari, Gioberti*
	(Reinforced by: *Vivaldi, Malocello*
	Premuda
Battleships:	*Littorio* (Admiral Iachino)
	Vittorio Veneto (Div-Admiral
	Fioravanzo)
Heavy Cruisers:	(Div-Admiral Parona)
3rd Division:	*Gorizia, Trieste*
Light Cruisers:	(Div-Admiral de Courten)
8th Division:	*Garibaldi, Duca d'Aosta*
Destroyers:	
7th Flotilla ⎫	
13th " ⎬	Twelve
11th " ⎭	

ITALIAN AND GERMAN U-BOAT DISPOSITIONS

Italian:	
Two Groups	of 5 boats each stationed to the north of Algerian coast
3rd Group:	5 boats in the Malta-Lampedusa area
4th Group:	5 boats in the Ionian Sea
5th Group:	comprising 2 Italian and 6 German U-boats
German E-Boat Flotilla:	(Lieutenant Wuppermann)
3rd Flotilla:	*S 54, S 55, S 56, S 58, S 59, S 60*

above compelled all crews to remain at action stations day and night. Wave after wave of aircraft arrived overhead in streams. The freighter *Bhutan* was sunk and another was damaged, but managed to keep up.

Even the darkness of night brought no rest. Aircraft lit the scene with flares and E-boats prowled like Formula One racing cars seeking a chance to make a killing.

It was one such snatched opportunity that put the cruiser *Newcastle* temporarily out of action, to which Leading Coder Norman (Nick) Carter (later Petty Officer) had been drafted. The dual operation, he understood, had been

> "in the hope that at least some ships would get through from either end of the Med with much-needed supplies. The attack on the Vigorous convoy began during the Dog Watch on Sunday 14th June and continued throughout that night. My action station was in the wireless office directly below the bridge. I did manage a brief spell on the upper deck and it was a terrible sight to see several of the merchant ships under attack and in flames in the darkness. In the early hours of the 15th *Newcastle* was struck in the bow section by a torpedo from an E-boat putting a hole through from the starboard to the port side ... which made us heavy by the head. We returned to Alex."

One of the last casualties of the operation was the cruiser *Hermione*. One of the ship's company was L.A. Warnes. He was one of the survivors and he left this report:

> "The cruiser was torpedoed at approximately 2355 on 16 June, 1942. The torpedo hit the after engine room and the ship started to list right away. I was lucky to be alive. I had been operating the after air compressor to supply compressed air for the guns and turret. Having charged the bottles to full pressure I left the compartment at 2345 to go forward to the mess deck. I had just got there when there was a loud explosion and the ship shuddered. ... The ship listed badly and next came the order to abandon ship. We all made our way to the upper deck. Water was already coming over the side of the ship. There were Carley rafts beside the funnel but we were unable to release them."

CIVILIAN CASUALTIES

Siege casualties as published by *The Times of Malta* on 11 June, 1942 immediately before Operations Harpoon and Vigorous

Killed 997

Died of Injuries 218

Seriously injured 1493

Slightly injured 1437

(Died of injuries should be deducted from the figure for Seriously injured.)

DAMAGE TO CIVILIAN PROPERTY.

Unofficially it is listed as follows:

Houses totally destroyed . . . . about 4350

Badly Damaged . . . . about 4300

Damaged but repairable 20300

CHURCHES AND PUBLIC BUILDINGS

78 Churches

13 Hospitals

21 Schools

8 Hotels

10 Clubs

12 Theatres

5 Banks

44 Historical Buildings

Warnes described how the cruiser was nearly on her side, so the crew went over the high side and slid into the sea. Warnes inflated his life belt and swam away from the ship:

> "There was a large explosion aft. The shock was very bad. It was like someone hitting you at the base of the spine with a sledge hammer. Some died in the water then. Still swimming, I headed for a dark object in the water. It was a Carley raft full of survivors. I clung to the side all night and well into the next day, eventually being picked up by one of the Hunts. The *Hermione* did not last long. I saw her bows rise in the water and then she sank."

At first light on 16 June *Badsworth* entered Grand Harbour at slow speed, glad to secure alongside in the dockyard.

Lieutenant Gray of *Badsworth* reflected that only two merchant vessels reached Malta, the majority having turned back to base after the failure of Operation Vigorous. The two which got through were both from the Harpoon operation. One cruiser and five destroyers had been sunk and several more were damaged. It had been a gallant but expensive endeavour. On the credit side, the Italian battleship *Littorio* had been hit by bombs from an American Liberator aircraft and the heavy cruiser *Trento* had been torpedoed by a Beaufort of 217 Squadron and later sunk by the British submarine *Umbra*.

Even while the two convoy operations were being fought through *The Times of Malta* was publishing some statistics about the battle for Malta.

OPERATION PEDESTAL

Before you start on this operation the First Sea Lord and I are anxious that you should know how grateful the Board of Admiralty are to you for undertaking this difficult task. Malta has for some time been in great danger. It is imperative that she should be kept supplied. These are her critical months, and we cannot fail her. She has stood up to the most violent attack from the air that has ever been made and now she needs our help in continuing the battle. Her courage is worthy of yours.

We know that Admiral Syfret will do all he can to complete the operation with success, and that you will stand by him according to the splendid traditions of the Merchant Navy. We wish you all Godspeed and good luck.

First Lord of the Admiralty, A.V. Alexander, to Convoy Captains, 0800, 10 August, 1942.

Operation Pedestal was perhaps the most powerful fleet ever assembled for a supply convoy in the Mediterranean. It was essential that Malta should be relieved. The island was suffering her "supreme ordeal". Her 2,000th air raid had long gone. She was battered beyond recognition. In a single month 6,700 tons of bombs had screamed down on the islanders. The docks were devastated. Over 10,000 houses had been demolished. Reservoirs had been destroyed. Stores of food were gutted and gun emplacements blasted. Worse still was the havoc caused in the Grand Harbour of Valletta. The cranes and installations were pulverized, wharves blitzed and warehouses knocked flat. And all this occurred on an area the size of greater London.

However, Malta was beginning to enjoy improved defence in the air. The deliveries of fighter aircraft in the ferrying operations by aircraft carriers – the USS *Wasp*, the *Eagle* and *Argus* in particular – were taking their toll of enemy aircraft. *Eagle* made nine ferrying trips and delivered 183 aircraft in all.

Operation Pedestal, planned for August, 1942, was to prove a bitter, relentless defence of the fourteen large, fast merchant ships comprising the convoy while the Axis forces were remorseless in their savage bombing and torpedoing.

The thirteen freighters and one tanker carried mixed cargoes of kerosene, oil fuel, ammunition, petrol, flour and other foodstuffs. The tanker *Ohio* carried 11,500 tons of kerosene and oil fuel. The navy nursed her like a patient and the enemy targeted her like a stalker.

As early as 11 August, a Thursday, the British forces were sighted by a German aircraft and the Axis forces alerted. It was believed that as many as 400 aircraft were available to engage the British forces, together with torpedo planes, E-boats and submarines. It was an awesome prospect. Disaster was not long in coming.

HMS *Eagle* (Captain L.D. Mackintosh) was struck by four torpedoes from *U-73* (Lieutenant-Commander Rosenbaum).

A witness of the torpedoing was Stoker Petty Officer A.V. Ellis aboard the cruiser *Nigeria*. His action station was on one of the starboard 4" HA guns.

"During a lull in the action I was watching *Eagle*'s planes taking off. Then a muffled boom and she just slipped over. The planes on her deck began to slide into the water. The sea was like the proverbial mill-pond. Air Raid Message Red came over the Tannoy. I got a bit busy and the next time I glanced astern all I could see were a couple of destroyers picking up survivors."

Ellis adds with laconic composure: "Two days later we [*Nigeria*] were torpedoed."

175

OPERATION PEDESTAL
Convoy WS.5.21.S.

Convoy Commodore: Commodore A.G. Venables RN Ret'd.

Merchant ships			
USA	*Almeria Lykes*	7,773 tons	* Sunk
British	*Brisbane Star*	12,791 tons	Survived
British	*Clan Ferguson*	7,347 tons	* Sunk
British	*Deucalion*	7,516 tons	* Sunk
British	*Dorset*	10,624 tons	* Sunk
British	*Empire Hope*	12,688 tons	* Sunk
British	*Glenorchy*	8,982 tons	* Sunk
British	*Melbourne Star*	12,806 tons	Survived
USA	*Ohio*	9,514 tons	Survived
British	*Port Chalmers*	8,535 tons	Survived
British	*Rochester Castle*	7,795 tons	Survived
USA	*Santa Elisa*	8,379 tons	* Sunk
British	*Waimarama*	12,843 tons	* Sunk
British	*Wairangi*	12,400 tons	* Sunk

British Forces

FORCE Z

Battleships: *Nelson* (Flag Vice Admiral Sir Neville Syfret)

                      Rodney

Carriers: *Victorious* (Flag Rear Admiral Sir A.L. St A. Lyster)

                      Indomitable (Flag Rear Admiral D.W. Boyd)

                      Eagle

                      Furious

Light Cruisers:	*Phoebe, Sirius, Charybdis*
Destroyers:	*Laforey, Lightning, Lookout, Quentin, Somali, Eskimo, Tartar, Ithuriel, Antelope, Wishart, Vansittart, Westcott, Wrestler, Zetland, Wilton*

FORCE X

Light Cruisers:	*Nigeria* (Flag Rear Admiral H.M. Burrough) *Kenya, Manchester, Cairo*
Destroyers:	*Ashanti, Intrepid, Icarus, Foresight, Fury, Pathfinder, Penn, Derwent, Bramham, Bicester, Ledbury*

Escorts for:

Convoy + Escort:	*Matchless, Badworth*
Fleet Oilers:	*Brown Ranger, Dingledale*
Corvettes:	*Jonquil, Geranium, Spirea, Coltsfoot*
Tugs:	*Jaunty, Salvonia*
Carrier:	*Argus*
Fleet Oiler:	*Abbeydale*
Corvettes:	*Burdoch, Armeiria*

Attached from:

Western Approaches:	*Keppel, Malcolm, Amazon, Venomous, Wolverine*
Malta Escort Force:	17th Minesweeping Flotilla: *Speedy, Hebe, Rye, Hythe*
3rd Motor Launch Flotilla:	MLs *121, 126, 134, 135, 168, 459, 462.*
Submarines:	*Safari, Unbroken, Uproar, Ultimate, Unruffled, Utmost, United, Una, P-222*

Samuel Peffer was another eye witness. He was part of the DEMS gunnery contingent aboard the merchant vessel *Dorset*, a large well-armed ship carrying a number of RA soldiers to man the Bofors. Peffer recalls:

"The large merchant vessels were loaded to the gunwales, escorted by what seemed like the entire Home Fleet. My action station was up on the Monkey Island [a deck above the bridge] manning a 20mm Oerlikon gun on the port side of the ship. On this particular morning I went on watch at midday. From my position in the gun pit I had a splendid view of the ships. The carrier *Eagle* was steaming abreast of our ship. It was at about 1 pm when I heard four large explosions. They were a salvo of torpedoes striking the port side of the *Eagle*. Great columns of water spouted up and clouds of dense smoke erupted as she keeled over. Within a few minutes she was under the water. I could not get it out of my mind."

Harry Brown was a stoker aboard the destroyer *Keppel* (Commander J. Broome) who went right alongside the *Eagle* as she went down. She picked up a few survivors.

ERA Stuart Tilford (later Warrant Engineer) was serving in the Hunt class destroyer (*Zealand*). He had just come off the forenoon watch and went up top for a breather:

"I was taking in the panorama of the convoy and as I looked over at the *Eagle* she suddenly turned on her side and sank. I could hardly believe what I was seeing. She disappeared in a matter of minutes."

Stoker Eric Knight also witnessed the sinking and, like Tilford, had just come off watch and went up top for a breath of fresh air. As he stepped up on deck he noticed two or three huge water spouts by the side of the *Eagle*. She had been torpedoed and went down in five or six minutes.

Stoker Jack Martin refers to "the grand old lady", HMS *Eagle*, in which he served, and the floating ditty box *Argus* with affection. He was a stoker in B boiler room, but when on watch assigned to assorted gun crews on the upper deck:

"On the Pedestal convoy I happened to be on the upper deck when the *Eagle* was torpedoed. Lots of us saw the whole thing, heard the bangs, saw the ship on one side, and then disappear, all in about eight minutes. Something spectacular to watch but awful to realize the large number of navy lads losing their lives or being maimed."

Alan Reid (ex RNVR) was serving aboard the destroyer *Venomous* (Commander H.W. Falcon-Steward). He remembers the convoy being shadowed all the time. The prize the enemy sought and won was the *Eagle* and her Swordfish. *Venomous* picked up a large number of survivors by scrambling nets and hand-to-hand grabbing, but many slipped away on the point of rescue.

Rosenbaum was awarded the Knight's Cross of the Iron Cross for his achievement. He later commanded a U-boat flotilla in the Black Sea and was killed in an air crash.

After the *Eagle* went down *Furious* had a narrow escape. She was hit in the bows by a torpedo and quickly took on a list. But this was corrected and she managed to limp back to Gibraltar. The convoy continued on its way. Peffer recorded in his diary that it was a brilliant day, the sun beating down from an azure sky. He recorded:

"Every ship was on full alert, expecting to hear the drone of aircraft. In a few hours it would be dusk, the most vulnerable time for the ships. The sun began to sink, a huge ball of red slowly descending towards the sea. Then they came . . . little shapes in the distance. . . . All hell broke loose as they began to dive and the ships began their firing. The noise was deafening, the guns pounding, the roaring of the engines and torpedoes exploding. Worst of all the scream of the Stukas diving. Darkness descended. The guns cooled down. The enemy departed."

The following morning the attack was renewed. Peffer reported his Oerlikon getting red hot. This was probably the attack that Ward referred to as coming in like bees swarming. He went on:

"The two battleships *Nelson* and *Rodney* loaded their 15" guns with shrapnel warheads and fired while the enemy aircraft were approaching, six miles away. The effect caused pandemonium among the attacking pilots and other ships close to the battleships. Their crews suffered temporary shock. As well as the shellshock waves, both battleships disappeared under a pall of smoke. This must have been the first time the monstrous anger of the 15" guns had been used as anti-aircraft shells."

The immediate thought of eye-witnesses was that both ships had been bombed. When they came through, majestically riding the waves, a terrific cheer was to be heard from all nearby ships' crews. It was a cry of relief. The enemy formations were broken up. But trouble lay ahead. An ammunition ship in the convoy, the *Clan Ferguson*, seemed to disappear in a flash. The report on the *Clan Ferguson* is not quite right. E.D. (Ernie) Tough was a DEMS (Defensively Equipped Merchant Ship) soldier serving as a gunner. He was aboard the vessel and survived the experience:

"The ship had already made a number of runs to Malta, but the preparations on board suggested that this run was something special. We also took on board several skilled personnel, making a total complement of 114. During the late evening of the Thursday *Clan Ferguson* was hit by a huge explosion, believed to have been caused by a torpedo fired by an Italian submarine, the resulting detonation igniting a supply of petrol."

Abandon ship was ordered. Tough was in the water for some hours before a *Clan Ferguson* lifeboat plucked him from the sea.

On the same day that Tough survived the blaze aboard the *Clan Ferguson* the carrier *Indomitable* took a bomb on the forward AA gun turrets. Seventy-two sailors lost their lives. The ship, however, was saved, its list corrected by judicious flooding.

Another casualty was the merchant ship *Deucalion*. She was the leading freighter on the port-side column. She was severely damaged by an aerial torpedo and by bombs which exploded on impact with the water, buckling her plates and flooding her holds. She limped away from the convoy under the protection of a destroyer, but she caught fire and was blown up. *Empire Hope* was bombed and set ablaze. The destroyer *Bramham* rescued survivors.

It is convenient at this stage to follow the fortunes of the activities of other ships of the convoy, which, incidentally, was styled Convoy WS 215 (a bogus number for the sake of security). The WS prefix stood for Winston Specials; he purred contentedly when he learnt this.

The ships of the convoy brought together an impressive 139,992 tons of cargo ships of modern naval construction.

The disastrous losses of the convoyed ships continued unabated. *Wairangi* was torpedoed and sunk by an Italian E-boat. All her crew were saved by the destroyer *Eskimo*. *Glenorchy* was bombed then sunk by torpedo from an E-boat.

Santa Elisa and *Almeria Lykes* were soon to follow. The *Rochester Castle* also succumbed and was able to be got under way again. She managed to reach Malta.

Waimarrama was less fortunate. She was struck by aerial torpedoes in quick succession. Her cargo of cased aviation spirit and ammunition blew up in a sheet of flame.

Melbourne Star was showered with debris as the sea blazed with fire all around. Twenty of her crew were rescued by HMS *Ledbury*, but eighty-seven were lost.

The sinking of the *Wairangi* was especially distressing. Mrs Joan Allen has written of her husband's experience as an engineer officer aboard the freighter which was torpedoed on the night of 12–13 August by "a dirty little Italian E-boat". This was after he had watched the sister ship *Empire Hope* sink. Depth charges had to be used to finish off the *Wairangi*. The surviving crew members were rescued by the *Eskimo* who was preparing to rescue the ship's company of the *Manchester*.

Waimarama was a sister ship of both the *Empire Hope* and the *Wairangi*. She was hit by three or more bombs which clustered near the bridge and exploded in quick succession, killing everyone there. The explosions set fire to her part cargo of petrol in drums. Soon the ship was in flames from end to end. Within a few minutes she was out of sight.

* * *

The aircraft carrier *Indomitable* is lightly dismissed as having been damaged, as if of little consequence. The fact is she was severely damaged, so extensively that she was almost lost. While *Nelson* and *Rodney* were in the throes of shelling enemy aircraft with their 16" guns *Indomitable* was selected as a prime target for the mass attacks. Syd Whitfield, a Leading Cook, was aboard the carrier. He records:

> "Our captain, Tom Troubridge, said over the tannoy: 'Today grouse shooting starts in Scotland [the Glorious Twelfth]. We shall be shooting before the day is out'."

B.G. Rees BEM provided a Report of *Indomitable*'s experiences:

> "Twelve Ju 87s appeared out of the setting sun and out of a smoky blue sky. . . . They made a concentrated attack on *Indomitable*. All the carrier's guns opened up in a desperate attempt to deter the plummeting planes. . . . Astern of her the protecting cruiser HMS *Phoebe* (Captain P. Frend) was fully engaged with her main armament of 5.25 inch guns . . . while the bombs rained down in a concentrated onslaught."

Indomitable became obscured by the splashes and smoke pouring from her flight deck fore and aft as she circled painfully at slow speed. She was turning away from the wind in an effort to master the flames which swept her hangar decks.

> "One bomb landed near her forward lift and penetrated the upper gallery deck and exploded above the main hangar deck. A hole some 20 feet by 12 was blown in the upper deck. Severe structural and splinter damage occurred . . . but the carnage aboard the carrier was terrible. The wardroom had been crowded with off-duty pilots and observers . . . and one of the near-miss bombs had wrecked it, killing every man there. In all, casualties amounted to six officers and 44 men killed and a further 59 seriously wounded. The men killed included the Royal Marine detachment manning guns: they had suffered particularly when both turrets had been destroyed."

Two huge columns of black smoke blossomed from her flight deck and it looked to eye-witnesses as though she could never survive. The last seen of her by many was the column of smoke still rising from her as she sailed to the west and the darkness of night shrouded her.

Arthur Lawson was a Leading Telegraphist aboard the carrier. He reported that at about 1930 *Indomitable* was under intense and continuous bombing while fighting back tooth and nail. Suddenly the carrier shuddered from stem to stern. A strange hush then prevailed, followed by the bedlam of damage control parties going about their grisly work. "My most vivid memory," Lawson related, "was seeing an officer finishing a drink he was having with half his head blown away."

Another Telegraphist was Charles McCoombe aboard the cruiser *Sirius*: He told Rees:

"She looked a right mess with the flight deck rolled up under the extreme heat. She was hit by several bombs and looked like an old-fashioned sardine can with the lid rolled back on the key."

Indomitable mastered the damage, increased speed and headed for Gibraltar which she reached safely.

Another ship which suffered damage was the escorting cruiser *Nigeria*. It was 12 August, a day of disaster, when *Nigeria* suffered the loss of fifty men and the AA cruiser *Cairo* was sunk. It was the day, too, when the tanker *Ohio* received her first hit, by torpedo. Among the *Nigeria*'s crew was Boy Seaman H.D. King, whose action station was with a gun's crew. He tells how the cruiser took two torpedo hits with the loss of a number of lives. He reports that there was no panic, although he was well aware that flooding was occurring three decks down.

Chief Technician Baker's steering station aboard *Nigeria* was the Forward Engine Room and he was also in charge of the After Damage Control: "We had just gone from First degree of readiness to Second." Baker opened up the quarterdeck hatches to ventilate ship. He had been battened down for 48 hours:

"I remember a tremendous flash and bump. My lungs filled with the acrid fumes of cordite and I was lifted bodily off my feet by a gigantic wall of water and carried aft."

He was deposited under the port torpedo tubes. Badly battered, he then noticed the list to port. He clambered to the starboard side and was horrified to see the *Cairo* going down stern first and the *Ohio* burning furiously. Within minutes arrangements were being made to transfer Admiral Sir Harold Burrough to the destroyer *Ashanti*.

Baker, looking like a drowned rat, made his way forward where everything was a shambles. When a semblance of order had been restored course was set for Gibraltar.

Thursday 13 August was another day of savage ordeals. The destroyer *Foresight* was immediately ahead of the destroyer *Tartar* in the screen when she took a torpedo aft. *Tartar* was ordered to stand by her and preparations were made to take her in tow.

Mrs Tabb reports that her husband served in the *Tartar* and has left a memoir of the incident of *Foresight*'s torpedoing and subsequent tow.

"*Foresight* could not steer and could only steam at about 2 knots. Tow was passed at 1930 and five minutes later we took the weight of the tow when five Beaufighters attacked and the tow was parted. Tow was passed again at 2040 and a westerly course achieved. A cruiser and two destroyers were then sighted in the darkness. We had no knowledge of friendly forces, so slipped the tow and stationed ourselves between *Foresight* and the unidentified ships, ready to engage. Speed was increased and the attack commenced. The captain shouted from the bridge, 'This may be the end of the glorious *Tartar* but we shall engage the enemy. I intend to torpedo the cruiser, sink one destroyer by gunfire and ram the other!'"

A challenging signal went unanswered. In a moment of impending catastrophe Tabb had a feeling of quiet pride for the ship and her splendid crew. At the very last moment a faint blue light responded to the challenge. The force was the damaged *Nigeria* and two escorting destroyers.

Tartar's attempt to tow *Foresight* failed. She was abandoned and torpedoed. The damaged ships all retired to Gibraltar. Tabb saw the *Indomitable* already in her berth. *Kenya* limped into harbour with her bows blown off. They were a sorry sight.

Another serviceman aboard the *Tartar* was James Fairhurst, an Ordinary Seaman, later Leading Seaman. He was a loader on X gun aft. He recalls a newspaper report of the time relating to *Tartar*:

> "When the action was at its height and all eyes were turned skywards one of the lookouts, Able Seaman Frederick Henry Tong, saw torpedo tracks, gave the warning and the captain was able to take avoiding action. He then signalled to the flagship: ABLE SEAMAN TONG HAS SAVED THE SHIP."

That same day, 12 August, saw the loss of the freighter *Deucalion*. Soon after noon she was attacked by a massed Italian air onslaught. She was struck and spewed smoke from a direct hit which brought her to a stop. The destroyer *Bramham* was ordered to guard her. After about 20 minutes she got under way again. The convoy was now well ahead. *Deucalion* and *Bramham* set off for the African coast hoping to sneak eastwards unobserved. The ploy was unsuccessful. At sunset she was sighted by some Ju 88s which set on her. She was hit several times, came to a stop and sank. She was abandoned and her crew rescued by *Bramham*.

Dawn found *Bicester*, *Wilton* and *Derwent* escorting the *Nigeria* slowly and painfully out of E-boat Alley, with an alarming list and down by the bows. The destroyers circled her, alert for any air attacks.

Able Seaman (AA3) G.H. Ward aboard HMS *Lightning* recalls watching a German pilot's dive bomber being hit by AA fire and diving in flames into the sea.

> "To be truthful I felt sorry for him and I thought of his mother, which seems a curious feeling to have, given that he was trying to kill British seamen. Other members of *Lightning*'s crew who were on the upper deck cheered, which is probably more sensible. I didn't tell anyone my feelings. They would have thought me mad."

What was left of the convoy was now approaching the Sicilian Narrows where Italian submarines had been given billets. The destroyer *Ithuriel* sighted a periscope and conning tower. She raced in to attack with depth charges and blew the submarine to the surface. She was rammed and sank, some of her crew being rescued. It was at this time that the *Foresight* had her stern blown off and had to be sunk.

On the evening of the 13th *Nigeria*, *Cairo* and *Ohio* were all hit. Two managed to survive, but the gallant light cruiser *Cairo* was lost.

Guns fired in wild confusion, but nothing seemed to stop the enemy aircraft. This was when the *Empire Hope* was bombed and set ablaze. She acted as a beacon till nearly midnight when an Italian submarine put her out of her misery and sank her.

Brisbane Star was also hit and shuddered to a stop. She managed to get under way again. Her master was Captain Frederick Neville-Riley DSO, described in the press as a tall Irishman. His nephew, Alan Rively, says he was neither tall nor Irish! The ship also carried a signalman, later Acting Yeoman of Signals John Mills who survived the Pedestal convoy. Another correspondent from the ship was Radio Operator Roy Heginbottom.

Mills wrote in his diary of the sinking of the *Eagle*, of the thunderous barrages fired by *Rodney* and *Nelson*, and the fearsome Stuka raids: "It's peaceful in Hell compared with tonight." Captain Riley was nearly 'wiped out' by a piece of shrapnel which missed him by a couple of inches.

The next day Mills witnessed the loss of *Empire Hope*. He recorded:

> "On fire but not sinking yet. Will be OK if she doesn't blow up. Fire getting worse. Poor devils. Two or three ships on fire but whether RN or MN can't tell yet. . . . Planes flew right through barrage. Good going. Must be Germans. Two ships ahead hit. Almost drowned in the spray. Felt like hell. One Yank on our right beam burning. Am writing this by light of burning ship . . . ship down by bows. Just arranged for dumping confidential books. Flags has just told me to put on lifebelt."

Mills railed against the government, the RN, admirals, staff officers, even democracy: "If I ever get back to England I shall do time in cells before I do another trip like this." Once the air raids diminished and the ship set course for Malta Mills modified his opinions. With an escort provided he wrote: "Funny how everyone feels now we have an escort."

Philip Perry was an assistant steward aboard *Empire Hope* and was serving lunch when the *Eagle* was sunk. "We all felt the shock waves" but when the air raids increased in intensity he recorded:

> "We slept in our clothes – pyjamas were put away. The catering staff stationed themselves close to the saloon, ready to do anything the 2nd and Chief Steward required – stretcher bearers, messengers, fire fighters, store suppliers to life boats if time or conditions allowed."

Empire Hope's end came after a blistering air raid developed and she seemed to be singled out for punishment. No fewer than eighteen near-misses thundered all around her for 30 minutes. The Master, Captain Gwilym Williams, handled the ship brilliantly but it seemed inevitable that she should be hit. The bomb burst which brought her to a standstill ripped a 15-foot hole in her side. Perry recalls the intensity of the bombing once the ship was stationary. He can remember actually seeing the bombs leaving the aircraft. Then at 8.50 in the evening two bombs made direct hits, after which the ship was doomed. One bomb penetrated No. 4 hold with its cargo of explosives. The fire which followed spread to the bridge deck. The high-octane spirit exploded and the after part of the ship became engulfed in flames. The blazing aviation spirit spread over the ship and the surrounding sea, engulfing all before it. One lifeboat was got away, half-filled with coal from her cargo, blown there by the explosions. The destroyer *Penn* (Lieutenant-Commander J.H. Swaine) made valiant efforts to rescue all the crew despite the blazing inferno. Gradually the ship sank and the waters doused the flames.

The struggle to reach Grand Harbour continued throughout the 13th. Only five vessels were to complete the operation. One of the early arrivals was the *Port Chalmers* flying the flag of the convoy commodore, barely showing signs of the ordeal behind them.

Rochester Castle, on the other hand, displayed a huge, gaping hole in her side. The reception given by the crowds on the bastions of Valletta was frenzied.

That same afternoon the *Melbourne Star* made her entrance. She had suffered grievously. So far only three of the merchant ships had arrived out of the fourteen which set out.

It was the next day, Friday 14 August, that the *Brisbane Star* arrived, carefully nursed into harbour by Captain Riley. The fifth, and last, merchant ship of Operation Pedestal to reach harbour was the tanker *Ohio*.

It was about 1515 when *Brisbane Star* made her entrance. Mills recorded in his diary:

"Everyone in Malta, people in boats, soldiers and all the school kids cheered like mad, and a band played on the castle's side. Messages of congratulation were received including one from the Vice Admiral, Malta, and three other ships of our convoy including our sister ship *Melbourne Star*. Not many people without a lump in their throat. Old Man [the master] had tears in his eyes. . . . It must mean everything to the people here to see ships arrive with stores and ammunition."

Brisbane Star had already undergone bombing attacks, but the climax of her ordeal came on 12 August. By that time the convoy's fortunes were critical. The old faithful, *Clan Ferguson*, veteran of eleven Malta convoys, had gone. *Empire Hope*, as we have seen, was ablaze and sinking, as was *Glenorchy*. *Almeira Lykes* (US) and *Santa Elisa* (US) had both gone. *Ohio* was still struggling to keep afloat, while *Brisbane Star* was falling away with her bows severely damaged. But she got under way again. The resourceful Captain Riley realized that survival lay in following the Tunisian coast with the mountains forming a black backdrop and blurring the ship's silhouette.

Able Seaman Bob Sanders was a young quartermaster aboard the *Brisbane Star* and, apart from steering the ship, he was a lookout and was qualified to man a lifeboat. He was a lad of sixteen, had been torpedoed once already and was to experience it a third time. Sanders recorded later:

> "They threw everything at us. The planes came in droves of a hundred, and submarines tried to get us too. There were a few poor souls going to heaven that day. . . . Nobody slept. You did your watch then went straight to getting ammunition for the gunners from the lockers. People ask if you were scared. You went past that stage. You went on automatic."

On the 13th *Brisbane Star* was struck by a torpedo in the bows. It blew a hole big enough to run a bus through – no explosion, no fire – but she kept afloat. Sanders was treated for a leg wound in the ship's sick bay, but quickly returned to his duties: "I could not stand people dying."

The fifth, and last, merchant ship of the convoy to reach Malta was the tanker *Ohio*, a tribute to her American constructors. Captain D.W. Mason, the youngest master in the fleet, commanded the 14,000-ton tanker belonging to the Texas Oil Company, one of the fastest tankers then afloat. She started the operation with a cargo of 13,000 tons of petroleum products.

Mason had helped select a special crew. His chief engineering officer was Mr J. Wyld, a man of exceptionable engineering experience. To him went the credit of re-starting the ship's engines after a particularly severe attack which brought her to a standstill. Despite the gaping hole in her side Wyld managed to achieve a speed of 16 knots. She even rejoined the convoy, which had forged on ahead.

During a day of almost continuous attacks when *Ohio* was near-missed by two parachute mines she suffered two extraordinary experiences. A Stuka dive bomber, rent apart by the stream of 20 mm shells from *Ohio* and the destroyer *Ashanti*, failed to come out of its dive and crashed hard into the side of the ship, after bouncing off the sea like a skimming stone. It wrought havoc. Flames and smoke obscured the scene, but the tanker emerged still intact, though virtually a wreck. Yet another German bomber, shot to pieces, bounced onto *Ohio*; other explosions blew out the boilers. She came to a stop while the other ships ploughed on to Malta.

HMS *Penn* and *Ledbury* were detached from the convoy escort to locate *Ohio* and to render all assistance.

As dusk fell a huge explosion shuddered through the ship. A column of water shot up to masthead height and cascaded over the ship. The chief officer, D.H. Gray, had just finished his watch and was still on the bridge. He later recalled:

> "When the torpedo struck the ship she shook violently. The steering gear broke and all communication with the engine room and the after end of the ship was cut off with the exception of a telephone."

Ohio now had a gaping hole in the main deck, the pumproom was completely open to the sea. Bulkheads were torn and tank lids buckled and open. The crew were mustered to help keep the ship afloat, extinguishing fires which were in danger of spreading. Down below in the engine room the engineers toiled to get the engines running again.

Events were now coming to a head. Malta lay over the horizon. The remaining ships of the convoy were approaching their destination. It was 13 August and word had got around Valletta that the great battle of survival was reaching its climax. Crowds by the thousand were already assembling.

By 1015 on the morning of the 14th the *Ohio* was under way again, a sagging, broken wreck. She made a remarkable sight. Towing her was the *Rye*. On each side of her the *Penn* and *Bramham* were lashed in order to give more buoyancy, as someone described it, like two huge surgical splints, and the *Ledbury* secured aft coaxing and guiding her in the right direction. Gathered around, forming a protective screen, were the minesweepers *Speedy*, *Hebe* and *Hythe*. But even at this late hour an attack by aircraft developed and another bomb nearly sank *Ohio* where she was. She was barely afloat, a floating wreck with a crashed plane on her deck, her back broken, her rudder carried away. She had been abandoned twice, then re-boarded. She was sinking slowly by about six inches an hour. It was

Saturday 15 August when this crazy little collection of ships hobbled into harbour.

A cruiser squadron's admiral signalled by Aldis lamp:

TO CAPTAIN DUDLY MASON: I AM PROUD TO HAVE KNOWN YOU.

Vice Admiral Malta signalled:

I AM VERY GLAD TO SEE YOU AND YOUR FINE SHIP SAFELY IN HARBOUR AFTER SUCH A HAZARDOUS AND ANXIOUS PASSAGE. YOUR CARGO WILL BE INVALUABLE IN THE WAR EFFORT.

The Admiralty signalled with traditional brevity:

SPLENDID WORK   WELL DONE

Operation Pedestal ended on 15 August, a Saturday and the Feast of the Assumption, and *Ohio* was the last of the convoy to reach her goal. It was to a tumultuous welcome. It was a feast of colour and the noise of the Royal Marine band, smartly uniformed, as ever, playing patriotic tunes.

There are two or three small anecdotes to bring this chapter to an end.

Her cargo, much depleted, was discharged and *Ohio* was moored in Rinella Bay where she broke in two and settled in shallow water. As it was impossible to join the two halves, each was made watertight and put to good use, one half for storage purposes and the other as a base for small units of the navy.

Eventually the two halves were disposed of after the war. The fore part was taken to a point ten miles off Grand Harbour and sunk by the destroyer *Virago*'s gunfire. That was on 19 September, 1946. Two weeks later the stern half was sunk by explosive charges. The *Ohio* had at last been put to rest.

The crews of the destroyers which towed the *Ohio* into harbour were subsequently awarded salvage money. Young Ordinary Seaman J.P. Kippin of the *Bramham* was awarded his share of £2 12s 6d.

But the cost to the Royal Navy had been high. The aircraft carrier *Eagle* had been lost, so had the destroyer *Foresight* and the AA cruiser *Cairo*. The cruiser *Manchester* had been damaged and then sunk. Ships damaged were the *Indomitable*, the *Nigeria* and *Kenya*. The Italians for their part lost the submarine *Cobalto*.

THE RELIEF OF MALTA

Taken together, the Malta Convoys of 1941-2 succeeded in their purpose, for the island held out, as it certainly could not have done without them. Yet the cost had been very heavy, especially in the British Maritime Services and to the people of Malta.

Captain S.W. Roskill, *The War at Sea,*
Vol II. 1956.

Operation Pedestal registered the high-water mark for Malta's fortunes. Thereafter it was downhill. Never again was the Royal Navy and the Merchant Navy to be subjected to the intensity of bombardment from the air, from under the sea and from the high-speed E-boats' torpedoes as they had been for the past 27 months.

After Pedestal the scenario in the Mediterranean changed. British convoys continued to be attacked from the air and the gauntlet had to be run. But by November, 1942, Operation Torch, the invasion of North Africa, and victory at the Battle of El Alamein in the Western Desert, completely changed the character of the war in the Mediterranean theatre.

In the twenty-seven months leading up to September, 1942, the Italians had lost 1,378 aircraft destroyed and 420 damaged. By September, too, with Pedestal behind it, it was becoming evident that Malta would be relieved: the future looked bright for the British forces for the first time in years.

November and December 1942, saw, the passage of more

convoys. The first was Operation Stoneage (often wrongly called Stonehenge). On 15 November four merchant ships assembled at Port Said. The convoy comprised the following: *Denbighshire* (British), *Bantam* (Dutch), *Mormacmoon* (USA) and *Robin Locksley* (USA). They were provided with a substantial escort of four cruisers (*Orion* – Flag, *Cleopatra*, *Euryalus* and *Arethusa*,) and seventeen destroyers. The convoy was subjected to air attacks but the venom of the past had gone. After nearly a day of desultory bombing the *Arethusa* took an aerial torpedo which did considerable damage. After a stern-first long tow and a battle with serious fires and a rising gale she was got back safely to Alexandria, but it had cost her dearly. No fewer than 155 men aboard *Arethusa* had lost their lives.

The convoy reached Malta safely: the freighters formed line ahead and stood into Grand Harbour. By the 25th the ships were unloaded and Malta was at least adequately supplied with aviation spirit.

Submarine trips to and from Malta were discontinued.

The arrival of the Stoneage convoy marked the final and effective relief of Malta. 35,000 tons of supplies were disembarked. December proved even more rewarding. Operation Portcullis (approximately 55,000 tons) and the two Quadrangle convoys in December (120,000 tons) brought the year's end to a satisfactory conclusion.

The navy, as so often in Britain's past had influenced the course of battles and had demonstrated once again its abiding power to do good.

Appendix I

BRITISH, ALLIED AND NEUTRAL MERCHANT SHIPPING LOSSES IN THE MEDITERRANEAN

1939

January–December	Nil	

1940

January–April	Nil	
May	(1)	2,568 tons
June	(6)	45,402
July	(2)	6,564
August	(1)	1,044
September	(2)	5,708
October	(1)	2,897
November	Nil	
December	Nil	
1940 Total	(13)	64,183

1941

January	Nil	
February	(2)	8,343
March	(2)	11,868
April	(105)	292,518
May	(19)	70,835
June	(3)	9,145
July	(2)	7,897
August	(2)	5,869
September	(4)	15,951
October	(6)	22,403
November	(4)	19,140
December	(9)	37,394
1941 Total	(158)	501,363

1942

January	(1)	6,655
February	(4)	19,245
March	(4)	19,516
April	(6)	12,804
May	(6)	21,215
June	(16)	59,971
July	(3)	5,885
August	(13)	110,423
September	(4)	813
October	Nil	
November	(13)	102,951
December	(3)	5,649
1942 Total	(73)	365,127

Summary:	1940	(13)	64,183 tons
	1941	(158)	501,363
	1942	(73)	365,127
	Total	(244)	930,673 tons

Appendix II

Joseph Caruana is the recognized authority on the convoys to and from Malta. He has kindly allowed me to reproduce his Tables for which I am extremely grateful.

CONVOYS			TO	MALTA		
FLEET OPERATION	CONVOY	ARRIVED MALTA	FROM	SHIPS		REMARKS
				SAILED	ARRIVED	
MB-3	MF-2	1- 9-40	East	3	3	(MW-1)
MB-6	MF-3	11-10-40	East	4	4	(MW-2)
MB-8	MW-3	9-11-40	East	5	5	
MB-9	MW-4	26-11-40	East	4	4	
COLLAR	-	29-11-40	West	2	2	
MC-2	MW-5	20-12-40	East	8	8	
MC-4	MW-5½	10- 1-41	East	2	2	
EXCESS	-	10- 1-41	West	1	1	
MC-9	MW-6	23- 3-41	East	4	4	
MD-3	-	21- 4-41	East	1	1	
MD-4	MW-7	9- 5-41	East	7	7	
SUBSTANCE	GM-1	24- 7-41	West	7	6	1T
HALBERD	GM-2	28- 9-41	West	9	8	1S
MF-1	-	18-12-41	East	1	1	
MF-2	-	8- 1-42	East	1	1	
MF-3	MW-8	19- 1-42	East	4	3	1S
MF-4	-	27- 1-42	East	1	1	
MF-5	MW-9	----	East	3	0	1T + 2S
MG-1	MW-10	23- 3-42	East	4	3	1S
HARPOON	GM-4	16- 6-42	West	6	2	4S
VIGOROUS	MW-11	----	East	11	0	9T + 2S
PEDESTAL	GM-5	13- 8-42	West	14	5	9S
STONEAGE	MW-13	20-11-42	East	4	4	
PORTCULLIS	MW-14	5-12-42	East	5	5	
T O T A L	24			111	80	11T + 20S

T = Turned Back   S = Sunk

UNESCORTED SOLO SUPPLY-RUNS : 7
Arrived 1;   Sunk 3;   Captured 2;   Turned Back 1.

CONVOYS	FROM	MALTA			
FLEET OPERATION	CONVOY	DEPARTED MALTA	TO	SHIPS	REMARKS
MA-5	MF1/MS1	10- 7-40	East	8	(ME-1)
MB-6	MF-4	11-10-40	East	2	(ME-2)
MB-8	ME-3	10-11-40	East	4	
MB-9	ME-4	29-11-40	East	5	
HIDE	--	20-12-40	West	2	
MC-2	ME-5	20-12-40	East	4	
MC-4	ME-5½	10- 1-41	East	2	
MC-4	ME-6	10- 1-41	East	6	
MC-8	--	23- 2-41	East	2	
MD-3	ME-7	19- 4-41	East	4	
SALIENT	--	28- 4-41	East	1	
SUBSTANCE	MG-1	23- 7-41	West	7*	
MINCEMEAT	--	21- 8-41	West	2*	
HALBERD	MG-2	26- 9-41	West	3*	
---	MG-3	Oct.41	West	4*	1 Sunk
MD-8	--	5-12-41	East	1	
---	ME-8	26-12-41	East	4	
MF-2	--	6- 1-42	East	1	
MF-4	ME-9	25- 1-42	East	2	
MF-5	ME-10	13- 2-42	East	4	
ASCENDANT	MG-4	10- 8-42	West	2	
MH-2	ME-11	7-12-42	East	9	
TOTAL	22			79	1 Sunk

* Unescorted, in singles or groups.

Appendix IV

CUNNINGHAM'S ADMIRALS

BAILLIE-GROHMAN, Harold Tom, Vice-Admiral (1888–1978). Commanded 1st Destroyer Flotilla, Mediterranean Fleet 1934–36. Commanded battleship *Ramillies* 1939–40. Attached to the staff of GOC Middle East 1941. Rear-Admiral Combined Operations 1942. FOIC Harwich 1944.

BOYD, Admiral Sir Denis William (1891–1965). Commanded the carrier HMS *Illustrious* 1940. Rear-Admiral commanding aircraft carriers Mediterranean Fleet 1941. Commanded Eastern Force Aircraft Carriers, 1942. Fifth Sea Lord and Controller of the Navy, 1943–45. Admiral (Air) 1945–46. C-in-C Far East Station 1948–49. Retired List 1949.

BURROUGH, Vice-Admiral Sir Harold Martin (1888–1977). Went to sea as a Midshipman 1904. Specialized in gunnery. Commanded HMS *Excellent*, the Whale Island naval gunnery school. Assistant Chief of Naval Staff. Commanded the naval element of the Vaagso Raid 1941. Malta Convoy Operation Pedestal, August 1942, with his flag in *Nigeria*. Awarded KBE. In HMS *Kenya* he was awarded the DSO. Promoted Vice-Admiral 1943. Took part in the 'majestic enterprise' of Operation Torch, the invasion of North Africa, and awarded the CB for his command of the Eastern Task Force.

CRESSWELL, Rear-Admiral George Hector (1889–1967). Served in WWI and earned DSC, and in WWII the DSO and the CB.

CUNNINGHAM, Andrew Browne, First Viscount Cunningham of Hyndhope (1883–1963). Admiral of the Fleet. Known throughout the navy as ABC. The foremost British naval commander of World War II. Born in Dublin of Scottish parents. Entered Britannia as a cadet in 1897. Midshipman in HMS *Doris* in Boer War (1899–1902). First saw action with Naval Brigade 1900. Promoted Lieutenant 1904. First command in 1908 HM Torpedoboat No. *14*. Commanded destroyer *Scorpion* 1911–18 for practically the whole of WWI. Helped shadow the German battle-cruiser and cruiser *Goeben* and *Breslau* in the Mediterranean and later served in the Dardenelles. Commander 1915. Won the DSO. Dover Patrol: was present at the raids on Zeebrugge, 1918. Awarded bar to DSO in 1919 and a second bar in 1920 for service in the Baltic. Captain 1920. Captain (D) 6th Destroyer Flotilla 1922, and 1st Flotilla 1923. Flag Captain and Chief Staff Officer to Admiral Sir Walter Cowan on American and West Indies Station 1926–28. Commanded battle-ship *Rodney* 1929. Naval ADC to King George V. Rear-Admiral Destroyers Mediterranean 1933. CB 1924. Vice-Admiral 1936. Commanded battle-cruiser squadron 1937–38. Admiral and C-in-C Mediterranean 1939. Awarded KCB. Victory in attack on Italian battlefleet at Taranto 1940: Greek/Crete convoys 1941. Battle of Cape Matapan 1941. Malta Convoy battles. Headed British Admiralty Delegation to Washington 1942. C-in-C of all Allied Naval forces in Mediterranean – named Allied Naval Commander Expeditionary Force covering North Africa, Sicily and Italy landings. Accepted surrender of Italian Fleet of 1943. Admiral of the Fleet 1943. First Sea Lord 1943–45. GCB 1941. Baronet 1942. Baron 1945. Viscount and OM 1946. Awarded KT – Knight of the Thistle. Responsible with Churchill for British maritime strategy. Attended summit conferences at Quebec, Yalta and Potsdam. Although buried at sea he is commemorated in the crypt of St Paul's with other great naval commanders. Arthur Bryant called him "the first seaman of the age".

CUNNINGHAM, Sir John Henry Dacres (1885–1962). Admiral of the Fleet. Entered the navy via *Britannia* in 1900.

Midshipman in *Gibraltar*. Lieutenant 1905. Specialized in navigation. Served as navigator in *Berwick*, *Russell* and *Renown* in WWI. Commander 1917. Navigator in *Hood* 1930. Captain 1924. Variety of posts including Director of plans at the Admiralty. Commanded *Resolution* 1933. Rear-Admiral 1936. Assistant Chief of Naval Staff (Air) 1936, Fifth Sea Lord and Chief of Naval Air Services 1938. Vice-Admiral 1939. Commanded 1st Cruiser Squadron in the Mediterranean 1938–41. Fourth Sea Lord 1941–43. C-in-C Levant 1943. Succeeded Viscount Cunningham of Hyndhope (no relation) as First Sea Lord and Chief of Naval Staff 1946–48. Admiral of the Fleet 1948. Chairman of the Irak Petroleum Company 1948–58.

CURTEIS, Admiral Sir Alban Thomas Buckley (1887–1961). Rear-Admiral 1938. Awarded CB 1940. Vice-Admiral 1941. KCB 1942. Vice-Admiral commanding 2nd Battle Squadron and Second in command Home Fleet 1941–2. Senior British Naval Officer Western Atlantic 1942–44. Admiral 1945.

EDELSTEN, Admiral Sir John Hereward (1891–1966). Cadet at Osborne and Dartmouth. Went to sea 1908. Lieutenant 1913. Commander 1926. Captain 1933. Rear Admiral 1942. Vice-Admiral 1945. Admiral 1949. GCB 1952. KCB 1946. CB 1944. GCVO 1953. CBE 1941. Imperial Defence College 1934. Deputy Director of Plans 1938. Chief of Staff to Cunningham 1941–42. Rear-Admiral (Destroyers) Pacific Fleet 1945. Commanded First Battle Squadron 1945–46. 4th Cruiser Squadron 1946. C-in-C Mediterranean 1950–52. C-in-C Portsmouth 1952–54. C-in-C Home Fleet 1952–54. Retired 1954.

FORD, Admiral Sir Wilbraham Tennyson Randle (1880–1964). Commanded *Royal Oak* 1929. Navigation School 1930–32. Rear-Admiral 1932. Commanded HM Australian Squadron 1934–36. Vice-Admiral 1937. Vice-Admiral in Charge and Admiral Superintendent Malta 1937–40. FOIC Malta 1940–41. Admiral 1941. C-in-C Rosyth 1942–44.

GLENNIE, Sir Irvine Gordon (1892–1980). Rear Admiral. Entered Navy via Osborne and Dartmouth. Served in Home Fleet and China 1910–14. Served in Grand Fleet destroyers 1915–18. Commanded destroyers 1925–27. Commander 1928. Admiralty 1930–32. Captain 1933. Commanded *Achilles* 1936–38 and *Hood* 1939–41. Rear-Admiral Mediterranean 1941–42. Home Fleet destroyers 1943–44. C-in-C American and West Indies 1945–46. Retired 1947.

HOLLAND, Vice-Admiral Lancelot Ernest (1887–1941). Educated at HMS *Britannia*, 1900. Assistant Chief of Naval Staff 1937–38. Rear Admiral 2nd Battle Squadron 1939. Commanded a cruiser squadron under Admiral Somerville with his Rear-Admiral's flag in the cruiser *Manchester*. She was sunk during Operation Pedestal August, 1942.

KING, Admiral Edward Leigh Stuart (1889–1971). Served in *Repulse* during the Prince of Wales' tour to Africa and South America 1925 and awarded MVO. Director of Plans, Admiralty 1933–35. Chief of Staff to C-in-C Home Fleet 1938 and in the same year ADC to the King. Awarded CB 1940. Commanded Mediterranean Cruiser Squadron 1941–42. Lord Commissioner of the Navy and Assistant Chief of Naval Staff 1941–42. Retired 1944. Deputy Lieutenant of Cornwall 1953.

LEATHAM, Admiral Sir Ralph (1886–1954). Joined *Britannia* as a cadet. Captain 1924. Commanded HM Ships *Yarmouth*, *Durban*, *Ramillies* and *Valiant*. Rear-Admiral 1st Battle Squadron 1938–39. Vice-Admiral 1939. C-in-C East Indies Station 1939–41. FOIC Malta 1942–43. Deputy Governor Malta 1943. C-in-C Levant 1943. Admiral 1943. C-in-C Plymouth 1943–45. Retired list 1946.

LYSTER, Admiral Sir Arthur Lumley St George (1888–1957). Commanded *Danae* 1932. Captain (D) 5th Destroyer Flotilla 1933–35. RN Gunnery School Chatham 1935–36. Director of Training and Staff Duties Admiralty 1936–37. Commanded *Glorious* 1938–39. Rear-Admiral Aircraft Carriers, Mediterranean Fleet – including the attack on Taranto 1940–41. Fifth Sea Lord and Chief of Naval Air Services 1941–42. Commanded carriers Home Fleet 1942–43. FO Carrier Training 1943–45. Retired List 1945. Awards: KCB, CVO, CBE, DSO.

PRIDHAM-WIPPELL, Vice Admiral Sir Henry Daniel (1885–1952). Born Bromley, Kent. Entered RN 1900. As a Lieutenant was aboard HMS *Audacious* when the battleship was sunk by a mine 1914. In 1915, as Lieutenant-Commander, commanded destroyers in the Mediterranean, including the Dardenelles and Palestine. Served two years as Commander in Operations Division of the Naval Staff. Captain 1926. Commanded cruiser *Enterprise* on East Indies Station. Commanded destroyer leader *Campbell* 1930. Director of Operations Division, Admiralty for two years. In 1936 was Commodore destroyer flotillas of Home Fleet with broad pennant in light cruiser *Cairo*, then *Aurora*. Rear-Admiral 1938. Director of Personal Services 1938–40. Awarded CB. Second in command to Cunningham in the Mediterranean.

RAWLINGS, Admiral Sir Henry Bernard Hughes (1889–1962). Entered RN 1904. Served throughout WW I 1914–18. OBE 1920. Commanded ships *Active*, *Curacoa* and *Delhi*. Naval Attaché Tokyo 1936–39. Commanded *Valiant* 1939. ADC to the King 1940. Rear-Admiral Commanding 1st Battle Squadron 1940. Commanded 7th Cruiser Squadron 1941. Awarded Hellenic War Cross and CB 1942. ACNS 1942–43. Vice-Admiral 1943. FO Eastern Mediterranean 1943–44. KCB 1944. Second in Command British Pacific Fleet 1944–45. KBE 1945. GBE 1946. Admiral 1946. Retired List 1946.

RENOUF, Vice-Admiral Edward de Faye (1888–1972). Joined HMS *Britannia* as a cadet in 1903. Served throughout WW I. Naval Attaché Buenos Aires 1930–33. Commanded HMS *Orion* 1934–36. Staff of Naval War College, Greenwich 1936–38. Commanded *Sheffield* 1938–40. Commanded Cruiser Squadron 1940–41. Retired 1943.

SOMERVILLE, Admiral of the Fleet Sir James Fownes (1882–1949). Brilliant commander of Force H in the Mediterranean. Entered the RN in 1897. Qualified as a torpedo specialist but changed to wireless telegraphy. Served throughout WWI in the Dardenelles and with the Grand Fleet. Fleet Wireless Officer on staff of Admiral de Robeck. He was a big ship man: all his time as commander and captain was spent in battleships. Director of Signals 1925–27. Staff of Imperial Defence College 1929–31. Commodore RNB Portsmouth 1932–34. Rear-Admiral 1933. Admiral (D) Mediterranean 1936–38. Vice-Admiral 1937. C-in-C East Indies 1938. Invalided out of the navy with TB. KCB 1939. Recalled to the navy and given command of Force H at Gibraltar 1940–42. C-in-C East Indies: by 1944 had a powerful fleet of carriers, battleships and cruisers. Bombarded Java and Sumatra. Head of Admiralty Delegation to Washington 1944–45. Admiral of the Fleet 1945.

SYFRET, Vice-Admiral Sir Edward Neville (1889–1972). Born near Cape Town. Entered RN 1904. Chief Cadet Captain at Dartmouth. Specialized in gunnery. Spent practically the whole of WW I in the North Sea as gunnery officer aboard cruisers of the Harwich Force – *Aurora*, *Centaur* and *Curacoa*. Commander 1922. Fleet Gunnery Officer, Mediterranean Fleet. Captained the naval gunnery school at Devonport. Commanded *Caradoc* on the China Station, then the *Ramillies* and *Rodney* in the Home Fleet. Naval Secretary to First Sea Lord 1939. Rear-Admiral 1940. Commanded cruiser squadron 1941 escorting Malta and Russia Convoys. In 1942 flew his flag as FO Commanding Force H in *Malaya*. Commanded occupying Force Madagascar 1942. Acting Vice-Admiral in *Nelson* during Operation Pedestal as Senior Officer Force F. Vice Chief of Naval Staff 1943. Awarded CB.

TOVEY, Admiral of the Fleet Lord (John Cronyn) (1885–1971). Entered RN as a cadet at *Britannia* naval college aged 14. Went to sea as midshipman 1901. Served in cruiser *Amphion*. He was a small ship man – mostly in destroyers. Commanded destroyer

Onslow at Jutland 1916. Awarded DSO. Served time at the Admiralty as Commander and Captain. Commanded destroyer flotilla. Commanded *Rodney*. Commodore RNB Chatham for 2½ years. Rear-Admiral Destroyers Mediterranean. Second in Command to Cunningham. C-in-C Home Fleet 1940. Pursuit and sinking of *Bismarck* in his flagship *King George V* May 1941. Awarded KBE, KCB and GCB. Created Baron Tovey 1946.

VIAN, Admiral of the Fleet Sir Philip (1894–1968). One of the Royal Navy's most successful tactical commanders of WW II. Educated at Osborne and Dartmouth. Served in destroyers in WW I (1914–18) and was at Jutland. Specialized as a Lieutenant in gunnery. Served in destroyers 1919–36. Commanded light cruiser *Arethusa* 1937–39. Commanded destroyer *Cossack* in 1940; intercepted prison ship *Altmark* and released 299 prisoners in Norway's Josing Fjord, captured in *Graf Spee*'s cruise. The boarding of the prison ship and the shout "The Navy's here!" was reminiscent of the days of the wooden walls. Vian commanded the Tribal class destroyer *Afridi* when she was sunk off Norway. He led the destroyer attacks in *Cossack* against the *Bismarck* in 1941. His shadowing and torpedo attacks on 26 May helped deliver the battleship to the C-in-C with the *King George V* and *Rodney*. He was Rear-Admiral in command of Force K escorting Russian convoys. It was his feats in the Mediterranean commanding the 15th Cruiser Squadron where he earned greater repute – a knighthood (KBE) and gained success in the skirmishes with enemy battle squadrons, and helped fight through Malta convoys. He served in Sicily and commanded a carrier force supporting landings in Italy. He won three DSOs in the Mediterranean. He commanded the Eastern Task Force to cover British landings at Normandy. Awarded the KCB. Commanded a carrier squadron in the Pacific 1944–45. Vice-Admiral 1945. Fifth Sea Lord and commanded Naval Aviation 1946–48. Admiral 1948. C-in-C Home Fleet 1950–52. Admiral of the Fleet 1952. GCB 1952. Stern disciplinarian and described as a man of forbidding silences.

WILLIS, Admiral of the Fleet Sir Algernon Usborne (1889–1976). Commanded *Warwick* 1927–29. Flag Captain HMS *Kent* on the China Station 1933–34. Flag Captain HMS *Nelson*, Home Fleet 1934–35. Captain of HMS *Vernon*, the Portsmouth Torpedo School, 1935–38. Commanded *Barham* 1938–39. Chief of Staff Mediterranean Fleet 1939–41. C-in-C South Atlantic Fleet 1941–42. Second in Command Eastern Fleet 1942–43. Commanded Force H Mediterranean 1943. C-in-C Levant Station 1943. Second Sea Lord 1944–46. C-in-C Mediterranean 1946–48. C-in-C Portsmouth 1948–50.

ACKNOWLEDGEMENTS

THE PRESS

The editors of the newspapers and magazines listed below have earned my gratitude for publishing appeals for participants in the Malta Convoys of 1940–42 to put their experiences on record. Their help was invaluable and the response enormous. Many other newspapers may have published my appeal but I have not been able to confirm this.

Aeroplane Monthly
Belfast Telegraph
Blackpool Gazette
Bristol Evening Post
Bournemouth Evening Echo
Burton Mail
Cambridge Evening News
Classic Boat
Coventry Evening Telegraph
Defender (George Cross Island Association)
Derby Evening Telegraph
Dorset Evening Echo
East Anglian Daily Times
Evening Argus (Brighton)
Evening Chronicle (Tyne and Wear)
Evening Despatch (Leith)
Evening Echo (Essex)
Evening Gazette (Tyneside)
Evening Gazette Colchester)
Evening Leader (Clwdd)

Evening News (Edinburgh)
Evening Telegraph (Grimsby)
Evening Telegraph (Northampton)
Evening Telegraph (Peterborough)
Express and Echo (Exeter)
Express and Star (Wolverhampton)
Gloucester Echo
Greenock Telegraph
Guernsey Evening Press
Hampshire: The County Magazine
Hartlepool Mail
History Today
Huddersfield Examiner
Jersey Evening Post
Lancashire Evening Post
Lancashire Evening Telegraph

Leicester Mercury
Listener, The
Liverpool Daily Post
Liverpool Echo
Liverpool Evening Post
Malta Images
Malta Remembered
Nautical Magazine
Navy News
Oxford Mail
Paisley Daily Express
Portsmouth News
Reading Evening Post
Scarborough Evening News
Sea Breezes
Sheffield Star
Shields Gazette
Shropshire Star

Southend Evening Echo
South Wales Argus
Sunday Independent
Sunday Mirror
Sunday Post (Glasgow)
Sunday Post and Dundee
Courier
Sunday Times of Malta
Sunderland Echo
Swindon Evening Advertiser
Times, The
Times of Malta, The
Uniform, The
Weekly News, The
Western Morning Mail
Worcester Evening News
Yorkshire Evening Post
Yorkshire Ridings Magazine

LIBRARIES, MUSEUMS
AND ASSOCIATIONS

I am grateful to the staff of the following for their kind help and patience: the Cambridge University Library; the Guildhall Library (the Lloyds Collection); the Naval Historical Branch of the Ministry of Defence; the Reading Room of the National Maritime Museum; the reference sections of the Essex County Libraries of Harlow and Chelmsford, and of the London Borough of Redbridge Reference Library.

I am especially indebted to Joseph Caruana, Curator of the National War Museum of Malta, who provided me with much information. Also to Dave Morrell of the North-West Branch of the George Cross Island Association: to L. McDonald of the HMS *Manchester* Association and Dick Paffatt of the HMSD *Cairo* Association. Also to the HMS *Eagle* Survivors Association.

For her demanding photographic work I am grateful to my daughter Valerie Thomas LRPS.

I am also pleased to acknowledge the help given by the Midland Branch of the George Cross Island Association and for allowing me to draw on some passages in their official *Newsletter* and Malta Images.

I also acknowledge the help given by the Department of Printed Books at the National Army Museum.

CORRESPONDENTS

I wish to express my debt and appreciation to the following correspondents without whose generous and willing help this book could not have been written.

Peter Adkin, N.C. Alderson, Mrs Joan Allin, Mrs Jean Amos, W. Andrews, Jill Arkley, William Ash, C.L. Asher, Alan R. Astley, H.H. Atkinson, Captain N.H.G. Austen DSO (RN Ret'd).

A.L. Baker, Mrs. I.L. Baker, F. Barkwitch, Lawrence Barrett, S. Barrett, J. Baron, Peter Bashford, Harry Beale, B. Bell, E.R. Bell, Jimmy Bell, F.W. Bennett, T. Bentley, Terry E. (Bish) Bishop, Mrs. Muriel Bland, F.W. Blaxill, Alf Bonsor, Commander M.C. Bourdillon, W. (Bill) Bradshaw, A. Bragg, Ken Briggs, Mrs F.C. Brooks, E. Brown, Mrs J. Brown, Dr. Kenneth Brown, George Brownlow, H.A. Bruce, W. Buckle, C.Y. Buist, Geoff Bullock, Elizabeth Bunyan, G.S. (Sam) Burlingham, A. Burnet, Anthony (Tony) Burns, Peter Byrne.

P.J. Cadge, H. Caffrey, P. Cain, Rev. Allan Campbell, A.E. Capon, George and Mrs. D. Cartwright, B.A. Chapman, William A. Charnoche, Bertha Clark, L.B. Clowes, A. (Tony) Coady, Charles Coates, Alf Cockburn, Mrs. E. Coe, John C. Coles, Ian Collin , Gerald Collins, R.G. Cook, Geoff W. Cooke, Victor A. Coombes, V. Copperstone, R.D. Croxon, William Corney, Joseph Caruana, Sadie Cowie, Lieutenant-Commander C.G. Crill, W.J. (Bill) Cross, B. Crossley, Commander H.J.P. Crusaz.

H. Dalby, Phillip Dalby, Mrs. V. Darker, Edward H. Davey, Sheila Davenport. A.D. Davie, Cyril G. Dawson, Lesley Day, J. Dean, E. Dearsley, Stan Deighton, Stan J. Dodd, John Donkin, Frank Donnely, Valerie Doty, G.V. Dougall, Commander R.M. Douglas, F. Downing, John (Jack) Doyle, Cliff Drake, Norman Drake, W. Draper, James Duckworth, Bert Duddle, J.L. Dupre.

G.W. Edis, Charles Edwards, F.J. Elgey, Hugh Elias, Bert Ellis, Evelyn English, Mrs Lindsay Eves, Jack Ewart.

Norman Fairfield-Jenkins OBE, James Fairhurst, R.W. (Bob) Ferry, Stan Filmer, Jack Flanagan, Mrs. P. Forder, Commander C.G. Forsberg, A.F. Foxon, H. Franklin.

Victor Gascoin, J.W. Gates, Bob Gillingham, Eric Gilroy, A. Goodenough, Mrs. G. Goodwin, R.W. Goosey, J. Gosling, Harry Gourlay, W.E. Gray, A. Green, Ben Green, R.A.C. Green, R.F. Green, John R. Grundy.

Mrs I. Hamilton, Innes Hamilton, Robert A. Hamilton, Sydney A. Hamilton, V. Healey, Ray E. Heginbothan, Leonard Hesketh, Herbert Higgs, Roland Hindmarsh, Mrs J. Hollington, Captain John H. Holman, Captain D. Howison, G. Hubbard, Maureen Hudson, Henry Hughes, Peter B. Hunt, W. Hyslop.

Tony Ireson.

Terry Jackson, Arthur James, Don James, Thomas Charles Jenks, Dr. Philip B. Jensen, Johnny Johnson.

D.J. Kellaght, H.D. King, Stephen Kingsbury, Colin Kitching, Jim Kitson, John William Kneale, Eric Knight.

Douglas C. Lane, Mrs L. Lankenam, James Larkin, Arthur Lawson, S.K. (Ken) Laycock, Admiral of the Fleet Lord Lewin, John T. Leech, Mrs Maureen Lewis, Tony Lewis, J. Liddle, F.C. Liles, G.A.D. Lindsey, H. Little, Alfred Longbottom, Mrs Diane Lonnia, George Love, J.E. Lucas.

D. McCarthy, Hector A. MacDonald, Robert McDonald, L. McDonald, Clive MacIntyre, John McHugh.

C.R. Maber, C.A. Makings, H.G.F. Male, Everard Mallinson, Frank Malton, John and Louise Mapley, C.E.S. Marchant, Mrs M.E. Marshall, A. Martin, Jack Martin, P.G. Mason, E. Masters, William J. Mathieson, S.J. Mead, John Samuel Mellor, C.H. and Mrs. E. Merchant, E. Merrey, John C. Middleton, James Miller, H. Mitchell, Terry Morgan, Ron Morham, D.W. Morrell, Denys L. Morrell, J.S. Morris, Robert Moss, John L. Mulligan, L. W. Munden, George Musso.

L. Newcombe, Harry J. Nicholls, James (Jim) Nicholson.

H.W. Outen, Ronald Overend.

Dick Paffitt, Mrs Pascoe, Rev. Ronald Paterson, S. Peffer, P. Perry, Reginald Plowman, William (Eric) Pitman, Dennis K. Pollard, P.J. Pond, Arthur (Stan) Potts, Mrs Beatrice Powell, Glyn A. Powell, G.F.T. Poynder, Fred Price, Kathleen Price, R. Proctor.

Ray Ratcliffe, H.A. Rawlings, Ronald R. Reed, B.G. Rees BEM, Allan F. Reid, David S. Reid, Mrs D. Richards, Alan Riley, Robert M. Ritchie.

S. Saggers, R.A. (Bob) Sanders, G.B. Sayers, Shadrach Scommell, George Senior, Frank Sharpe, Jim Sheehan, H.W. Shepherd, Derrik Shepherd, Ron Sloan, Alan Smith, E.F. Smith, John George Smith, Margaret E. Smith, Mrs P. Smith, Mrs Toni Smith, William John Smith, Ted Snowdon, J.H.S. Stephenson, A.J. Stevens, Paul B. Stevens, Roy Stevens, R.L.R. Stock, G.P. Stoddart, Ann and Ray Stone, W.R. (Dick) Sugden, M.K. Swarbrick, Dickie Sweet, George Swift.

L. and Mrs Tabb, Mrs Marjorie Tabbitt, Mrs L. Tait, G. Taylor, John Omar Taylor, Joe W. Temple, Alan Thipthorpe, Elizabeth Thacker, Stuart Tilford, Ernie D. Tough.

David (Tim) Ubsdell.

Monty C. Vealle.

Frank Wade, A.F. Walker, M. Walley, Douglas Ward, G.H. Ward, Peter Ward, L.A. Warnes, G.A.F. Watts, Mark D. Wells, Syd J. Whitfield, A.E. (Ted) Wicks, Florence Wicks, Joan and Enid Wignall, E.H. Willcox, Harry Wilks, Ron Williams, A.H. Wilton , Les Wright, Peter Wright, Albert Thomas Wyatt.

L.T. (Les) Yeo.

Sydney Zak.

SELECT BIBLIOGRAPHY

ALLAWAY, J., *Hero of the Upholder: The Story of Lieutenant-Commander Wanklyn*, Airlife Publishing, 1991.

APPS, Lieutenant-Commander Michael, *Send Her Victorious*, William Kimber, 1971.

ATTARD, Joseph, *The Battle of Malta*, William Kimber, 1981.

BAILEY, Captain E.A.S., *Malta Defiant and Triumphant: Rolls of Honour 1940–43*, pub. E.A.S. Bailey, 1992.

BARTON, Leonard R., *Lucky Me!* Nonsuch Productions, 1994.

BEESELY, Patrick, *Very Special Intelligence*. The Story of the Admiralty's operational intelligence, Hamish Hamilton, 1977.

BEHRENS, C.B.A., *Merchant Shipping and the Demands of War*, Official History of the Second World War, HMSO, 1955.

BEKKER, Cajus, *The Luftwaffe War Diaries*, Macdonald, 1964.

—— *Hitler's Naval War*, Macdonald and Janes, 1974.

BEEVOR, Anthony, *Crete, The Battle and the Resistance*, John Murray, 1991.

BELOT, Rear Admiral Raymond de, *The Struggle For The Mediterranean, 1939–45*, OUP, 1951.

BENNET, Ralph, *Ultra and Mediterranean Strategy*, 1989.

BRAGADIN, Commander Marc' Antonio, *The Italian Navy in World War II*, US Naval Institute Press, Anapolis, 1957.

British Vessels Lost at Sea 1939–45, HMSO, 2nd Edition, Patrick Stephens, 1983.

BROWN, David, *Warship Losses of World War II*, Arms and Armour Press, 1990.

—— *Carrier Fighters*, Macdonald and Janes, 1975.

—— *Carrier Operations in World War II*, Vol. 1: The Royal Navy, Ian Allan, 1968.

BUSCH, Harald, *U-Boats at War*, Putnam, 1955.

CAMERON, Ian, *Red Duster, White Ensign*, Frederick Muller, 1959.

CHURCHILL, Winston S., *The Second World War*, 6 vols. Cassell, 1948–54:

Vol. I The Gathering Storm, 1948.

Vol. II Their Finest Hour, 1949.

Vol. III The Grand Alliance, 1950.

Vol. IV The Hinge of Fate, 1951.

CIANO, *Ciano's Diary 1939–43*, edited with an introduction by M. Muggeridge, Heinemann.

CLARK, Alan, *The Fall of Crete*, Anthony Blond, 1962.

COLLEDGE, J.J., *see* LENTON.

COMMEAU, M.G., *Operation Mercury*, William Kimber, 1975.

COULTER, J.L.S. Editor *Medical History of the Second World War*: Royal Navy Medical Services, Vol. II, HMSO, 1956.

CRISP, Robert, *The Gods Were Neutral*, Frederick Muller, 1960.

CULL, Brian, *see* SHORES.

CUNNINGHAM, Admiral of the Fleet, Viscount Andrew B. of Hyndhope, *A Sailor's Odyssey*, Hutchinson, 1951.

DAVIN, D.M., *Crete: Official History of New Zealand in The Second World War 1939–45*, OUP, 1953.

DIVINE. A.D., *Destroyer's War*, John Murray, 1942.

DÖNITZ, Grand Admiral Karl, *Memoirs: Ten Years and Twenty Days*, trans. R.H. Stevens in collaboration with David Woodward, Weidenfeld and Nicolson, 1958.

EDWARDS, Bernard, *The Merchant Navy Goes to War*, Robert Hale, 1989.

FÜHRER *Conferences on Naval Affairs, 1939–45*. Editor Jak P. Mallmann Showell, Greenhill Books, 1990.

HAY, Ian, *The Unconquered Isle: The Story of Malta GC*, Hodder and Stoughton, 1943.

HILL, Roger, *Destroyer Captain: Memoirs of the War at Sea 1942–45*, William Kimber, 1975.

HINSLEY, F.H., *British Intelligence in the Second World War*, 1979.

HODGKINSON, Lieutenant-Commander Hugh, *Before The Tide Turned*, Harrap, 1944.

HOGAN, George, *Malta: The Triumphant Years, 1940–43*, Robert Hale, 1978.

HUNTER, Anthony, *see* SHANKLAND.

IACHINO, Admiral A., *Tramonto di Una Grande Marina*, Milan, Mondatori, 1959.

IRELAND, Bernard, *The War in the Mediterrenean, 1940–43*, Arms and Armour, 1993.

IRESON, Tony, *Old Kettering: A View From the Thirties*. Account of HMS *Badsworth*, pp. 119–124, published by the author, 1984.

JANES ALL THE WORLD'S FIGHTING SHIPS, Edited Francis E. McMurtrie, Sampson Low Marston & Co, 1941.

KEMP, Paul, *Malta Convoys 1940–1943*, Arms and Armour, No. 14 in the Warships Illustrated Series, 1988.

KEMP, Lieutenant-Commander P.K., *HM Destroyers*, Herbert Jenkins, 1956.

—— *Victory at Sea*, Frederick Muller, 1957.

KESSELRING, Field Marshal, *Memoirs*, William Kimber, 1974.

KIMMINS, Commander Anthony, *Half Time*, Heineman, 1947.

—— *It Is Upon the Navy*, Hutchinson, 1942.

LAMB, Commander Charles, *War in a Stringbag*, Hutchinson, 1977.

LANGMAID, Kenneth Rowland, *The Med: The Royal Navy in the Mediterranean 1939–1945*, The Butterworth Press, 1948.

LENTON, H.T. and COLLEDGE, J.J., *Warships of World War II*, Ian Allan, 1973.

LLOYD, Air Marshal Sir H., *Briefed to Attack – Malta's Part in African History*, Hodder & Stoughton, 1949.

LONG, Gavin, *Greece, Crete and Syria: Australia in the War of 1939–45*, Series 1, Vol. II, Canberra, 1953.

LUCAS, Laddie, *Malta – The Thorn in Rommel's Side*, Stanley Paul, 1992.

LUCAS, W.L., *Eagle Fleet*, Weidenfeld and Nicolson.

MACDONALD, Callum, *The Lost Battle: Crete 1941*, Macmillan, 1993.

MACINTYRE, Captain Donald, *Fighting Admiral*, Evans, 1961.

—— *The Battle for the Mediterranean*, Batsford, 1964.

MALIZA NICOLA, *see* SHORES

MARCH, Edgar J., *The British Destroyer*, Seeley Service, 1968.

MARDER, Arthur J., *From the Dreadnought to Scapa Flow*, OUP, 5 vols 1961–70.

MARS, Alistair, *Unbroken: The Story of a Submarine*, Muller, 1953.

—— *British Submarines at War 1939–1945*, William Kimber, 1971.

MAX, Oliver A.R.L., *Malta Besieged*, Hutchinson,

MORISON, Rear-Admiral Samuel Eliot, USN, *History of US Navy Operations in World War II*, Vol. II, OUP, 1947.

PACK, Captain S.W.C., *The Battle for Crete*, Ian Allan, 1973.

—— *Sea Power in the Mediterranean*, A. Barker, 1971.

—— *The Battle of Matapan*, Batsford, 1961.

—— *Night Action off Cape Matapan*, Ian Allan, 1972.

—— *Cunningham: The Commander*, Batsford, 1974.

—— *The Battle of Sirte*, Ian Allan, 1975.

PADFIELD, Peter, *Dönitz: The Last Führer*, Victor Gollancz, 1984.

PEROWNE, Stuart, *The Siege Within The Walls: Malta 1940–43*. Hodder & Stoughton, 1970.

PLAYFAIR, Major-General I.S.O., with Captain F.C. FLYNN, Brigadier C.J.C. MOLONEY and Air Vice-Marshal S.E. TOOMER, *History of the Second World War: The Mediterranean and Middle East*, Vol. II, "The Germans Came to the Help of Their Ally", HMSO, 1956.

—— Vol. III "British Fortunes Reach Their Lowest Ebb", HMSO, 1960.

POOLMAN, Kenneth, *The Kelly*, William Kimber, 1954.
—— *Illustrious*, William Kimber, 1958.
—— *Allied Submarines of World War Two*, Arms and Armour Press.
POPHAM, Hugh, *Sea Flight*, William Kimber, 1956.
PORTER, E.B., and NIMITZ, Chester W., Editors: *Sea Power: A Naval History*, Prentice Hall, 1960.
PULESTON, W.D., *Influence of Sea Power in World War II*, OUP, 1947.
RAEDER, Grand Admiral Erich, *Struggle For The Sea*, William Kimber, 1959. An abridged translation of the two vols. *Mein Leben*, published 1956, 1957, Tubingen, Schlictenmayer.
ROHWER, Jürgen, and JACOBSEN, Hans Adolph, Editors, *Decisive Battles of World War II, The German View*, Andre Deutsch, 1965.
—— and HUMMELCHEN, G., *Chronology of the War at Sea 1939–45*: Vol. I 1939–42: Vol. II 1943–45, Ian Allan, 1972. Revised and expanded edition, Greenhill Books, 1992.
—— *Die U-boote Erfolge der Achsenmachte*, Munich, 1968. Up-dated and published in English as *Axis Submarine Successes, 1939–45*, Patrick Stephens, Cambridge, 1983, see pp. 223–256.
ROSKILL, Captain Stephen W., *A Merchant Fleet at War 1939–45*, Vols I and II. All told four vols, HMSO, 1954–61. An indispensible book for a detailed study of the naval war.
—— *HMS Warspite*, Collins, 1957.
RUGE, Vice-Admiral Friedrich, *Sea Warfare, 1939–45*, Cassell, 1957.
SAINSBURY, Captain A.B., *see* SHRUB.
SCHOFIELD, Vice-Admiral B.B., *The Attack on Taranto*, Ian Allan, 1973.
SHANKLAND, Peter, and HUNTER, Anthony, *Malta Convoy*, Collins, 1961.
SHORES, Christopher, and CULL, Brian, with MALIZIA, Nicola, *Malta: The Spitfire Year, 1942*, Grub Street, 1991.
SHRUB, Lieutenant-Commander R.E.A., and SAINSBURY,

Captain A.B., Editors, *The Royal Navy Day by Day*, Centaur Press, 1979.

SIMPSON, Rear-Admiral C.W. (George), *Periscope View*, Macmillan, 1972.

SLADER, John, *The Fourth Service: Merchantmen at War 1939–45*, Robert Hale, 1994.

SMITH, Peter C., *Pedestal: The Malta Convoy of August 1942*, William Kimber, 1970.

—— *The Stuka at War*, Ian Allan, 1971.

—— and WALKER, Edwin, *Battles of the Malta Striking Forces*, Ian Allan, 1974.

SPENCER, John Hall, *Battle For Crete*, Heinemann, 1962.

SPOONER, Tony, *Faith, Hope and Malta GC*, Newton Publishers. *Supreme Gallantry: Malta's Role in the Allied Victory 1939–45*, John Murray, 1996.

STEPHANIDES, Theodore, *Climax in Crete*, Faber, 1962.

STEPHEN, G.M., *Fighting Admirals: British Admirals of the Second World War*, Leo Cooper, 1991.

STEWART, I. McD.G., *Struggle For Crete*, OUP, 1966.

STITT, Commander G., *Under Cunningham's Command*, Allen and Unwin, 1944.

TAFFRAIL, *Blue Star Line*, Gardiner, Liverpool, 1948.

TERRAINE, John, *The Life and Times of Lord Mountbatten*, Hutchinson, 1968.

THOMAS, David A., *Crete 1941: The Battle at Sea*, Andre Deutsch, 1972.

TREVOR-ROPER, H.R., *Hitler's War Directives 1939–45*, Sidgwick and Jackson, 1964.

VIAN, Admiral of the Fleet, Sir Philip, *Action This Day*, Frederick Muller, 1960.

WARNER, Oliver, *Cunningham of Hyndhope, Admiral of the Fleet*, John Murray, 1967.

WELDON, Lieutenant-Colonel H.E.C., *Drama in Malta*, nd.

WINTERBOTHAM, F.W., *The Ultra Secret*, Weidenfeld and Nicolson, 1974.

WINGATE, John, *The Fighting Tenth*, Leo Cooper, 1991.

WINTON, John, *Ultra at Sea*, Leo Cooper, 1988.

WINTON, John, Editor *Freedom's Battle: The War At Sea*, Hutchinson, 1967.

——, John, *Cunningham*, John Murray, 1998.

Action Against a Convoy, 15–16 April 1941. Supplement to the *London Gazette*, July 14th 1947.

The Air Battle of Malta, HMSO.

Ark Royal: The Admiralty Account of Her Achievement, HMSO, 1942.

Battle of Crete, Admiral Cunningham's *Despatch*. Supplement to the *London Gazette*, May 24th 1948.

Battle of Matapan 1941, Admiral Cunningham's *Despatch*, Supplement to the *London Gazette*, July 31st 1947.

The British Empire, BBC TV Time Life Books No. 77: *Malta: Prize of the Mediterranean*, Nigel Nicholson, 1973.

The Campaign in Greece and Crete, HMSO, 1942.

East of Malta, West of Suez, the official Admiralty Account of the Mediterranean Fleet, 1939–45, HMSO, 1943.

Einsatz Kreta, XI Air Korps Battle Report, June 11th 1941.

Fleet Air Arms Operations against Taranto, November 1940, Supplement to the *London Gazette*, July 14th 1947.

Fleet Air Arm, The Admiralty Account of Naval Air Operations, HMSO, 1953.

His Majesty's Submarines, HMSO, 1945.

Letters of Proceedings, in particular those by:

> Rear-Admiral H.B. Rawlings
>
> Rear-Admiral I. Glennie
>
> Rear-Admiral E.L.S. King
>
> Vice-Admiral H.D. Pridham-Wippell

Malta Images, compiled and edited by Bert Mason and Dick Squires, published by the George Cross Island Association, North-West Branch, n.d.

La Marina Italiana Nella Seconda Guerra Mondiale, Vol. IX, "La Difesa del Traffico con L'Albania, La Grecia e L'Egeo," Ufficio Storico Della Marina Militare, Roma, 1965, and Vol.

XIII "I Sommergibili in Mediterraneo, Roma, 1967.

Mediterranean Convoy Operations 1941–42: Supplement to the *London Gazette*, carrying Reports by Cunningham, Curteis, Somerville and Syfret. August 11th 1948.

The Mediterranean Fleet, Greece to Tripoli, the Admiralty Account of Naval Operations April 1941 to January 1943, HMSO, 1944.

Military History (incorporating *War Monthly*) "HMS *York* is Sunk" by Charles H. Bogart, pp. 70–75, February 1983.

Operation Pedestal, Supplement to the *London Gazette*, May 10th 1948.

HMS Penelope, by Her Company, George G. Harrap, 1943.

The Story of HMS Glengyle, 1940–46. Glen Line Limited, n.d.

Transportation of the Army to Greece and evacuation of the Army from Greece, 1941. Admiral Cunningham's *Despatch* together with *Reports* from Vice-Admiral H.D. Pridham-Wippell and Rear-Admiral H.T. Baillie Grohman. Supplement to the *London Gazette*, May 19th 1948.

War Monthly, published by Marshall Cavendish:

Issue 6 "Stuka" by Peter C. Smith, pp. 22–30.

21 "Crete Invasion" by William Fowler pp. 16–23.

24 "Fighting Warspite" by Captain S.W. Roskill, pp. 34–4

30 "Corvettes" by John Lambert, pp. 39–48.

44 "Gulf of Sirte" by David A. Thomas, pp. 41–48.

60 "Ark Royal" by Brenda Ralph Lewis, pp. 21–29.

68 "The Clean Sweep" by Brian Perrett, pp. 30–35.

71 "Destroyer Hotspur in WW II" pp. 16–23.

79 "Italian Surrender" by Richard Lamb, pp. 30–37.

83 "How Ohio Saved Malta".

World War II Series edited by Peter Young, published by Orbis Publishing. Relevant articles appear in the following parts:

Vol. I Part 14, pp. 263–273.

Vol. II Part 15, pp. 287–289.

Part 16, pp. 310–213, 314–5.

ADDENDUM

Attention is specially drawn to the *Defender* series of the George Cross Island Association publication. There are too many to enumerate here. See, for example, the *Defender*, edition No. 5 pp. 1–4, September, 1989, "The Eagle Through the Periscope" attributed to Lieutenant-Commander Helmut Rosenbaum of *U-73*, translated by L.P.R. Wilson.

INDEX

223